SEXUAL JUSTICE

ALSO BY ALEXANDRA BRODSKY

The Feminist Utopia Project:
Fifty-Seven Visions of a Wildly Better Future
(coeditor)

SEXUAL JUSTICE

SUPPORTING VICTIMS, ENSURING DUE PROCESS,
AND RESISTING THE CONSERVATIVE BACKLASH

ALEXANDRA BRODSKY

Metropolitan Books
Henry Holt and Company   New York

Metropolitan Books
Henry Holt and Company
Publishers since 1866
120 Broadway
New York, New York 10271
www.henryholt.com

Metropolitan Books® and 🅜® are registered trademarks of
Macmillan Publishing Group, LLC.

Library of Congress Cataloging-in-Publication Data

Names: Brodsky, Alexandra, author.
Title: Sexual justice : supporting victims, ensuring due process, and
  resisting the conservative backlash / Alexandra Brodsky.
Description: First edition. | New York : Metropolitan Books, 2021. |
  Includes bibliographical references and index.
Identifiers: LCCN 2021002313 (print) | LCCN 2021002314 (ebook) |
  ISBN 9781250262547 (hardcover) | ISBN 9781250262530 (ebook)
Subjects: LCSH: Sex discrimination against women—Law and
  legislation—United States. | Women—Crimes against—United States. |
  Sexual harassment of women—Law and legislation—United States. | Sexual
  abuse victims—Legal status, laws, etc.—United States. | Due process of
  law—United States.
Classification: LCC KF4758 .B76 2021 (print) | LCC KF4758 (ebook) |
  DDC 342.7308/78—dc23
LC record available at https://lccn.loc.gov/2021002313

Our books may be purchased in bulk for promotional, educational, or business use. Please
contact your local bookseller or the Macmillan Corporate and Premium Sales Department at
(800) 221-7945, extension 5442, or by e-mail at MacmillanSpecialMarkets@macmillan.com.

First Edition 2021

Designed by Kelly S. Too

Printed in the United States of America

1   3   5   7   9   10   8   6   4   2

*For the women who have shaped my
feminism through their friendship,
and for Alec*

CONTENTS

PART III. EXCEPTIONALISM

PART IV. CO-OPTATION

SEXUAL JUSTICE

Introduction

First there was Harvey Weinstein in the *New York Times*. Then there was Kevin Spacey in *BuzzFeed*. In the *Los Angeles Times*, director Brett Ratner. Then Louis C.K. and Jeffrey Tambor. Roy Moore and Al Franken. Charlie Rose. Garrison Keillor. Matt Lauer. Lorin Stein. Mario Batali. James Franco. R. Kelly, again. Woody Allen, again. Blogs started lists to keep track of the allegations, sometimes numbering in the hundreds, depending on who mattered enough to count. It didn't take long for the accumulation of names to pass the stage where anyone could plausibly pretend this was about the downfall of a few bad apples.

The accusations of sexual abuse that made the headlines were usually about famous men, and many of their victims were famous as well. Plenty of the allegations recounted abuses on movie sets or in the penthouse suites of luxury hotels. But ordinary people saw themselves in the stories, too. The boss who offered you extra shifts in exchange for a date. The dinner when you told your mom who touched you, and she said never to tell anyone again. The meeting when you told the principal a classmate had raped you, and he suspended you instead. That time when you felt you could not say no. That time you said no and it didn't matter. So we said "Me Too."

Others recognized themselves in a different aspect of the stories. They could be one of those men. They could be a name on a list.

Almost as soon as the flood of stories broke, critics and commentators raised concerns about the men accused. *What about due process?* they asked. I heard that question in two different tones. One was the even, perplexed voice of a real questioner, searching in good faith for answers: *What is the best, fairest way to respond to troubling allegations?* The other was indignant, loud, interrupting: *How dare we threaten a man's good name? How could that ever be fair?* To these critics, any consequence at all was a violation of due process.

While awaiting trial on rape charges, Weinstein attended a monthly performance night at a New York City bar. During her time onstage, one young comedian, Kelly Bachman, pointed out the "Freddy Krueger in the room." "I didn't realize we have to bring our own mace and rape whistle to Actors Hour," she joked. After the set, two other performers directly confronted the Hollywood producer. Both were escorted out. One, Zoe Stuckless, later recalled: "This guy was leading me out the stairs, just repeating 'due process, due process' to me." A Weinstein rep would echo the objection in a public statement, decrying the incident as "an example of how due process today is being squashed by the public."

FOR THOSE OF us who had been involved in the campus sexual assault movement, this backlash was familiar. At the time the Weinstein story broke, I was a year out of law school, working at the National Women's Law Center, a feminist nonprofit based in Washington, D.C. As a law student, I'd split my time between feminist advocacy and criminal defense. After graduation, I started a fellowship with the Law Center, focusing on discriminatory student discipline meted out against girls of color.

I connected to the girls with whom we worked partly because I, too, had been introduced to the law as a student in need of legal help. In 2011, when I was an undergrad at Yale, I had joined fifteen friends to file a complaint against our college with the U.S. Department of Education. By tolerating sexual harassment, including violence, against students like us, we said, the college had violated the law that prohibits sex discrimination in schools: Title IX of the Education Amendments of 1972, popularly known as just "Title IX." The Department of Education investigated Yale and spurred it to change its policies. The school abandoned its opaque, labyrinthine set of reporting systems and debuted a clearer process for survivors to come forward. It also started publishing regular reports about what kinds of sexual harassment complaints it had received and their outcomes, giving the community some insight into behind-the-scenes decisions. The process still wasn't perfect, but it was much improved.

Around the same time, a friend of a friend named Dana Bolger was organizing against Amherst College's abysmal handling of sexual abuses. We talked on the phone, and then frequently over email and Facebook. Online, we connected with students and young alumni of other colleges who had faced similar issues. In those conversations, we swapped advocacy strategies, pooled our experiences, and came to see common threads. One was that few of us had known about our legal rights under Title IX when we needed them. Over the summer of 2013, Dana and I decided to put together accessible legal explainers for student survivors. We called the project Know Your IX. In collaboration with other activists, we wrote up the basics of Title IX's protections against sexual harassment and offered tips about organizing on campus. We published those resources on a website and disseminated them on social media. Our plan was to wrap up before the fall. Dana still had a semester of college to finish. I was about to start law school.

We did not wrap up. Know Your IX grew from a summer project to a national campaign. I wish I could say it expanded because of some strategic insight our team shared. But the truth is that the scope of the problem and the need for an organized student voice was much greater than we had anticipated. Know Your IX did not only need to bring the law to students; we also needed to bring student voices to lawmakers. Our first big action was a protest outside the Department of Education at which we delivered a petition with over 175,000 signatures pushing the department to enforce Title IX and hold schools accountable for wrongdoings. Although we initially met resistance from government officials, over the next few years many of our demands became federal policy. At our urging, the department started publicly announcing when its investigations turned up Title IX violations; finally, schools might see a reason to follow the law. We sought and received guarantees that undocumented survivors could file Title IX complaints with the government without risking deportation. We pushed officials to provide clear instructions that schools needed to offer survivors services like mental health care free of charge. We helped legislators pass good laws and defeat bad ones, like proposed statutes that would have forced schools to turn over all reports to the police. (More on that later.)

The Know Your IX team worked alongside students across the country who were organizing to change their schools for the better, such as Columbia undergraduate Emma Sulkowicz, who made front-page news with her visually stunning "Mattress Performance (Carry That Weight)." Students at other colleges as well as ones still in high school investigated their schools' policies, drafted reforms, and demanded change that would make their classrooms safe and equitable. The work was hard, but often the students won. Schools created proper channels to report harassment. They changed policies to recognize, for the first time, male survivors and violence within queer relationships. They opened offices to provide free support for victims. They began programs that taught students basic principles of sexual respect.

As would later happen with Me Too, the successes of the Title IX movement came with critics—professors, lawyers, and pundits who found fault with both the student movement and the new policies schools were implementing. They worried that colleges, in particular, had "overcorrected." Where once it was survivors who faced mistreatment, they opined, now alleged assailants were the ones who had to fear injustice. In particular, critics complained that disciplinary procedures—the rules laying out each step in the adjudication—often failed to protect the rights of students accused of sexual assault. Some of the stories reported were deeply disturbing. A student at Wesley College, for example, was invited by administrators to what he believed was a preliminary conversation about a serious allegation against him. When he arrived, he learned it was instead a formal disciplinary hearing for which he'd had no opportunity to prepare. School administrators failed to provide him with full information about the accusation, or even with correct material about the school's policies. That hearing earned Wesley a public reprimand from the U.S. Department of Education. Similarly, the University of Southern California faced a lawsuit from a student, identified as John Doe, who had been suspended after being found responsible for facilitating a gang rape of his sexual partner. A state court ruled against the university, holding that its process was unfair because Doe was never informed of what, exactly, he was accused of doing, and never given the opportunity to challenge the evidence against him. As a result of this deficient process, the court found, Doe was denied a meaningful chance to defend himself.

I struggled with how to respond to these stories. I worried that critics would wrongly attribute schools' procedural mistakes to the important progress student activists had made for survivors, putting our victories at risk. But I also saw criticism of disciplinary procedures as a natural part of our project. Our whole purpose was to make schools respond to reports of sexual harassment fairly, so that no student would be unjustly deprived of the chance to learn and thrive. And I was hardly shocked that schools were sometimes mistreating students accused of sexual harms—after all, they had been doing the same to survivors for so long. In law school, I spent a year reviewing lawsuits from students who claimed they were wrongly suspended or expelled for sexual assault. Their complaints of procedural defects echoed those I had long heard from survivors, and also from students facing disciplinary charges that had nothing to do with sex. They were unaware of their rights. They never got the chance to tell their full story. The decision-making process was opaque and, to the extent it was discernible, appeared biased—either toward one side over the other, or toward protecting the university's own interests. Of course, I thought, those problems should be fixed—for everyone's sake.

In her excellent book *Down Girl*, the philosopher Kate Manne describes what she calls "himpathy": the common knee-jerk concern for men accused of wrongdoing that casts aside the women they may have hurt, women who are automatically seen not as victims but as untrustworthy threats to the good names of good men. I share her concern and disgust. Yet I still had, well, empathy, or at least sympathy, when I read accounts of accused students who struggled to navigate disciplinary proceedings. I felt this with some discomfort, because the line between valid compassion and misguided "himpathy" is all too easily crossed. I felt—I feel—constantly uncertain about whether I'm on the right side of that divide.

But the fact is that sexual harassment is too prevalent for any of us to feel confident that we can maintain a cool distance. Whether or not we're aware of it, we all love people who have been harassed, just as many of us have been. And many of us love someone who has been the harasser, likely without our knowing. This combination of prevalence and ignorance means most of us, I think, have had a flash of a nightmare question: *What if someone I love were accused of harassment? Of rape?* What would I do, how would I feel, if someone named my college roommate? My husband? I like to think I would live my politics. I would want those I love held accountable if they had sexually abused someone. In the process, though, I would want them to be treated fairly, and have the chance to present their account of what had happened, too.

I don't mean to invite false equivalency. Harassment is so much more likely to occur than an accusation, let alone a false one. And I am wary of feeding a narrative that accused harassers are the true victims, the most deserving of our concern. But we can care about multiple things at once. We must.

Because of our overlapping interest in fairness for all students, Know Your IX was sometimes able to forge fruitful relationships with members of "the other side." Away from the media, with room to admit ambiguity and uncertainty, we had tough conversations with advocates for alleged student harassers. When it came down to it, we could often find substantial agreement and distill what we actually disagreed about to no more than a few logistical questions. Those conversations gave me hope that, with enough care and good faith, consensus was within reach. We could build procedures that treated all students equitably and with dignity.

But not all the critics of campus reforms were acting in good faith. Some spoke of "due process" when their real goal was impunity. In public, one Georgia state representative complained that state schools needed better procedures to investigate students accused of sexual assault. Privately, he bullied schools into letting particular accused students off the hook. As though that was a fair process!

Many of these critics misrepresented the facts on the ground, claiming hysterical feminists had pressured schools to adopt policies where mere allegations warranted expulsion. *If you don't call a girl back the next day, she'll report you to the dean and you'll be out by noon!* They repeated lies—including basic inaccuracies about the law—so many times that the inaccuracies made their way into national reporting as fact. If I had a dollar for every article claiming the Obama administration invented the idea that Title IX applies to sexual assault, required schools to use a lower standard of evidence than most did before, or prohibited accused students from hiring attorneys, I could fund the fact-checkers those newspapers need.

Anti-feminist zealots are, of course, infuriating. But if I'm being honest, I had a harder time dealing with the moderates and progressives whose procedural objections seemed rooted in sexist assumptions. They demanded that schools provide special protections to students accused of sexual harms, protections unavailable to peers accused of other kinds of misconduct—as though sexual allegations were uniquely suspect. As though a student who said she'd been raped was more likely to be lying than a student who said his roommate had punched him in the face, or berated him with racial slurs, or committed any of the other forms of misconduct schools are regularly called on to address. Some critics on the left never acknowledged the young survivors on the other side of the table. They seemed to forget that *two* students' educations were at stake, not just one. Prominent attorneys with progressive credentials openly dismissed sexual violence as trivial or the victim's fault, the kinds of myths I'd naively thought the left would not tolerate.

I knew that we couldn't dismiss all concerns about student discipline for sexual harms simply because some of the most vocal critics had dubious methods or motives. But it was often difficult to distinguish between the good-faith actors and the bad. The result was that some Title IX advocates abandoned complexity, dismissing concerns about due process out of hand, or rejected reasonable reforms because they came from "the other side." Some used low rates of false reporting to excuse mistreatment of the accused, or were cavalier about the stakes for a student facing suspension. In light of the anti-feminist backlash, that skepticism of procedural criticisms was understandable. But it was still wrong.

THE TOXICITY OF the debates about school harassment procedures made me wary when a similar response emerged, perhaps inevitably, in the wake of the Weinstein story. With the rise of the Me Too movement, the conversation about harassment stretched past the confines of campuses to the workplace and our broader communities. In a way that felt new and long overdue, wrongdoers—overwhelmingly men—were starting to face consequences for the harm they caused. But many people seemed to believe that accountability for sexual abuses is per se unfair. And again, the more sophisticated right-wing voices knowingly wielded the language of due process to pursue impunity.

Having seen this fight play out before in the campus wars, I knew that we needed to proceed thoughtfully. Fair process is crucially important in responding to sexual harassment allegations; and yet concerns about fair process are often co-opted and weaponized to thwart progress. We need to recognize both these truths to respond to sexual harms in an effective way—to make a lasting contribution to equality, to safety, and, fundamentally, to the way we treat one another.

There is no single blueprint for how every institution—businesses and nonprofits, social clubs and political organizations, places of learning and places of worship—should handle allegations of wrongdoing. But there are common principles and values that can guide us. Those can help promote fairness to all and simultaneously resist reactionary movements that seek to roll back advancement on sexual harassment.

That common understanding starts with recognizing what sexual harm is and what victims need. Many people think of sexual assaults as crimes and crimes alone. A common response to a public accusation of sexual violence is that the victim should have called the cops, as though a criminal trial were the only path to truth and justice. But sexual abuse is also a civil rights violation. Among other things, that means a victim can bring her own civil lawsuit, seeking monetary damages and policy changes. That kind of legal action contrasts sharply with a criminal prosecution, which is brought by the government to vindicate its interests, not the victim's, and seeks to send the defendant to prison—an outcome that a victim might not even want.

Putting the legal mechanics aside, understanding sexual harassment as a civil rights issue is also about reframing the problem. The civil rights lens recognizes that by keeping survivors from participating fully in workplaces, schools, politics, and other public spheres, sexual harm serves to cement inequalities that permeate our society. Once we are focused on the many ways sexual abuse holds victims back, we can recognize that criminal prosecution is ill-suited to help many survivors in the wake of violence. The remedy it offers—incarceration—simply cannot address their needs.

Because of the danger and inaccessibility of legal proceedings, the vast majority of victims do not turn to the law in the wake of harassment, at least not in any formal sense. Some tell a few friends but never seek any redress. Many tell no one. And of those who do pursue some sort of accountability, remarkably few ever file either a criminal complaint or a civil lawsuit. Instead, they may turn to institutions to respond, filing complaints with their company's human resources department, for example, or their school's Title IX coordinator. These options exist in the shadow of the law, informed by it and sometimes required by it. But they are not legal proceedings themselves. The first part of this book explores the different ways that survivors can seek remedies and why they might choose institutional responses over courts.

I'm aware that starting off with a discussion focused on survivors may alienate readers who have come to this book primarily concerned with the rights of the accused. But I feel strongly that we cannot have a conversation about how to respond to sexual harms without a shared understanding of why those harms require an institutional response—who is hurt, and how, and why legal systems fail victims. Despite the many Me Too headlines, our national debate has proceeded on a paper-thin understanding of these injuries, one that cannot provide the foundation for the difficult conversation of *what comes next?*

I promise that we will get to that question. As I discuss in the second part of the book, any response to sexual abuses must grapple with how we can treat all parties with dignity and keep our worst prejudices at bay. Law doesn't have all the answers, but the ethical principles that underlie the legal concept of "due process" can provide important guidance for what fairness means and how to achieve it.

These principles also make clear that we are wrong to regard accusations of sexual harm as requiring special skepticism and safeguards.

To get right hard questions about process and harassment, we must understand why so many think that fairness is particularly fraught in the context of sexual allegations. Why do so many critics, for example, demand *uniquely* robust procedural protections for people accused of sexual harassment, unavailable to those accused of any other harm? The answer, I explain in the book's third part, largely boils down to misogyny. And in the final chapters, I show how bad actors, including lawmakers, have been using common misunderstandings about harassment and process to protect abusers—not from unfairness, but from any accountability at all.

DESPITE THIS BOOK'S title, there is certainly far, far more to "sexual justice" than these pages can cover. So I want to say a little bit about what is not in here. First, this is not a book about what does, or what should, count as sexual harassment. There are crucial conversations happening across the country, from college campuses to workplaces to the American Law Institute, about how current definitions fail to account for many forms of sexual harm, and how we can best fix them. (Perhaps the most controversial part of the conversation has been the idea of "affirmative consent"—that our laws should move from defining rape by the presence of a "no" to the absence of a "yes.") These are vital questions, but not ones I seek to answer with this book. My focus is the steps by which people can vet an accusation of sexual harassment, rather than the matter of what *constitutes* sexual harassment. Of course, those two issues are inevitably intertwined, and injustice along one axis can exacerbate injustice on the other. For example, a vague policy that leaves open what, exactly, is prohibited can make an unfair process even more daunting for both the victim and the accused, and is likely to result in inconsistent and discriminatory outcomes. But in order to avoid biting off more than a single book can chew, I'll leave the question of defining sexual harms for another time.

I also don't attempt to say exactly what consequences institutions should impose on sexual harassers. In truth, there is no one-size-fits-all solution. At various points, I discuss sanctions that companies and schools may employ when they've substantiated reports of harassment, ranging from office reassignments and dorm transfers to terminations and expulsions. I believe such remedies are sometimes necessary for safety and equality, and also that a proportionate response, rather than an overly punitive one, is necessary for fairness. In each case, striking that balance—one that will vary based on the specific circumstances of each case—is critical. That's not, however, my focus here.

On a similar note, this is not a book about restorative justice. For decades, feminists have imagined ways to address sexual abuses that focus on rebuilding rather than punishment for its own sake. Restorative justice is one such method. That process depends on the wrongdoer's willingness to acknowledge and rectify the harm he has caused. Through a series of facilitated conversations, the victim and other community members help the wrongdoer understand the impact of his conduct and how he can address the victim's needs while ensuring that the injury isn't repeated. Such work is crucial; I hope to see restorative options for survivors dramatically expanded. And even apart from formal restorative models, the principles behind this approach certainly have much to teach us about responding to harm. But my project here is a different one: How can today's institutions fairly handle allegations that the accused *denies*—when he says no harm occurred, so nothing needs to be restored?

I should explain, too, that although this book considers a broad range of groups that might be called upon to respond to allegations, there are a few I have intentionally left out. One is families. This book's discussion might help other institutions respond to sexual harms that occur between relatives—for example, a synagogue may be called upon to consider an allegation of intimate violence between spouses when one says she cannot safely worship in the other's presence. But as for how families themselves should investigate alleged wrongdoing within their close ranks, different dynamics are at work, with which I lack sufficient expertise. I'm eager for someone else to write on this topic. As I explain in more detail in a later chapter, I also do not venture into institutions like prisons and immigration detention centers, which are so inextricably tied to criminal law that a firm line between criminal prosecution and any internal procedures is perhaps impossible to draw.

Finally, this is not a book about famous men, or at least not primarily so. I use examples drawn from the headlines, such as the accusations against Weinstein and Brett Kavanaugh, to examine how our beliefs about harassment, gender, and process play out. But I'm far more concerned with how those dynamics affect the vast majority of people, whose interactions with violence, either as victims or as alleged perpetrators, are unlikely to be of interest to anyone outside their communities. To put it simply, there are many more not-famous people than famous ones. Assuming that this is true of this book's readership as well, I hope any insights or lessons you draw from these pages will equip you to better understand harassment and process in your own lives—which probably, like mine, look very different from Hollywood. Some of the questions posed by celebrity allegations are relevant to the rest of us (for example, how much proof does an employer need before cutting ties with an employee?), so there is certainly reason to discuss such cases in this book. But many others (for instance, how much proof does a newspaper need before it should run with a story?) are not directly relevant to most of our situations.

A FEW QUICK notes about vocabulary. I've already referred to "process" many times, and, unsurprisingly, will continue to do so. I use that term to mean the series of steps by which an investigation and adjudication takes place. In popular discussion, the term "due process" is often used to refer both to specific legal principles and to an ethical commitment to fairness. I will parse this distinction later in this book, but as a general matter, I use "due process" when I refer to legal rules and "fair process" when I refer to procedures that conform to moral commitments, which often exceed the low floor set by the law.

Another unsurprisingly frequent term: "sexual harassment." I use this umbrella language to refer to a wide range of sexual and gender-based abuses, physical and verbal alike, including everything from inappropriate comments to rape. I sometimes will refer to these same abuses using other capacious terms, like "sexual harms." And when I discuss specific forms of violence, like intimate partner abuse or sexual assault, I'll use those labels. But I primarily use "sexual harassment" because it is the term used in civil rights law to encompass all these actions, which are united not by the precise form they take or by their severity but by the way they threaten the equality and dignity of their targets. So, although sometimes people reserve "harassment" to refer only to verbal abuses, I use it to describe a broader range of harms.

Throughout the book, I discuss both "criminal" and "civil" laws. Later on, I will say more about why that distinction matters. All that readers need to know from the start is that criminal prosecution occurs when the state seeks to vindicate its interests, usually by sending someone to prison. (This is the kind of thing you see on *Law & Order*.) A civil suit is a legal action filed by a person on their own behalf, seeking some kind of compensation or policy change; prison is not on the line. Separate and apart from both criminal and civil litigation are institutional responses—for example, a workplace conducting its own internal investigation of an allegation. Institutional processes seek to maintain the group's collective well-being; they might be motivated by profit, the desire to avoid a lawsuit, or genuine care for the community. The institutional remedy is not a replacement for criminal or civil legal action, nor does it pretend to be. Instead, each of these three approaches has different, if sometimes overlapping, purposes.

When discussing people affected by sexual harassment, I switch back and forth between "victim" and "survivor." Often "survivor" is used as a term that acknowledges the strength and resilience of people who experience harassment, where "victim" focuses on the harm they have experienced. Some people prefer one over the other because it fits better with their experiences. Others reject the dichotomy between the two terms, which they see as suggesting a particular linear narrative: someone is harassed, they are a victim, they grow and thrive, and then they are a survivor. As writers like my friend Dana Bolger have pointed out, for many people, healing is not so straightforward. We get better, but then sometimes we get worse. You might be a victim one day, a survivor the next, and then a victim again. You might be both at the same time. Because these terms are loaded, and because people have different preferences, I use both words in an attempt to acknowledge that experiences and reactions to harassment vary widely. That's not a perfect solution, but it's the best I have.

Similarly, I vary the pronouns I use to refer to both wrongdoers and victims, though I disproportionately refer to "him" hurting "her" or "them." In doing so, I want to reflect the reality that people of all genders hurt people of all genders, but male violence against women and other gender-oppressed people is the most common. My hope in deploying pronouns in this way is to make it explicit that this work is for all survivors without erasing the gendered causes and effects of sexual harassment. I also want to make clear that although harassment and the politics around it are deeply gendered, this is not a simple fight between men and women. As I'll discuss later in the book, men are more likely to be sexually assaulted than falsely accused of sexual assault. In the words of Me Too founder Tarana Burke, "men's first role in this movement is as survivors." And plenty of other men care about sexual harassment because it has hurt or threatened those they love.

Finally, anyone picking up this book presumably knows they will be reading about deeply upsetting forms of abuse, which many readers have experienced firsthand. So, rather than a warning, I offer a note of care. I've made a very purposeful effort not to dwell on the gory details of wrongdoing. I don't want to treat trauma like pornography. At the same time, I often find the subjects in this book infuriating and depressing, and perhaps some of you will as well. In fact, I hope you do.

PART I

REPORTING
SEXUAL HARASSMENT
IN THE REAL WORLD

1

The Story of After

DarbiAnne Goodwin had always loved Pennridge School District. She had been an enthusiastic student since she'd enrolled as a preschooler in the rural Pennsylvania district, which her older siblings attended, too. At the end of her freshman year of high school, she had a near-perfect GPA and a résumé full of extracurricular commitments. She hoped to be president of the student council someday.

Over winter break her sophomore year, a classmate sexually assaulted Darbi in the parking lot of a local restaurant, the Country Place. The young man, "H.," was a year ahead of Darbi at Pennridge High School. When Darbi returned to school in January, she saw H. and his friends everywhere. A classmate told her that these students had started a rumor that, on the night of the assault, Darbi had consented to sex with multiple boys. She could no longer stand to step foot in the school she had once loved.

Darbi needed help. She told her mother about the assault, and together they approached Pennridge administrators. More than anything, Darbi just wanted H. and his friends to leave her alone. She did not want to worry about seeing them between classes or in the lunchroom. She didn't want to hear the rumors they spread about her. She wanted to feel safe enough to focus on school again.

There was a lot Pennridge could have done after receiving Darbi's report. Administrators could have arranged Darbi's and H.'s schedules so that they didn't have to see each other all the time. They could have offered Darbi free counseling services and a tutor to help her catch up on any work she missed because of her anxiety. They could have investigated the allegation by interviewing Darbi, H., and anyone the two students had told about that night. (Those conversations may have easily resolved the matter: H. later admitted to the basic facts of the assault.) If the school determined that the evidence proved Darbi's claim, they could have suspended H. Even more importantly, Pennridge could have connected him with rehabilitative services to change the way he treated women and ensure Darbi would be his last victim. They could have assembled the whole school to learn about sexual respect.

Pennridge pursued none of these options. Instead, administrators told Darbi and her mom that the sexual assault was a police matter, not a concern for the school. It even put H. in the same study hall as Darbi and assigned her to the same lunch period as his friends, who continued to harass her. As a result, Darbi ended up missing months of high school. "If I got up the courage to go to school, by third period, I would just leave," she told a journalist. "I would break down and cry and go home. I probably spent one to two full days at school a week, and most of my days were spent either in a bathroom stall, covering my mouth and trying not to let people hear that I was crying, or in the guidance counselor's office, crying. . . . Every day was the same routine."

Darbi's GPA plummeted. She avoided the cafeteria, where she knew she'd see her harassers. She finished her sophomore year at home, trying to teach herself the material she should have learned in class, and then ultimately completed her junior year through an online school that didn't offer the advanced courses she should have taken. She was nominated for student council president but had to turn it down: she didn't feel safe enough to attend meetings at school.

I met Darbi when she called the National Women's Law Center for legal assistance. She was one of my first clients as a young attorney, and my colleagues and I represented her and two other young women in lawsuits against Pennridge. (The case settled before trial.) Pennridge was right, of course, that sexual assault is a crime. But it is also a threat to the victims' educations and opportunities—a threat that exacerbates and entrenches systemic inequalities.

SURVIVORS DO NOT feel or experience or mourn or suffer or heal as a group. They live as individuals, and their experiences of harm differ from one another. Violence marks us all in different ways, to different degrees.

Despite this variety of reactions, victims often speak in similar ways about how harassment stops them from living full lives, especially if they don't receive the support they need to feel safe. Unaddressed harassment forces them to withdraw from communities and opportunities they most value, and fundamentally shifts the way they move through the world. This harm is one that most women and gender-nonconforming people can understand. Anyone who has ever been catcalled or followed home from work knows how a stranger can make you feel like the streets do not equally belong to you. In the same way, survivors learn that their schools, their workplaces, and their communities are not theirs, either. This has material impacts on survivors' educations, careers, economic security, and even their freedom.

In Darbi's case, because she no longer felt safe at school, she had to finish her classes at home. That experience is all too common. While the problem is under-researched, data shows that over a third of college sexual assault survivors quit school. If they stay, they are less likely to participate in class discussion, and are more likely to avoid parts of the campus, skip class sessions, or drop a course. Their academic performance suffers. One study found that women who were raped in their first semester of college finished their freshman year with lower GPAs than those who were not; they were about 2.5 times more likely to end their first year with a GPA under 2.5. "These deflated GPAs have a rippling negative impact on survivor's graduate school options and access to professional opportunities," notes Cari Simon, a Title IX lawyer. "Those lost opportunities are devastating. . . . Individual students miss out on what they had worked hard to achieve." Sexual harassment in school, then, can depress a survivor's wages over their lifetime. Some victims lose scholarships when their GPAs decline, or end up saddled with student debt from degrees they were never able to complete.

A similar pattern can be seen among workers. According to a 2017 study, women who were sexually harassed at work were 6.5 times as likely to leave their job as their unharmed colleagues. Those victims often leave for a worse job with lower pay. And those who stay may be financially penalized as they struggle with the abuse and its aftermath. "Many women who experience sexual harassment at work report increased anxiety and depression, which is associated with lower productivity and poorer performance at work," explains a report by the National Partnership for Women and Families. Plus, "women in workplaces that do not address sexual harassment may feel less empowered to negotiate salaries and raises, depressing their long-term earnings and advancement."

Women are not the only ones to experience such effects. A man recently wrote to the *New York Times* about an incident that had occurred many years before. "I was on the receiving end of an unwelcome sexual advance," he wrote, "when an older man with whom I worked invited me to his apartment for lunch. I agreed, innocently enough, but when I saw that he had prepared a meal only for me, I quickly realized that I was to be his lunch. As his advances became more and more aggressive, I froze—couldn't move, couldn't speak— until he unzipped my fly, took my penis in his hand, and pulled it into his mouth. The shock of that sensation in that situation stimulated a fight-or-flight response, and I bolted for the door. I quit my job that afternoon so that I would never again encounter that man."

Beyond threatening their success at school and work, sexual harms put survivors' very liberty at stake. A startling number of women in prison are victims of sexual violence. A 2012 report commissioned by the Department of Justice concluded that 86 percent of women in jail had been sexually assaulted at least once in their lives; 77 percent had been abused by a partner. These trends start early. A 2006 study of girls involved in Oregon's juvenile justice system found that more than three in four had been sexually abused before they turned thirteen. (The rates among boys are not as high, but far too many boys in the juvenile justice system also have histories of sexual trauma.) No wonder advocates speak of a "sexual abuse to prison pipeline." The chain of causation between sexual assault and incarceration may not be as clear as the case of a worker who gets fired the day after turning down her boss's advances, but it is just as undeniable. Studies show that trauma—when unaddressed by proper support and treatment—can lead girls and women to drug and alcohol abuse, mental health struggles, and violent behavior. Young survivors may skip school to avoid their harassers, and then end up in trouble with the law for truancy or crimes of poverty.

Once inside a prison, survivors face a harrowing likelihood of further abuse. And when they leave, they must try to rebuild relationships, find an employer willing to hire a worker with a record, and secure housing, which may exclude people convicted of certain crimes. All the while they must grapple with the compounding traumas of abuse and incarceration. Those forms of instability—social isolation, poverty, homelessness, mental illness—in turn make them vulnerable to further violence.

The devastating effects of harassment on its individual victims thus combine to reinforce and exacerbate existing societal inequalities. The groups most vulnerable to harassment are those who already face marginalization. Women are sexually assaulted far more often than men are. Queer people and people who are transgender or non-binary (that is, those who do not identify as a man or a woman) are more likely to be sexually assaulted than their heterosexual or cisgender counterparts. People with disabilities are also subject to unusually high rates of sexual abuse. Native American women are assaulted at astronomical rates, double that of all other racial and ethnic groups. The population of women in prison, who are likely to suffer sexual abuse both before and during incarceration, is disproportionately made up of women of color. And between 2012 and 2016, Black women filed harassment complaints with the Equal Employment Opportunity Commission (EEOC) at nearly three times the rate as did white, non-Hispanic women.

Harassment compounds the obstacles that members of these marginalized groups already struggle to overcome. It systematically deprives them of educational opportunities—either because they feel unsafe at school, like Darbi, or because they become entrapped in the criminal legal system at a young age. The scars of discrimination accumulate and limit their entry points to the working world, itself still rife with harassment. In their jobs, workers from marginalized groups are denied by harassment the opportunities to build wealth and to climb up the ranks that their white, straight, cisgender male peers enjoy. That, in turn, means fewer women, queer people, trans people, and people of color in leadership positions, where they might shape policy and, if needed, support younger workers who face harassment themselves. The effect is generational. If Darbi's career is stunted by her deflated high school grades, who will pay for her daughters' educations? What lessons about who this world is for, and how they can expect to move through it, will they inherit? Over and over again, in all these different contexts, abuse operates in the same ways: it targets the vulnerable and keeps them vulnerable. Inequality ensures its own survival through violence.

WE RARELY HEAR these stories about survivors' lives after abuse. We read about the lurid details of back-alley rapes and "casting couch" coercion. But to the extent we think about the future, we focus entirely on the accused, debating whether their downfalls were deserved and what the terms of their redemption might be. Missing entirely are the years the victim lost following the harm, the costs large and small, what never came to be. Because the story stops when the assault is done, those lasting ramifications rarely factor into our understanding of the harm wrought by sexual harassment. I think often about an administrator at the prestigious Deerfield Academy who, according to a lawsuit filed against the school, told a young woman that the decision not to punish the boy who sexually assaulted her was based on "the very difficult choice" between "a boy's future and her feelings." As though only her *feelings* were at stake, and her own prospects—surely shaped by her assailant's continued presence in her small rural school—were of no consequence. As though only men get futures.

The erasure of victims is no accident. It is a direct result of the impact sexual harassment has had on so many, derailing their educations, careers, and rise to community leadership. When victims are excluded from public life, our world is shaped in their absence, by their absence. Legislative staffers tell of dropping out of politics because of rampant harassment in Washington and state houses. What laws were never passed because these survivors were not in the room? What could have been if they had kept their seats at the table? The actors blackballed by Weinstein, the comedians intimidated by Louis C.K., the women who left media after working for Charlie Rose—all these survivors lost the opportunity to tell their stories, to influence public consciousness. The result is that, in ways we will never appreciate, we have seen the world through Weinstein's lens but never theirs.

One might fairly ask: Why should we care about missing stories when the stakes are survival? But part of what violence does is rob us of the opportunity to do more than survive. To describe the world as we see it and build one where this does not happen again. To write our collective future.

That is the story not only of harassment but of inequality and injustice writ large. Some years back, the writer Reina Gattuso, then a student, wrote about wandering around her college library. Some-times, she wrote, walking through the stacks, "I feel the incredible pressure of the books that are not there":

There is a ghost [library] full of books that did not get written.

There is a book I did not write when I put all my energy into not-eating, and there is a book I did not write when I felt weird because I was in love with a girl. There is a book I didn't write when I was dodging sexual comments, and there is a book I didn't write when I was feeling inadequate for not receiving sexual comments. There is a book I didn't write when I was sick with what I thought was love.

There are books that you didn't write, either.

There are books you didn't write because you were waiting for someone to make a racist comment, and there were books you didn't write because someone made a racist comment. There were books you didn't write because you were trying to figure out if it was really a racist comment and everyone said you were being too sensitive, and you wondered if maybe you were.

There were books you didn't write because you are sensitive, because of course you are sensitive, because the half-slights and the full slights wear you down and all the books in you start rioting and say: Hey! I am a book! Let me out, let me out of here!

2

A Civil Right

In America, the middle of the twentieth century was marked by widespread protests against racial and sexual inequality. Slavery was over, as was the male-only vote. But discrimination persisted, ensuring that white men continued to dominate the public sphere—in politics, schools, workplaces, and elsewhere. Black people could not eat at a lunch counter or buy a house on equal footing. Women were not allowed to take out a credit card without their husband's permission or, in many states, serve on a jury.

Advocates called for the federal government to pass civil rights laws that would forbid such unequal treatment. Despite much resistance from white men (including many elected officials) eager to hold on to their power, in the 1960s and '70s Congress passed a series of important antidiscrimination statutes. Among these were the Civil Rights Act of 1964 and the Education Amendments of 1972. Together, these statutes officially prohibited sex and race discrimination in many workplaces and schools. It fell to the courts, though, to interpret these laws, defining exactly which forms of unfair treatment they do and do not cover. It took until 1986—not so long ago, really—for the Supreme Court to consider whether the scope of the civil rights laws encompasses sexual harassment.

Mechelle Vinson started work as a teller at a bank in 1974, when she was not yet twenty years old. She was hired by Sidney Taylor, a former janitor at the bank who had risen through the ranks to become manager. At first, Taylor acted "fatherly," providing Vinson advice and generous bonuses. The two sometimes ate dinner together at a local Chinese restaurant. It was there, Vinson testified, that Taylor first propositioned her. In a dodge familiar to many workers, Vinson deflected her boss's come-on, demurring while insisting she was grateful for all his help. "I don't want appreciation," Taylor reportedly replied. "I want to go to bed with you. . . . Just like I hired you, I'll fire you, and just like I made you, I'll break you, and if you don't do what I say then I'll have you killed." The threat worked. That night, in a motel room connected to the restaurant, Vinson, crying, lay "stiff like a board, almost like I was dead," as the man she depended on for her livelihood "did what he wanted to do."

The abuse intensified. When Vinson balked on later occasions, Taylor used more force to rape her, at least once injuring her to the point that she required medical care. Vinson's appetite disappeared, her hair began falling out, and she could not sleep—but she saw no way out. She needed the job. Besides, even if she could have afforded to leave, Taylor continued to threaten to kill her if she did not obey his orders. She had no reason to believe he would not follow through.

Given that very real fear, it's all the more remarkable that, after connecting by chance with a sympathetic lawyer, Vinson sued the bank. Through Taylor's harassment, she said, her employer had violated civil rights law. Shortly after she filed the lawsuit, she was fired; the bank insisted she had misused her sick leave.

Despite the severity of the abuse, it was not obvious Vinson would win her case. At the time, courts were still grappling with a then novel theory identifying sexual harassment as a form of discrimination. Even if a court believed every word Vinson said, it might still determine that nothing the bank had done was against the law.

ONE OF VINSON'S attorneys was Catharine MacKinnon, a pioneer in trying to convince scholars and courts that sexual harassment was a form of illegal discrimination. Shortly after graduating from Smith College in 1969, MacKinnon had enrolled in Yale's graduate program in political science, and then also in its law school. New Haven, a working-class industrial city that plays host to a liberal university, was fertile ground for the feminist projects of the 1960s and '70s. Consciousness-raising groups, which gave women of all backgrounds a chance to discuss how private indignities connected to larger inequalities, were a key element of the women's movement. In one of those groups, MacKinnon heard stories from female secretaries about abuses they suffered at the hands of their male employers, a long-accepted practice that had only just started to become known as "sexual harassment."

Those accounts, among others, inspired what eventually became MacKinnon's first book, published just two years after her graduation from Yale Law. *Sexual Harassment of Working Women* introduced lawyers and legal academics to a new vision of workplace abuses as a civil rights violation. Sexual harassment, MacKinnon proposed, came in two often overlapping forms: quid pro quo harassment, where workers were offered professional advancement (or safety from professional retaliation) for sexual favors; and "hostile environment" harassment, where sexually demeaning behavior, comments, and attitudes pervade the workplace.

The theoretical heavy lifting of MacKinnon's book builds on a couple of key premises. First, she stressed the importance of power and social context for understanding harassment. A judge or juror might be tempted to view abuse like Taylor's as an inherently private matter, a dispute between a young woman and her disappointed suitor in which courts should not intervene. But sexual harassment occurs in a world dominated by men, in spaces and situations where men so often have outsize influence and power, especially over subordinates.

Second, and relatedly, MacKinnon argued that victims were targeted for sexual harassment "on the basis of sex." This was critical as a legal matter, because Title VII of the Civil Rights Act of 1964 only made it unlawful for an employer to discriminate against an employee "because of such individual's race, color, religion, sex, or national origin." Other civil rights laws also focused only on such special aspects of a person's identity. Discrimination based on something else—a person's musical tastes, for example—just isn't the concern of civil rights legislation, no matter how abusive or distasteful it may be.

It might seem obvious from statistics about sexual harassment (as described in the previous chapter) that it has a disproportionate impact on girls and women. But as a technical legal matter, that wasn't enough. MacKinnon needed to show that when a woman was harassed, she was harassed *because she was a woman*. To do so, MacKinnon argued that sexual harassment expresses and reinforces social meanings of what it means to be a woman or a man. In other words, when Taylor harassed Vinson, he did so because he understood women to be first and foremost sexual objects, not workers. And in making her employment contingent on sex, he solidified those social meanings, "perpetuat[ing] the interlocked structure by which women have been kept sexually in thrall to men and at the bottom of the labor market."

In the decades since the publication of *Sexual Harassment of Working Women*, other feminist theorists have built on MacKinnon's work, offering various additional theories that explain why sexual harassment is a form of sex discrimination. In my view, the diversity of these academic opinions underscores just how many forms discrimination can take. Some scholars make the commonsense observation that gender is often a key element in sexual desire—that is, when an abusive boss desires women, he will not attempt to sleep with his secretary unless she is a woman. Other theorists elaborate on MacKinnon's central observation that sexual harassment serves to reinforce a gendered hierarchy. They emphasize the connection between sexual harassment and sex-based stereotypes of all kinds—a helpful framework for understanding harassment against people of all genders. After all, everyone, not just women, faces sexist stereotypes about how they "should" act.

As law professor Katherine Franke puts it, "sexual harassment is a technology of sexism." It is both an *example* of sex discrimination and a *tool* to further entrench gender-based roles. And that tool can work in different ways to put victims "in their place." The "sex" in sexual harassment might be clearest in a case like Vinson's, where a male boss saw his female employee not as a full human or valuable colleague but as a means of gratification. The resulting abuse served to push Vinson out of the workplace and into women's traditional sphere, the home. Not all sexual harassment, though, centers on sexual desire. For example, some women, especially those in male-dominated fields, are subjected to sexually explicit comments not as expressions of lust but as a means of showing them that they do not belong in the workplace, a man's domain.

Take the experience of Barbara Steiner, the first female floor manager at a Las Vegas casino. The industry was characterized by a strict gendered hierarchy, with men comfortably at the top. Female employees were seen first and foremost as objects of desire, and required to dress the part. Even though Steiner had been promoted into a traditionally masculine position, her male manager called her gendered epithets and yelled that she was "not a fucking floor man"—even though being a "floor person" was, quite literally, her job. "You are a fucking casino host," he told her. "Why don't you go in the restaurant and suck their dicks?" As Franke explains, "What made it sex discrimination, was . . . that he used sexual harassment to put Steiner in her 'proper place,' thereby diminishing her authority and role as a floor person. In this sense, the sexual harassment feminized

Steiner, rendering her less competent and more sexual, while at the same time it masculinized the male supervisor as someone who possessed both the will and the power to render his female subordinate a sex object." To borrow from the philosopher Kate Manne, this kind of misogynistic harassment "primarily targets women because they are women in a *man's world*."

And it's not only women who suffer. People of all genders may be sexually harassed because they do not conform to gendered expectations. Non-binary people may be harassed because their very existence challenges the whole framework: they fit in neither box. Men may be sexually harassed by colleagues who think they are insufficiently masculine. In one case in Illinois, a man who worked at a paper plant was targeted because he lived at home with his mother and blushed easily when the other men talked about sex. As Franke puts it, "By asserting their proper masculinity through . . . sexual harassment, [the victim's] male coworkers humiliated him because he held a man's job without acting manly."

VINSON LOST HER case at the trial level, and appealed it all the way up to the Supreme Court. In the meantime, some lower courts considering other suits ruled that sexual harassment *was* sex discrimination. Other judges, as the attorney Gillian Thomas puts it in her book *Because of Sex*, had "responded to complaints about abusive bosses with a collective shrug that conveyed, 'You can't blame a guy for trying.'"

Confusion reigned until the Supreme Court stepped in and decided Vinson's case. In an important victory, the court unambiguously acknowledged sexual harassment as a form of sex discrimination, a civil rights violation. Its opinion recognized that abuses like the ones Vinson survived are not only crimes but also threats to equality and dignity. As a result, the court made clear, employers are required to do their part in stopping harassment and addressing its impact on the victim after it occurs. Six years later, in a different case, the Supreme Court extended its reasoning to the context of schools: it held that Title IX, which prohibits sex discrimination in educational programs that receive federal funding, requires schools to respond to sexual harassment as part of their general legal responsibility to ensure gender equality.

In ruling for Vinson, the Supreme Court relied in part on the better-established principle that racial harassment constituted race-based discrimination for purposes of Title VII and similar laws. That analogy reflected the insights of civil rights pioneer Pauli Murray, who had first argued that sex discrimination suits could be modeled on race discrimination claims. MacKinnon had noted this parallel in *Sexual Harassment of Working Women* and then again as a part of Vinson's legal team, and feminist groups drew the same analogy in "friend of the court" briefs filed in support of Vinson. It's meaningful that a Black woman, Vinson, was the plaintiff whose case established that antidiscrimination law prohibits sexual harassment: the fight for gender justice has been inextricably tied to the fight for racial justice, and Black women have led the way.

With all that said, the Supreme Court's opinion in Vinson's case was far from perfect. It stated that a complainant's "sexually provocative speech or dress" were "obviously relevant" to whether "he or she found particular sexual advances unwelcome"—an invitation for courts to blame victims for their treatment. The court also rejected Vinson's argument that the bank was automatically liable for Taylor's misconduct because he was the bank's employee and manager. Instead, Vinson had to prove that the bank had failed to intervene to stop the abuse. As a result, today the general rule is that an employer is only liable for harassment about which it actually knew or should have known, and which it fails to address—a requirement that frequently allows employers who operate hostile work environments to avoid liability. The court's test for Title IX claims is even less friendly to victims. A student can only win their suit if the school had "actual knowledge" of the abuse and was "deliberately indifferent," which excuses school responses that are poor but not "clearly unreasonable." Obviously, the Supreme Court hasn't ended sexual harassment—both because it has invented ungenerous standards and because, ultimately, there is only so much that law can do. As an attorney, I am under no illusion that courts alone will save us.

Still, Vinson's win and its Title IX sequel were major victories, especially given the alternatives for survivors. Without the Supreme Court's rulings, many victims would have no legal recourse at all. This is partly because a lot of sexual harassment—especially verbal abuse—does not violate any criminal law. A boss who subtly conditions an employee's promotion on a date is likely not committing a crime. Neither is the student who sits behind a classmate's desk every day and makes explicit, sexualized comments about his body. But even where sexual harm is a criminal offense, most violations never lead to prosecution. Of sexual assaults that are reported to the police, only about 20 percent lead to an arrest and around 4 percent are referred to prosecutors. Those rates do not reflect how many victims want their case to move forward. Rather, the issue is that survivors don't get to decide what comes of their police reports.

As I noted before, a criminal case is brought by the government, not the victim. In other words, it is a contest between the state and the defendant. The victim is, at most, an important witness, not a party to the case. She does not get to determine whether and how the case proceeds, and she typically doesn't receive any kind of personal remedy if the defendant is convicted: he goes to jail, while she attempts to struggle on with her life. The intent of prosecution is to vindicate the state's interests, not to assure the survivor's well-being. Under American legal theory, the four purposes of a criminal prosecution are supposed to be retribution (making sure the wrongdoer gets what he deserves), rehabilitation (helping the convicted become a law-abiding member of society), deterrence (discouraging the defendant and others from violating the law in the future), and incapacitation (separating the defendant from society so he can't offend again for some time). The welfare of the victim simply is not in that mix.

In contrast, a civil rights case is usually brought by the victim. She gets to decide whether to initiate the lawsuit and, with her attorney, makes strategic calls about how to proceed. Brought against an institution, such a suit also offers remedies that the criminal prosecution of individual wrongdoers cannot. Not every victim wants her assailant to go to prison, and even those who do may also have other needs and goals that punishment alone can't serve. If a survivor wins a civil rights suit, the court may order the institution to take specific actions—for instance, reinstating an employee who lost her job when she spoke up about her boss's harassment. The court can also order the institution to make bigger, systemic improvements that will help others avoid harassment, such as changes to company policies. And that is to say nothing about the significant financial awards that a judge or jury may order the defending institution to pay a victim. Those damages can go toward therapy or other medical expenses, allow her to pay off debts incurred after leaving work or school, and help her get back to her life. (While monetary support is sometimes available through the criminal justice system, it's usually only as compensation for a set of specific expenses victims may incur as a result of the crime.)

Theoretically, before Vinson's case established sexual harassment as a civil rights violation, victims could have brought a different kind of civil suit: a "tort" claim for money damages, either against an institution or against the individual assailant. A tort is what many people think of when they picture a classic civil proceeding—the lawsuit that follows after person A injures person B with their car, or with medical malpractice, or with a public lie. Because torts are civil, not criminal, claims, a victim gets to stay in charge of the case. But there are a number of reasons a survivor might prefer to file a civil rights suit instead of a tort claim. Chief among these is that tort laws, like criminal laws, are very focused on the assault itself, but don't have much to say about what institutions have to do to remedy that harm after it occurs. If Darbi's school had *caused* her assault, for example, it might have been on the hook under tort law. But because Darbi challenged the school's failure to protect her education *after* the rape, she needed a civil rights statute. Plus, in some states, public institutions like schools are immune from tort suits altogether.

Instead of suing an institution, a victim could always try to bring a tort claim against an individual perpetrator. (By contrast, civil rights claims under Title IX and Title VII only permit suits against the school or workplace.) But tort suits only cover a narrow set of physical harms, and rarely result in remedies beyond money damages. Even financial awards might prove elusive, since individual defendants, unlike institutions, often simply can't afford to pay out a significant sum. A jury's verdict ordering the defendant to pay the victim, then, could be a symbolic victory only. For that reason, it can be hard for a survivor to find a lawyer for a tort suit against her harasser if he doesn't happen to be rich. Civil rights suits, in contrast, go after institutions that often have deep pockets or insurance. And civil rights laws include special provisions to provide financial compensation for attorneys to encourage them to take on these important cases.

VINSON'S HARASSMENT KEPT her from being able to do her job. It threatened her and her economic livelihood. It deprived her of the opportunity to show up at work on the same footing as everyone else. In fighting back, she proved that sexual harassment is a civil rights issue, a profound injustice for individual victims and for society.

For me, learning to think about responses to sexual harms outside the criminal system isn't just about the mechanics of law. It's a philosophical shift. Earlier, I observed how rarely we hear about survivors' lives after harassment. Instead, we focus on the assailant and his punishment alone. We fail to center survivors in their own stories, in the action of their own lives. As I see it, this is a criminal law mindset: the victim falls out of the picture, just like in a criminal prosecution. Thinking about sexual harassment as not just a crime but also a civil rights issue expands our view. Social justice movements fought for civil rights legislation to root out inequality, both to help wronged individuals rebuild their lives and to end systemic injustice. So when we approach sexual harassment as a matter of civil rights, we see violence in its full context—the circumstances that give rise to it, the material impact it has on survivors, and the effects that ripple out afterward. We are guided not by the state's simplistic thirst for punishment, but by what victims need to ameliorate the harm and build a more just world.

I think we should bring the civil rights lens to every question about harassment, whether it be how to design a smart policy or how to best support a friend. As I see it, our communities and institutions can choose to embrace the values that motivate civil rights legislation, or they can adopt criminal law's narrow, punitive approach. Consider Darbi's story. All of us should want H. to understand that what he did was wrong and, yes, to be held accountable. But if all we did was punish him, we would lose the chance to provide Darbi with what she needed to learn and thrive in the wake of the assault. We would also lose an opening to teach students to treat each other with respect—a lesson that would serve H. and his friends well as they become adults. And we would squander the chance to make sure Pennridge students never face obstacles to learning because of their gender, so that all of them can go into the world with the same education, opportunities, confidence, and recognized dignity.

What Institutions Can Do

The Supreme Court opinion in Vinson's case opened up the courthouse for survivors. But its most important effect was to tell institutions what they had to do to avoid a lawsuit: address sexual harassment allegations internally, just as they dealt with other forms of discrimination. If they did not, they could face a suit like Vinson's. In response, human resources departments in companies and Title IX offices in schools have built structured grievance processes. These are not part of the court system, but they are required by law.

Grievance procedures can take many different forms, but many readers who have worked at a job or attended school will have seen some version of how an institution can look into misconduct (sexual or not). Often, designated personnel conduct a formal investigation. This usually involves giving each party the opportunity to tell their side of the story. Interviews by HR or an outside investigator, as well as written statements, frequently follow. Generally, witnesses identified by the two parties will be questioned, too, and any available evidence—text messages or medical records, for example—will be reviewed. If the allegation is determined to be true, internal decision-makers will develop a plan, which might include both support for the victim and consequences for the perpetrator. Depending on the underlying conduct, that sanction may be fairly minor, like a note in a record or a transfer out of the survivor's department. For more severe misconduct, the institution might decide that suspension or termination is the appropriate remedy, especially if that's the only way to keep the community safe and for the victim to stay in school or on the job. Many employers and schools also offer informal processes that give victims an opportunity to ask for help without triggering an investigation or any repercussions for the assailant. For example, a victim might be allowed to change her shift so she doesn't have to see her harassing boss, or a student might be provided free mental health services. The through line: these remedies, varied and flexible, seek to ameliorate the threat harassment poses to equality.

Addressing serious, even criminal misconduct like sexual assault might seem like a heavy responsibility for a workplace or school. But these institutions didn't need to start from scratch when Vinson won her case. Even where civil rights law doesn't require it, institutions have always had to make decisions about allegations of misconduct within their ranks. If an employee punched a coworker or a customer in the face, all of us would be surprised if the bosses shrugged it off and just told the victim to report the incident to the police. That punch may be illegal, but it also threatens the healthy functioning of the company. The victim may want assurance that if he shows up tomorrow, he won't be punched again. Without that guarantee, talented employees might quit; customers might stay far away. All that unchecked punching would ultimately hurt the bottom line. From the company's perspective, the problem isn't just that a law was broken: it's that the conduct is bad for the group.

In other words, even setting aside any legal requirements, employers and educators have their own interest in ensuring a safe community where everyone can do what they came there to do, like work or study. As a result, they regularly investigate allegations of all kinds to determine what happened and who was responsible, and then make decisions about what should be done as a result, including whether someone should be sanctioned. "They have disciplinary codes, and they enforce them in all areas, and they need to keep doing that," Naomi Shatz, a lawyer who represents employees and students on both sides of sexual harassment allegations, told me. "The same way employers have handbooks and rules, and say, 'Okay, this is a smoke-free work environment,' they can decide what happens in their workplace and then enforce that."

Speaking of smoke: during my last year of high school, a bunch of kids set a trash can on fire in our "senior lounge," a section of the cafeteria with beat-up couches and a PlayStation. The school investigated who was responsible by talking to witnesses and looking at camera footage, and then suspended the students who were involved, independent of any criminal arson prosecution. Regardless of whether that was the appropriate punishment—it seems a bit harsh to me in retrospect—of course administrators had to do *something*: you can't really have a school where kids freely go around setting things on fire. The same goes for less serious forms of misconduct, like sharing answers to a Spanish quiz, and also more serious transgressions, like physical violence. The school's interest in intervening would have been even higher if the students' pyromania had threatened their classmates' civil right to learn free from discrimination—if, say, they had set crosses, rather than trash cans, aflame.

At most schools and workplaces, internal rules may reflect some definitions drawn from the law. They might say, for example, that sexual harassment is "unwanted conduct of a sexual nature" that is "severe or pervasive." But the policies will also usually encompass some behaviors that, on their own, would be unlikely to give rise to a successful criminal action or civil suit. The policies are there to define what is acceptable within the community, and some forms of misconduct—such as plagiarism or low-level harassment—may be legal but still not internally acceptable.

Where internal rules and external laws do overlap, a sexual

harassment victim doesn't have to choose between legal options and reporting to the institution. He could, for instance, simultaneously report to the police seeking criminal charges, initiate a civil suit against his assailant for money damages, and file a complaint with HR to make sure he'll be safe at work. These systems all operate independently and serve different goals. And because each option provides different remedies, a victim can decide to cobble together something that feels like justice to him, or at least like a decent way to get back on his feet.

THERE ARE PLENTY of reasons why a sexual harassment victim might want to use an institution's internal procedures in addition to, or instead of, external legal options. For one, in many cases—I'd wager *most*—they are the only option available. A police report will probably never result in charges, and many victims cannot afford to hire a lawyer for a civil suit against the assailant. What's more, criminal prosecutions and tort suits can take years. By the time a legal action is resolved, a worker may have left her job because of her abusive boss, and a student might have graduated—that is, if she managed not to drop out. In contrast, schools and workplaces have to respond in some way to every report, and they can do so quickly. Of course, these institutions don't always live up to their responsibilities, and I'll talk more later about their failures. But plenty do get it right, at least in part.

Perhaps most importantly, institutions can provide community-specific protections and remedies a court cannot. Usually, the only remedy a criminal trial can offer is incarceration, and victory in a tort suit against a harasser almost always means just money damages. An institution, by contrast, can't lock up an abuser or order him to pay his victim. But it can do so much else. A school can give a student an extension on the paper due the week after she was raped. It can make sure to never schedule her and her attacker in the same class or lunch period. An HR office can assign a worker to a new supervisor so he doesn't have to depend on his harasser for a promotion. Prosecution and lawsuits simply cannot provide these kinds of swift, flexible, and light-touch solutions.

Even when significant sanctions are needed to keep the victim and community safe, many survivors prefer the ones available to an institution rather than (or in addition to) punishment by a court. Many victims are uninterested in criminal prosecution in the first place, as I'll discuss more in the next chapter. A worker might want the boss who raped her to be fired but not sent to prison. Only her employer can help her achieve that.

I spoke to a number of survivors for whom relatively small accommodations made a world of difference. Tara Tyrrell, a college classmate of mine, told me she was "definitely" glad she was able to report a classmate who sexually assaulted her to a school authority. When her assailant refused to leave her dorm room, she and her roommate initially contacted campus police. But she feared a lengthy criminal investigation and worried that she would be an unsympathetic victim: she had been drinking the night of the assault, and had flirted with the guy before their encounter turned violent. So in the wake of her assault, she turned to a man she had shared dinners with in the dining hall and already thought of as an ally: the dean of the dorm where she and her assailant lived. What Tara most appreciated was that the dean laid out her options—pursuing criminal charges, formally reporting to the university's disciplinary system, having the dean confront the assailant more informally, or some combination—and let her choose the path she wanted to take. At her request, the dean spoke to the classmate, who quickly confessed and expressed remorse. Because he was willing to accept responsibility, Tara was satisfied with the dean requiring the man to attend counseling, and did not pursue a disciplinary investigation. Looking back, Tara told me, she thinks she may have chosen a nonpunitive response out of misplaced concern for the man who had hurt her. But she's still glad the choice was hers, and that she had been able to pursue it within a community she trusted.

The benefits of a familiar system separate from the police also meant a lot to another woman, whom I'll call Selena. In her junior year of college, she was assaulted by an ex-boyfriend after she broke up with him. The man graduated that semester, but came back to campus often and frequently contacted her. Seeing him gave her panic attacks, and she started to avoid her dorm's dining hall out of fear of encountering him. So she spoke to her dean, who connected her to the college's sexual harassment response office. Selena told me repeatedly that she felt grateful that school administrators were generous with their time and explained her options; she trusted them. She chose to pursue a remedy through the school because she could "retain ownership" over the process. "Having an institution that wasn't the law was actually really meaningful," she told me, "both because the process felt perhaps more connected to me personally and also because I have trust in the system in the way I might not if there are just a bunch of cops taking my underwear to test." The school eventually worked out an arrangement in which her ex would be able to visit the university but not her dorm. "It took me years of therapy to come to terms with my assault and not have a panic attack at the mere mention of the guy's name," she told me. "If there hadn't been an institutional capacity to help me feel safe on campus again, I'm not sure I would have completed my degree. I can't help but feel grateful that institutions can and do respond to assault cases like mine."

A woman named Megan shared with me her account of reporting sexual harassment in the male-dominated audiovisual field in which she worked. She had seen her boss harass other employees before, and had tried to tolerate it. When he loudly remarked on the color of her bra and asked Megan if she was wearing "matching panties," she felt shaken. "I was humiliated," she remembers. "I started spending twenty extra minutes each morning getting dressed, ensuring there was no way to even catch a glimpse of my undergarments. I began having anxiety attacks driving to the office and couldn't wait to get out of there every day." The boss kept up his harassment, and a friend convinced Megan to report the incidents to the company's vice president, whom she knew and liked. She worried her boss would get off easy, and that she would have to continue working with a man who not only harassed her but knew she had reported him. But after interviews with Megan, coworker witnesses, and the boss, the company fired him. "While going to work didn't get immediately easier," she says, "it got better every day."

A man who worked in a restaurant kitchen told me about his experience of being harassed by a chef there, much higher up in the workplace hierarchy. He had no idea what to do. "Someone else reported it," he told me, "saying it made them very uncomfortable, and I'm glad they spoke up. That chef was disciplined and apologized to me, and nothing like that ever happened again. If not for that random unknown coworker, who knows what would've happened." Another food service worker told me that after she reported that a colleague had rubbed himself against her inappropriately, she spoke with the restaurant's owner. She requested a shift change, which the owner immediately granted. Eventually, the harasser was fired, she told me. "I was really impressed that they took me so seriously," she remembers.

I also heard likely rarer, but equally moving stories: people accused of sexual harassment who told me an institutional response had changed their behavior for the better. One, a nurse named Mike, told me, "Having an individual go to HR with a detailed complaint was the best thing that happened to me. I cooperated, answered truthfully, and was fired. I took time, worked on things, and I'm a fundamentally healthier person than I was before, and I would not act in the ways I have in the past." Another man who was accused of harassment as a young student found the process deeply painful, but also told me it spurred him to rethink how he treated others.

FORMAL INSTITUTIONS WITH legal responsibilities, like schools and workplaces, are not the only ones who respond to sexual harassment. Some religious congregations, for example, have their own policies for handling complaints. And more casual groups have been making efforts to establish such policies as well. Gotham Volleyball, a recreational LGBTQ volleyball league in New York, includes an anti-harassment policy in its league bylaws. I have found similar efforts by dance clubs, labor unions, commercial gyms, and amateur biking clubs. In my experience, these groups may lack the technical skill of an HR specialist, but are more likely to respond out of genuine care, because the community is motived by a commitment greater than mere legal obligation.

Some of the most interesting efforts come from activist and political groups. In 2017, for example, the Democratic Socialists of America passed an anti-harassment policy in order "to ensure," as the resolution explained, "that everyone is able to organize without fear of harassment, abuse, or harm." The document explained what kind of behavior might constitute harassment: for example, "unwelcome attention," "slurs or jokes," and "inappropriate physical contact or proximity" might cross the line if "such conduct has the purpose or effect of creating a hostile environment interfering with the individual's capacity to organize with DSA." And it laid out a process by which complaints would be received. Each DSA chapter with over one hundred members was required to appoint "harassment grievance officers" to accept complaints and investigate them if the accused denies the allegations. The officers would also produce regular reports outlining, in general terms, how many complaints were received and how many resulted in disciplinary action. Remedies for wrongdoing might include expulsion from DSA, but the policy suggested first considering other alternatives, such as removal from leadership positions and the creation of a plan for the wrongdoer to stop his damaging behavior. As I'll discuss later, the organization's implementation of this policy has come under criticism as lackluster. But, at least on paper, the process is thoughtful, fair, and well suited for DSA's decentralized model—an important first step.

Reading the DSA policy, I recognized a name among the drafters: Allison Hrabar, whose work as a college Title IX activist I had followed years before. When I reached out to her, Hrabar readily acknowledged that her experience working to reform her school's internal procedures informed the way she approached helping to create DSA's policy. But she also stressed to me that while the DSA drafters drew inspiration from harassment law, they deliberately sought to go beyond it. They began by copying language from the Equal Employment Opportunity Commission (EEOC) reflecting what kinds of harassment are prohibited by federal civil rights law—for example, harassment based on race, sex, and disability. "And then we said, what is missing?" Hrabar told me. They added prohibitions on harassment based on class, profession, and physical appearance, to acknowledge harms that civil rights laws do not (yet) recognize.

Hrabar told me that the need for a DSA harassment policy was obvious to her from the time she joined the organization. "When you are sexually assaulted or when you are harassed . . . and you say what are my options, going to the police is rarely the best option on the list, it's usually one of the poorer options. So a lot of people go to their institution," Hrabar noted, drawing analogies to her experience as a student advocate. "And they say 'I don't really want to report my professor, or my classmate, or my boyfriend to the police. I want to deal with it through this common institution we have. . . .' And I think DSA is very similar. DSA is a large political organization with 50,000 people, but we're also a social organization. We're people who see each other a lot; we're people who drink together; we're people who live together. So I think an institutional response to that, as opposed to having to go to the police on your neighbor or friend or comrade, was a natural choice."

In part, the commitment to expanding support options for survivors reflected the DSA's own ideology. "The entire idea of DSA is that we want a socialist nation because it will make people free from harm," Hrabar explained. "If you're being discriminated against, that's obviously the opposite of being liberated." But in addition to the lofty political goals, the policy was also deeply practical. The drafters wanted to ensure, Hrabar said, that "the people who are doing the work" don't find themselves having to leave the group "because they're being discriminated [against], assaulted, harassed." DSA has not yet achieved that goal. But it has rightly taken on the responsibility to do so.

Hrabar and DSA are part of a long tradition of political communities looking to put their values into practice when it comes to responding to sexual harms outside of the criminal legal system. This work had been pioneered by radical grassroots groups led by women of color, many of which are committed simultaneously to stopping interpersonal violence, especially within intimate relationships, and to ending abusive policing and incarceration.

A particularly encouraging case study comes from women of color organizers at Communities Against Rape and Abuse (CARA), a project based in Seattle that helped local groups respond to internal reports of sexual harm. A young woman named Marisol turned to CARA for support after she was sexually assaulted by Juan, a fellow member of Unido—a Chicano rights activist group—while the two were at a conference. Soon after, Marisol learned that Juan had abused other women within Unido's ranks. With CARA's guidance, Marisol organized a plan alongside her fellow Unido survivors "to confront Unido's largely male leadership about the problem of sexual violence in general and Juan's behavior specifically."

Because of the negative effects the criminal system had in their community, the activists did not want to pursue criminal prosecution. The young women instead demanded "that Juan step down from leadership positions in Unido, that he pursue counseling and that his friends support him to go to appropriate counseling, and that Unido pursue intensive educational work on sexual violence." Unido's leadership agreed on all counts and made good on those commitments. The leadership also decided to prioritize ending sexual assault as part of Unido's national agenda.

I want to be very, very clear: the community-based, transformative, explicitly anti-carceral efforts by radical communities of color are in no way interchangeable with the kinds of practices I mainly focus on in this book, such as workplace HR proceedings, simply because they all occur outside the courts. To overdraw the parallel would be an insult to a rich radical tradition, and an obvious false equivalence. CARA was motivated by deep political commitments; HR departments are invested in avoiding liability, and generally focus on investigating individual allegations rather than instigating broader community change. Yet to ignore the influence of CARA and similar groups on the work of DSA and others today would be to erase vital history. And institutions would do well to draw inspiration from the way that radical groups, past and present alike, seek transformation and broad accountability.

I GOT TO see an informal institutional response in practice when my brother Jason's science fiction society dealt with an abuse accusation by one member against another. The Harvard-Radcliffe Science Fiction Association was a big part of Jason's college years. He met many of his lifelong friends there; he met his now wife; and he found a home of like-minded gamers, who could together celebrate passions that hadn't been shared by others back home. Many members were queer or trans and used the group's role-playing games as opportunities to experiment with different genders and sexualities. The community was important enough that Jason and other HRSFA members continued to regularly meet up after college graduation.

A few years ago, Jason was serving as the president of HRSFA's alumni association, HRSFANS. During his tenure, a woman whom I will call Monica reported to him that a fellow member had sexually abused her. Monica considers herself "weird" but does not identify as a "geek," as some other members do. And parts of geek culture turned her off. "There's this idea that you have to invite everyone and everyone's quirks must be tolerated," she told me. "There's a positive version of this. You have a bunch of people who don't quite fit anywhere, and here's a place where they can go and people are happy for them to be kind of weird. But the flip side to that is the things that count in this umbrella of weird properties . . . including men being kind of creepy at women." Men making women uncomfortable was often dismissed as just a blameless lack of social skills. "There's the agreement they seem to make with each other: I won't tell you to change if you don't tell me to change," Monica explained. "But some kinds of change are good."

Still, Monica stayed in the HRSFANS orbit. She liked many of the members. Their events, including the big annual conference and frequent house parties, were a good way to see some of her closest friends.

Monica later told me that Simon had always creeped her out. (I have changed his name to protect the privacy of all involved.) He was never good with boundaries. Once, she recalled, when she wore a backless dress to a party, Simon approached her from behind and ran his hand up her bare back. Other members, however, including her then boyfriend, encouraged her to take Simon's behavior in stride. Sure, Simon was odd, they said, but he was harmless. Plus, he was married, and although many HRSFANS members were polyamorous, he was a vocal proponent of monogamy.

Or, at least, he was a *public* proponent of monogamy. Simon decided he wanted a relationship with Monica. They lived in different states and rarely saw each other, but, she recounted, Simon started to message her constantly, contacting her at all hours. She wasn't interested, but that did little to discourage him. In retrospect, Monica realized she had little practice shutting down men. She had been taught since childhood that it would be rude to do so.

In the lead-up to HRSFA's annual convention, Simon proposed they share a hotel room. The prospect made Monica nervous, but when he promised he wouldn't try to have sex with her, she agreed. Once they were there, though, Simon propositioned her; she relented, unenthusiastically. Then, in the middle of the night, she woke up to Simon masturbating over her face. She had not consented to this. Monica couldn't tell if Simon had realized she had woken up—and she was afraid that if he did, the incident might escalate. So she "played dead," as she later put it.

Monica never considered reporting the masturbation to the police or filing a civil suit. She knew that few would see her as a "perfect victim": she was sexually active, had struggled with her mental health, and had agreed to share a room with Simon and then have sex with him. But, concerned for the HRSFANS community, she felt she had to do *something*. So she wrote up her experience with Simon and sent it out to the HRSFANS board and membership.

When Monica's message went out, the board had recently started to draft an anti-harassment policy and grievance procedure. Suddenly, their task became much more urgent. Putting their brand-new process to the test, they solicited a statement from Simon, and gave both him and Monica a chance to object in writing to any points contained in the other's account. Then the board invited the larger community (which was already clued in to the allegations) to provide any other relevant information. In response, it received reports of other women's experiences with Simon, which pointed to a pattern of bad behavior. As with Monica's report, Simon was given the opportunity to deny or rebut these accounts. Ultimately, the board decided Simon posed a threat to its membership and banned him from HRSFANS events for ten years.

Monica was happy with the result. No longer would the community vouch for a misbehaving man, and no longer would he be able to hurt others in their ranks. "I would do it again," she told me about going through the process, although she hopes she never has to. Despite Simon's absence, she does not plan to attend further HRSFANS events, either. But she hopes she left the community better than she found it.

Why Not the Police?

Those of us who advocate for student survivors' Title IX rights will tell you the question we get asked the most, bar none, is why schools have any business responding to rape reports, beyond perhaps placing a call to 911. That was, of course, the reaction of Darbi's principal at Pennridge, too. The association between rape and the police is so strong that a survivor's decision not to file a criminal report is often seen as evidence that they're lying. In 2018, when Christine Blasey Ford accused then Supreme Court nominee Brett Kavanaugh of sexually assaulting her when the two were teenagers, many, including the president, cited the fact that she had not made a criminal complaint as evidence that her account was not trustworthy.

I get the instinct. As an undergrad, I applied to a summer job at a New York nonprofit that provides legal services to domestic violence victims. I don't remember much about the interview, but one moment has stuck with me. The attorney I hoped would hire me spoke about the kinds of help they offer spouses fleeing domestic abuse. I naively commented, *Of course, you tell them to report to the police.* I was surprised by her answer: *No.* Sometimes, she explained, that is not the right choice. I did not get the job.

For me, the exchange illustrates how even those with the best intentions can misunderstand survivors' needs and overstate the usefulness of the criminal legal system. By the time of my interview, I knew from my studies that sexual assault is the most underreported serious crime: only 23 percent of sexual assaults are reported to the police, compared to over 60 percent of batteries and robberies. And I had, by that point, experienced sexual harms myself, and had not once considered calling the police. Nevertheless, it seemed obvious to me that reporting was the right course for someone else. It took years of work with survivors for me to understand why they—why we—do not come forward in the ways everyone else tends to expect. I had viewed a victim's choice not to seek police help as a mistake, if an understandable one. But I have learned that it is, instead, a decision based on a reasoned cost-benefit analysis about what good, and what harm, might come from the criminal legal system.

For the majority of survivors, criminal law is an incomplete and sometimes dangerous "solution" to rely on in the wake of violence. I've discussed some of the reasons already. Perhaps most importantly, there are plenty of remedies that police and prosecutors simply cannot provide, and not everyone wants to see their assailant in prison. Plus, much sexual harassment (for example, most verbal abuse) does not violate any criminal laws. And many victims prefer to turn to an institution they already know and trust.

But there's also another fundamental mistake made by the people who instinctively assume that we should leave sexual harms to the criminal legal system: they assume, as I did during that ill-fated interview, that police and prosecutors serve sexual violence victims well. That common belief, though, could not be further from the truth. When survivors report, they often face skepticism, abuse, and even the risk of imprisonment, all for a minuscule shot at some imperfect vision of justice. To even try to cover all of the ways criminal law fails victims would take a book of its own (as the many existing books on the topic show). But I'd like to discuss, at least briefly, some of the most notable issues.

TO BEGIN WITH, victims who turn to the police in the wake of sexual assault encounter a system that is startlingly unlikely to convict reported assailants. Readers will remember that very few sexual assault reports lead to arrest (20 percent) or are referred to prosecutors (4 percent). Even fewer—only about 2 percent—result in felony convictions. Reported sexual assaults are about three times less likely to result in convictions than nonsexual assaults and batteries.

I find these numbers significant even though I don't see convictions as a true and straightforward measure of justice, given the horrors of incarceration and its incompleteness as a remedy for victims. Regardless of my values, low conviction rates reflect the criminal system's failures on its own terms. And if we are asking what criminal law can provide victims, these statistics demonstrate the unlikelihood that the system will be willing or able to make good on its promises.

So what's driving these low rates of arrests, prosecutions, and convictions? It's not, as many believe, that reports of sexual assault are far more likely to be false than reports of other crimes. Instead, dropped cases are largely the product of biases that permeate police stations, judges' chambers, and jury boxes, and inform the decisions prosecutors make. Survivors hear those messages loud and clear.

Law enforcement skepticism of sexual assault reports is rooted in police acceptance of "rape myths"—common misconceptions that shape how society views victims. A 1997 study of police officers found that half adhered to victim-blaming ideologies and obsolete legal definitions. For example, one officer stated that "the 'man in the bushes' is a much bigger threat to the community than the date that got carried away," even though the vast majority of perpetrators target people they know. Another pondered, "What if someone has had sex twenty or thirty times over a three-month period. Then one night they say 'no.' Should this be rape? I don't think so." A third officer explained, "Sometimes a guy can't stop himself. He gets egged on by the girl. Rape must involve force—and that's really rare." And a fourth veered into fantasy territory: "Rape is just rough sex that a girl changed her mind about later on. Technically, rape is a sex act done by the use of force, but so many girls are into being forced, that you can't tell the difference and you wouldn't want to convict an innocent guy." All of these statements are false as a matter of both ethics and law.

And while police views may have evolved in more recent years, research suggests those changes have been insufficient. In a 2010 study, less than half of surveyed officers said they were likely to believe a woman who said she was raped by her husband, even though marital rape is now illegal in all fifty states. (In light of these attitudes, it is perhaps not so surprising that police officers themselves commit sexual violence at alarmingly high rates.)

Police officers are particularly unlikely to believe survivors who deviate from our popular model of the "perfect victim"—generally, a white, heterosexual, cisgender, virginal, middle-class (or richer) woman, who was not drinking, using drugs, or selling sex, who did not know her assailant, and who fought to get away, ideally under the threat of some kind of weapon. Almost none of us are described by such a portrait. One "requirement" alone knocks three-quarters of survivors out of the running: the vast majority know their abuser. Yet many police officers still expect victims to fit the narrow mold.

The role these biases play in police decision-making isn't subtle. For instance, a 2007 study found that 44 percent of officers felt they would likely not believe a report of rape from a sex worker. Survivors can feel this kind of skepticism. Almost half of the women in one study who had called the police about partner abuse felt that officers had discriminated against them. Most felt that this discrimination was due to "not being a 'perfect' victim" because of, among other things, their "income, reputation, disability, [or] sexual identity."

Many police officers also endorse another common myth: that all victims are women and all perpetrators are men. In a 2010 study of several dozen detectives who dealt with sexual assault, none "had heard of female-on-male rape"—even though thousands of such assaults occur each year. And 34 percent of officers surveyed in another study published that same year did not believe the statement "any man can be raped." Not unexpectedly, then, male victims are less likely than women to report intimate partner violence, especially to police.

In light of this widespread incredulity and ignorance, it should come as no surprise that police officers tend to overestimate the prevalence of false rape reports. For any crime, it's hard to know exactly what percentage of reports are untrue. After all, people generally don't tell you they're lying. But all methodologically rigorous studies converge on rates between 2 and 8 percent of all rape reports, a range similar to that for other crimes. (I'll get further into the weeds of this research in a later chapter.) Yet a 2014 study drawn from interviews with law enforcement officers found that more than 80 percent believed false rape reports are more common than that. Most startlingly, the majority of officers believed *most rape reports were false.* Who could blame survivors, then, for deciding not to report?

AND WHAT IF a survivor does make her way past police officers' ingrained skepticism? Then she can expect a trial that may end up more about her than about the conduct of the defendant. As scholar Louis Trosch put it before he became a North Carolina judge, "Rape trials traditionally have stood alone among criminal proceedings as examinations not of the defendant's actions, but of the victim's conduct, lifestyle, and personal history." During cross-examination, victims are asked, usually in open court, what they wore when they were abused, whether they had been drinking, why they did not fight back harder, and whether they "really wanted it." Name a common rape myth, and it will almost inevitably emerge in any given sexual abuse trial.

Defense attorneys use these tactics because they work—and not only on untrained juries, but on judges, too. In 2014, a Dallas County judge explained why she gave a probation-only sentence to a man who confessed to sexually assaulting a fourteen-year-old: the girl was not a virgin, and "wasn't the victim she claimed to be." The year before, a Montana judge commented that a Latina girl raped by her teacher "seemed older than her chronological age," a common stereotype associated with Black and Latina girls, and was "as much in control of the situation" as the adult. The young victim killed herself during the trial.

Ugly defense tactics are hard to reform away because they are, at least to an extent, inherent to our adversarial criminal system. Lawyers have a duty to advocate zealously on behalf of their clients. And since rape myths hold real sway with judges and juries, many defense attorneys believe they are ethically obligated to use them. (I think this is a tremendously difficult ethical question.) Adversarial confrontation may be a hallmark of our criminal justice system, but that's cold comfort for victims who have to live through it. For many survivors considering whether to report, a trial that calls their credibility and moral fiber into question is simply too bleak a prospect.

The risks are compounded by victims' lack of control within the criminal legal system, where decisions about whether and how to proceed are made by prosecutors and police rather than complainants. Take, for instance, the headline-making case against Jacob Walter Anderson, the president of a fraternity at Baylor University. In 2016, after he allegedly raped a woman at a frat party, a grand jury indicted Anderson on four counts of sexual assault. Armed with that indictment, McLennan County prosecutors could have brought him to trial. Instead, to widespread dismay, they entered into a deal under which Anderson pleaded guilty to a single lesser charge and would serve no time in prison.

In a letter to the victim and her family, prosecutor Hilary LaBorde later explained why she had agreed to the compromise. LaBorde, an experienced sex crimes prosecutor, told them she thought that a jury would likely acquit the fraternity president because of rape myths, citing the outcome of another case she had tried recently to justify her decision. There, she recounted, a jury acquitted a college student who had admitted to penetrating a woman too intoxicated to consent. Three male jurors in that case told LaBorde "they would not send anyone to prison for that." And a female juror "said she didn't think the defendant 'looked like a rapist'"—as though a young white man could never rape anyone. A plea deal, LaBorde said, would ensure that Anderson faced at least *some* repercussions.

She may well have been right about that calculation. In the wake of a disappointing plea agreement, it's easier to be mad at an identifiable prosecutor than a hypothetical jury. But an experienced attorney's assessment of a case has to take account of how ordinary jurors and, in some cases, judges will respond to the allegations. No matter how strongly you disagree with their prejudices, they can pose real obstacles to conviction. Still, it's notable that LaBorde initially didn't even inform the victim about the plea deal, never mind consult with her about it: the survivor and her family first learned of the arrangement when it was reported in a local newspaper.

Ultimately, prosecutors' decisions not to bring hard cases often come down to personal ambition. To put it simply, they don't like to lose. Whether they are low-level prosecutors fresh out of law school or elected district attorneys aspiring to higher office, their careers often depend on maintaining a good track record, which means a high ratio of convictions to cases brought. (When then district attorney Kamala Harris was campaigning to be California's attorney general, she touted her office's high conviction rate as a key qualification.) For most purposes, a plea deal like the one that LaBorde secured counts as a win, while a report that never leads to charges doesn't count at all and so doesn't risk damaging the ratio. But risk aversion can end up a self-fulfilling prophecy. When the only assaults brought to trial are those that conform to popular notions of what a "real" rape is, those assumptions get solidified. We associate rape so strongly with criminal law that when criminal law turns its back on victims, we assume they were not victims at all.

THE SAME SKEPTICISM that leads police to do nothing in response to victim reports can sometimes lead to a much more drastic response: a decision to punish the survivor herself. The story of a woman named Kate, described in a report by Washington's King County Coalition Against Domestic Violence, is a typical one. Kate's boyfriend didn't like it when she talked to her friends. One day after she did so he beat her as her children watched, hitting her face and back and throwing her into furniture. "I wanted to get free so I grabbed him by the throat, and left scratches on his neck. He let go of me," she recounted. "I picked up the phone and dialed 911. He grabbed it and hung up. When the officers got there, he told them that I had been smoking marijuana, and that I had assaulted him. He showed [one of the officers] the scratches on his neck, and I was arrested." One study found that 24 percent of surveyed women who had reported sexual assault or partner abuse were either arrested or threatened with arrest after calling the police. Social service providers who work with male domestic abusers report that men in treatment tell each other to "get to the phone first": the police, they have concluded, are likely to believe whoever places the first call for help.

Victim arrests have become more common with the introduction of mandatory arrest laws—which, as the name suggests, require law enforcement to place someone under arrest when they respond to a domestic violence report. With these statutes, well-meaning legislators and advocates sought to address a very real problem: police showing up at a violent home, telling the abuser to take a walk around the block, and refusing to intervene in a "private" matter. But the unintended consequences of these laws have been devastating. A study in New York City concluded that mandatory arrest policies exacerbated two dangerous patterns: retaliatory arrests, where abusers call the police on their victims, and dual arrests, where police arrest the victim along with their abuser. In particular, when police cannot immediately identify who initiated the violence—most often because the victim caused some injuries to the attacker while acting in self-defense—they often arrest both parties. After all, *no* arrest is not an option.

Survivors who do not conform to the "perfect victim" mold are particularly likely to end up arrested. A 2008 study, for example, found that police responding to an intimate partner violence call were at least ten times more likely to arrest both partners in a queer couple than a straight couple. Because police are used to assuming that "the woman" is the victim and "the man" is the perpetrator, they often default to labeling violence in same-sex relationships as "mutual abuse" and arrest both parties. Another factor is that police often miss bruises and other injuries on dark skin. So, to them, an injured Black survivor may appear unscathed, while a white abuser—scratched up from the victim's self-defense—may appear to be the real victim.

Even if police and prosecutors believe a victim's initial report, she may still be jailed later if she refuses to testify or is unable to do so. In Harris County, Texas, a rape victim broke down on the stand when she was first called to testify against her assailant. The trial was delayed, and the woman was treated at a local hospital. When she checked out, she was greeted by an armed investigator from the prosecutor's office, who placed her under arrest and brought her to the local jail. She was not charged with committing any crime. Rather, the court had granted the prosecutor's request for what is known as an "attachment order" because they feared she would not appear to testify again. As a result, she was imprisoned for a month until the trial restarted. Certainly, a survivor's willingness to testify against the defendant might make or break a case. From a prosecutor's perspective, such testimony may be worth securing at great cost. But for a victim, incarceration is a terrible price to pay for reporting.

Immigration-related fears can also deter victims from filing criminal complaints, as the Trump era starkly illustrated. Domestic violence reports from Latino residents of many cities, including Houston, Los Angeles, San Diego, and Denver, dropped significantly from 2016 to 2017. ACLU researchers noted that 70 percent of prosecutors found sexual assault cases during that time "more difficult to prosecute as a result of an increase in fear of immigration consequences." Those fears were hardly misguided, despite the availability of special visas (known as U and T visas) to protect undocumented survivors. Irvin Gonzalez Torres, an undocumented trans woman, sought a protective order in El Paso against her abusive ex-partner. She received the order, but before she could exit the courthouse, immigration officers arrested her for being in the country illegally. Likewise, a legal services lawyer in Florida "described a case in which a survivor of domestic violence had called the police, who then came and arrested everyone in the household and never investigated the allegation of domestic violence. The woman, although a victim of a crime, is now in immigration proceedings with no documentation that an investigation was ever conducted, and thus no ability to apply for a U visa."

BEYOND THE HIGH likelihood of being brushed aside or mistreated by police and prosecutors, one of the most common reasons why sexual assault victims do not report to the police is fear of reprisal—by assailants, by family and friends, or the wider community. And once again, these fears are perfectly rational.

Fourteen-year-old Daisy Coleman and thirteen-year-old Paige Parkhurst were raped in 2012 while incapacitated in a popular football player's basement in their small hometown of Maryville, Missouri. A video of Daisy's assault was reportedly shared widely around her school. She went to the police, and one of the assailants was convicted in juvenile court after he confessed to raping Paige. But the conviction did nothing to protect Daisy from vicious harassment and bullying in her community, particularly on social media. "About 12 or 13 different girls came forward to make statements that something similar had happened to them," Daisy's mother, Melinda, told a reporter. "But one by one they fell away when they saw what was happening to Daisy. They were intimidated and I can't blame them." After prosecutors brought and then dropped charges against Daisy's alleged rapist, the harassment intensified, culminating in the Colemans' home burning down—the result of arson, Melinda believed. In August 2020, Daisy Coleman died by suicide. Melinda followed her four months after.

There are too many similar stories. Coleman's case is often compared to that of Audrie Pott, a fifteen-year-old who was raped while unconscious in Saratoga, New York. She took her own life after classmates circulated photographs of her assault. Lizzy Seeberg, a freshman at Saint Mary's College, told the police that she had been assaulted by a football player from nearby Notre Dame. One of the player's teammates texted her: "Don't do anything you would regret. Messing with Notre Dame football is a bad idea." Seeberg killed herself ten days after the reported assault.

Because of cases like these, the DOJ's National Crime Victimization Survey consistently finds that one of the most common reasons victims of sexual assault don't contact police is fear of retaliation. A participant in another study explained she was afraid that by calling the cops, she would be "making the situation worse. They might arrest my abuser, and when he is out, he will hurt me like he has threatened." Under the hashtag #WhyIDidntReport, Twitter users have shared their experiences; one recounted that "two of his fraternity brothers showed up at my dorm room the next day and threatened to kill me if I told."

Those victimized in prison face particularly high odds of retaliation. (These victims do not "call the police"—that is not an option—but they report to an arm of the criminal-legal system that can deliver potential criminal consequences to their abusers, so I consider this part of the same general pattern.) A report by Human Rights Watch states that "virtually every prisoner we interviewed who had lodged a complaint of sexual misconduct faced retaliation by the accused officer, his colleagues, or even other prisoners. In some cases, they also faced punishment by correctional officials." Some victims were written up themselves for engaging in sexual misconduct and suffered consequences that made it more difficult to get parole. And some were placed in solitary confinement after reporting—either under the guise of "protection" or explicitly as punishment.

FINALLY, SURVIVORS OFTEN do not report their abuse because they don't want their assailant incarcerated, or fear that police will mistreat him. This dynamic can be difficult for outsiders to understand. *Why would a victim protect her rapist?* But the truth is that many do—especially those among the vast majority of survivors who know their abusers. Who among us has not continued to love someone, perhaps a family member or longtime friend, who has hurt us? Perhaps it is not so surprising, then, that in one study, nearly half of intimate partner violence survivors who did not call the police reported that they "were concerned that the police would be rude to the offender or that calling the police would have negative consequences for the offender's life."

It's impossible to talk about victims' concern for their abusers without also talking about gender. A 2006 survey of college students found that when the wrongdoer was a family member or friend, survivors were likely to identify not wanting their assailant to be prosecuted as a deterrent to reporting. In that study, women ranked concern for their assailant higher as a deterrent than men did. It's hard not to assume that this impulse is rooted, at least in part, in the gendered expectation that good girls forgive—and that women must care for the men around them, even at the risk of their own health and safety.

The urge to protect an assailant may be especially strong when both parties are part of a group regularly targeted and abused by law enforcement, as Black people are. (There's also a long, ugly history of white people making false allegations of sexual violence against Black men, which I'll explore later.) Writing in *Time* about football player Ray Rice's abuse of his then fiancée, prominent activist and author Feminista Jones reflected on the specific deterrents to reporting that Black domestic violence survivors face. "For Black women, a strong sense of cultural affinity and loyalty to community and race renders many of us silent, so our stories often go untold," she wrote. "One of the biggest related impediments is our hesitation in trusting the police or the justice system. As Black people, we don't always feel comfortable surrendering 'our own' to the treatment of a racially biased police state and as women, we don't always feel safe calling police officers who may harm us instead of helping us."

For decades, feminists have engaged in rich debate about whether and how criminal law should address sexual violence. Should we try to reform a system that regularly fails victims and puts them at tremendous risk of future abuses, or should we abandon it? If the criminal system occasionally helps some survivors, can that justify the harms it inflicts on other victims, not to mention the damage wrought by hyper-incarceration? What alternatives can we build? I have no perfect, complete answers to offer here. The one thing of which I am sure is that the criminal legal system does not deserve the public's collective faith. It does not deserve the monopoly it has over our thinking about sexual violence—the unquestioned belief that rape is first and foremost a crime, that the solution will always come through law enforcement, that cops and courts will keep victims safe. To limit survivors' avenues for support, justice, and healing to the criminal system alone would be to abandon them, utterly and completely.

5

When Institutions Fail

The criminal justice system does not have a monopoly on mishandling reports of sexual harm. Workplaces and other institutions screw up all the time. If they did not, Dana and I wouldn't have started Know Your IX to reform campus responses, and I would not now need to represent student survivors mistreated by their schools. Me Too would not have taken off in the wake of the Weinstein allegations if millions of workers in much less glamorous jobs did not see themselves in the actresses whose allegations had been brushed aside by studio executives.

The good news is that none of these failures are inevitable. Using law, media, and other public advocacy, survivors have successfully pushed their institutions to do better. But, to do so, we have to be honest about how and why these institutions often abdicate their legal and moral responsibilities.

When Breauna Morrow worked as a teenage cashier at a McDonald's in St. Louis, an older male coworker propositioned her: "You have a nice body; have you ever had white chocolate inside you?"

When she reported the comment to a manager, she says, she was told that she would "never win that battle." Another McDonald's worker was fired, she said, for reporting that her manager had asked "how many penises she could take," and if she wanted to see his. "McDonald's advertises all over television saying it's 'America's best first job,' but my experience has been a nightmare," Morrow says.

Nightmares like those led McDonald's workers in ten cities across the country to strike in September 2018. Harassment is rampant in the fast-food industry: a 2016 survey found that 40 percent of women who work in nonmanagerial roles in fast-food restaurants have experienced sexual harassment. McDonald's is no exception, and its management refuses to address the problem, according to workers. As I'm writing, McDonald's faces several Title VII lawsuits for mishandling claims and retaliating against victims who report. The company's primary defense is that it is not responsible for what happens at its restaurants because, like many fast-food joints, they are franchises owned by middlemen. That is, McDonald's headquarters does not directly control each location but rather contracts with others to run them. McDonald's can tell a franchisee what kind of cheese it must put on a Big Mac, but it cannot—it says—make its franchisees take sexual harassment law seriously. If successful in the courts, that argument could devastate protections for fast-food workers.

The stories from McDonald's make clear that, just like reporting to the criminal justice system, reporting to an institution comes with risks for survivors. These stakes are particularly high for undocumented workers, whose angry harassers may call immigration authorities. Like other forms of retaliation for speaking up about harassment, that practice is illegal. But, of course, enforcement of rights requires knowledge of the law and, sometimes, money for an attorney. Often the threat of reprisal is enough to keep an undocumented worker silent. For that reason, among others, sexual harassment is rampant in agricultural industries that rely significantly on undocumented laborers.

Retaliation also sometimes comes in the form of disciplinary action. Survivors who report to institutions too often end up facing sanctions for rule-breaking—much like they face arrest and prosecution when they report to the criminal justice system. In 2016, Brigham Young University came under fire for suspending students who disclosed their violations of the school's honor code, like drinking or staying out after curfew, in order to report they had been raped. BYU has since instituted an amnesty clause for survivors to encourage them to come forward. But the problem is not confined to a single school. One of my young clients was suspended by her high school after reporting that she had been orally raped by a classmate. The assailant insisted that the two had had consensual oral sex. After asking why she hadn't bitten her classmate's penis to show she really didn't want to participate, the school concluded my client was lying. And because, according to the school's account, the girl had broken its rules by participating in sexual contact on school grounds, she was punished.

Other problems with institutional responses lack an analogue in the criminal system and arise because of their differences. Theoretically, anyone can file a police report or lawsuit. But not everyone has access to institutional procedures. Workers in informal industries— for instance, independent domestic workers who labor in private homes without meaningful oversight—have no central HR office to email. Nor do sex workers, whose efforts to offer mutual aid are often surveilled and incriminating. And abusive, misogynistic organizations and communities where harassment flourishes are probably the least likely to set up remedies for survivors, whether they are legally required to do so or not. Truly internal recourse is also often unavailable in institutions like prisons, immigration detention, and the military, where the line between reporting to the institution and filing a criminal complaint is, at best, porous. For example, prison officials are often required to turn over "internal" allegations to law enforcement. As a result, in those contexts it's difficult, perhaps impossible, to construct a formal, separate process by which victims can pursue support or accountability outside the reach of the criminal system.

There's also the problem that institutions often lack the power to force change that courts, for better or for worse, easily wield. Case studies from CARA, the organization whose work with Unido survivors I found so inspiring, also include a demoralizing account of trying to stop another activist from harassing young women in his community. This activist and his organization repeatedly refused to consider survivors' reports, mete out consequences, or work to prevent future violence. They even accused the women of undermining the cause by speaking up. And because neither CARA nor the young victims could compel the harassing activist to show up and engage with their allegations, as a court could, he simply did not.

THE OPACITY OF institutional responses also can contrast sharply with the openness of court proceedings. Privacy might be attractive to survivors who don't want their identity, or that of their assailants, publicly exposed. Indeed, the promise of confidentiality might be the only reason a victim is willing to come forward at all. But closed doors bring their own problems. Without public scrutiny, institutions can stick to bad habits without consequence.

Perhaps no company has proved this better than Uber. In 2017, Susan Fowler published a lengthy account of the harassment she had faced as an engineer at the company, and its HR department's utter failure to address her reports. On her first day on the job, her direct supervisor propositioned her via the company's chat system. "He was trying to stay out of trouble at work, he said, but he couldn't help getting in trouble, because he was looking for women to have sex with." She took screenshots of the message to show HR. "Uber was a pretty good-sized company at that time," Fowler writes, "and I had pretty standard expectations of how they would handle situations like this. I expected that I would report him to HR, they would handle the situation appropriately, and then life would go on—unfortunately, things played out quite a bit differently."

Differently, indeed. HR agreed with Fowler that her supervisor was sexually harassing her. But they told her this was her manager's first offense, and when Fowler then brought the complaint to upper management, she was told her supervisor was "a high performer." Executives explained that "they wouldn't feel comfortable punishing him for what was probably just an innocent mistake on his part." Fowler was then given a choice: she could switch to a different team or continue working with this manager—but if he gave her a bad review in retaliation for reporting him, HR warned, they could do nothing to protect her because she had "chosen" to stay. "I remarked that this didn't seem like much of a choice," Fowler wrote. Although she had been excited about her first team's work, which aligned with her significant experience, she transferred.

Over time, Fowler met more women at Uber, and heard from them more stories like her own. "Some of the women even had stories about reporting the exact same manager I had reported, and had reported inappropriate interactions with him long before I had even joined the company," Fowler wrote in her blog post. "It became obvious that both HR and management had been lying about this being 'his first offense,' and it certainly wasn't his last. Within a few months, he was reported once again for inappropriate behavior, and those who reported him were told it was still his 'first offense.'" Eventually, Fowler left Uber.

The year after Fowler published her account, another engineer, Ingrid Avendaño, sued Uber, alleging a similar pattern. Avendaño faced rampant harassment at Uber, she said. A senior colleague touched her inner thigh. A coworker talked about her ass. An engineer repeatedly told recruits that Uber was the "type of company where women can sleep their way to the top." Avendaño reported the harassment to HR multiple times, she alleged in her lawsuit, but it failed to investigate her complaints. And when she complained about HR's inaction to a senior executive, she was denied pay increases and promotions, leading to what HR called an "abnormally low" salary. Like Fowler, Avendaño left the company.

Ultimately, it took sustained public outcry in response to Fowler's and Avendaño's accounts, among others, to spur Uber to overhaul its broken human resources process. If the two women had not been willing to come forward, the rest of us would have known nothing about the company's dysfunction. And before they heard stories from similarly mistreated colleagues, even Fowler and Avendaño hadn't known how deep the rot went. Only Uber's management could see the extent of the problem, and without public consequences, they were happy to continue to prioritize the male "high performers" and see junior women engineers leave.

By contrast, had a court regularly botched cases in this way, its failures would be public record. Interested members of the public could watch the trials sitting just a few feet away from the witness stand, listen to jurors read their verdicts, and read the judges' opinions online. The openness of American courts has long provided fodder for legal reforms. Transparency allowed twentieth-century feminists to see how courts failed to appreciate the gravity of domestic violence, and permits today's advocates to track disproportionate and discriminatory sentencing patterns.

The story of Uber is one of corporate failure and abuse. But it's also a story of effective advocacy by survivors who forced the organization to pursue structural reform. In the wake of Fowler's blog post, a company-wide investigation by an external auditor led to the termination of at least twenty employees, including some senior officials. A team of lawyers, hired by Uber and led by former attorney general Eric Holder, released a set of public recommendations for improving the company's responses to sexual harassment. Shortly after, Uber's founder, Travis Kalanick, resigned. In 2019, Uber agreed to pay $4.4 million to settle charges of sexual harassment and retaliation brought by the federal Equal Employment Opportunity Commission. The costs to Fowler, Avendaño, and other victims who demanded that Uber do better were, undoubtedly, tremendous. But when advocates are willing to press forward anyway, they show that tolerance for sexual harassment isn't inevitable.

ONE OF THE more technical reforms that Uber implemented to improve its response to sexual harassment was to limit the use of a corporate practice common among tech giants: forced arbitration agreements, whereby workers are required, as part of their employment contracts, to sign away their right to sue their employer. These companies require that any legal grievances be handled by private arbiters—who are often chosen and paid by the company, and hired back if they perform "well." Their decisions are binding on the parties and, with only the rarest of exceptions, unreviewable by courts. That means if a survivor is mistreated by HR when she reports harassment, she cannot sue. Instead, she must take her claim before the arbitrator, essentially a private judge supplied and paid for by the corporation. What's more, arbitration often ends with a nondisclosure agreement, which prohibits the victim from talking about the underlying harassment or their company's process for addressing it.

To be sure, some employees might prefer arbitration to a drawn-out court battle, much for the same reasons that some would choose to report harassment to HR rather than report it to the police. But there is a vast difference between choosing a private, speedier option and being forced into it, with no option for oversight if the process is unjust. And there's considerable reason to think the arbitration system is rigged against workers. Employees required to submit to arbitration win their cases only 59 percent as often as those who sue in federal court, and just 38 percent as often as their counterparts who are free to sue in state court. That means, of course, that employers are less likely to face consequences through arbitration than they would through lawsuits.

Mandatory arbitration thus not only serves as an obstacle for individual workers who might do better in a lawsuit but takes the pressure off employers to follow the law in the first place. By insulating themselves from litigation, these companies can rest assured that their inadequate responses to sexual harassment are unlikely to hurt them later in the courtroom. So if they want to leave a harassing supervisor to his ways, why not?

One possible answer is the PR disaster that it invites. After Uber narrowed its use of forced arbitration agreements, a public outcry against Google's reliance on them, led by its employees, forced that company to do the same. Workers are not completely powerless in the face of corporate malfeasance—especially when, like tech employees, they have the cultural capital to force the public to listen. Still, forced arbitration undoubtedly silences many and gives corporations too much room to abandon their legal and ethical responsibilities.

Institutions may be particularly likely to protect abusers when senior leaders have personal relationships with the people accused of doing harm, like an HR manager who has long shared an after-work drink with other executives. (To be fair, the same dynamic of self-protection can play out in court systems, too. Police are notorious for looking the other way when they receive domestic violence calls about fellow cops.) And even a strong written policy is no guarantee that an institution will enforce it. Some members of the Democratic Socialists of America, for instance, have criticized the organization's implementation of the anti-harassment policy that it established in 2017. "Variations on this pattern have publicly played out twice in the last year," Allison Hrabar, one of the authors of the DSA policy, wrote in an April 2019 blog post. "A person in DSA (usually a man) abused another member (usually a woman). The member reported the abuse to someone in chapter leadership, or national leadership, or someone responsible for handling grievances. The grievance went nowhere, or resulted in a warning or short suspension. The abuser is still in DSA. The reporting member is not."

As Hrabar sees it, DSA's leadership was simply unwilling to put its policy into practice. "I am proud of what we tried to do," she wrote of the work she and her comrades did to write the policy. But despite their efforts, she says, "those of us that want to end abuse are forced to fight on two fronts: against both abusers themselves and leadership that is, at best, apathetic."

THESE HORROR STORIES might scare a reasonable person away from institutional responses altogether. But I think that's the wrong response. The corporate abuses at Uber and McDonald's are not the inevitable failures of institutions trying their best to address sexual harassment. After all, there are plenty of success stories out there. Rather, these accounts of retaliation and silencing are examples of institutions actively protecting wrongdoers from accountability. We should not say they "failed" to protect employees because they never tried.

The lesson from these cover-ups, then, is that institutional responses will not work if the people calling the shots don't want them to. So it's the advocates' job to make it so that people in power *need* these remedies to function. We must change the incentives so that ignoring abuses is more costly to institutions than facing them head on. By naming and shaming their companies, tech workers demonstrated that the public costs of forced arbitration agreements aren't worth the legal advantages. When I was at Know Your IX, we fought hard for the U.S. Department of Education to release the findings of its Title IX investigations publicly, so schools would know that mistreating students might damage their reputations. Looking back, I feel confident that transparency played a significant role in forcing a sea change in schools' responses to sexual harassment.

Some groups use both carrots and sticks. To address sexual harassment and other abuses of agricultural workers, the Coalition of Immokalee Workers (CIW) created a "Fair Food Code of Conduct." Tomato growers who opt in to those rules and pass an audit benefit from good PR, and can label their products as "fair." At the same time, farms that mistreat their workers face heavy financial consequences: thanks to CIW's advocacy campaigns, major stores like Walmart and Whole Foods will only buy tomatoes from compliant farms. One external evaluation found that "because of this market enforcement mechanism, the Fair Food Program has been able to virtually eliminate horrendous human rights abuses like slavery and sexual harassment from the fields in which they work."

When we successfully flip the calculus and force improvements, we should remain vigilant. An institution may appear to welcome reform efforts after a lawsuit or walkout forces them to do so. But that doesn't mean the changes will stick, or that they'll be implemented well. This is especially true for powerful, moneyed institutions whose interests are sure to diverge from those of their members. These institutions deserve neither our protection nor the benefit of the doubt. We certainly shouldn't confuse HR departments with the feminist movement. And university Title IX offices are not "on our side," either practically or politically.

Rather, they are *useful*. Although institutional failures make the news more often than successes, schools and workplaces have done far more for the survivors I know and represent than the police ever have. I've worked with hundreds of victims over the years, as either a colleague or an attorney. Many are prison abolitionists who see no role for law enforcement in addressing sexual harms, in large part because of their own traumatic, futile experiences with the criminal system. But I cannot think of a single survivor I've worked with who has called to end schools' or workplaces' role in addressing sexual harassment, even when those institutions let them down.

On the contrary, survivor-advocates have organized to expand the responsibilities of schools and workplaces to address sexual harms, even as right-wing actors have tried to limit those. (One such GOP campaign is the topic of a later chapter.) Victims recognize that to give up on these responses would simply excuse institutions' failures, condemning everyone to the same fate as those abandoned in the wake of violence. Should we design a world in which everyone is treated like Susan Fowler, like my client Darbi, or like the McDonald's workers who brought suits, all turned away when they sought help?

Or should we, instead, fight for institutions to live up to their legal and moral responsibilities?

I choose the latter. Instead of abolishing a useful tool for its imperfections, we should take on the hard work of sustained agitation. We should push for continued progress, both in policy and in culture. And institutional responses may, in many cases, be easier to reform and improve than our criminal justice system. Your boss might be more likely to meet with concerned coworkers than your senator is. Company policies can be changed by its management team; passing a law is much more onerous. Of course, not every institution will be responsive. But where they are, change may come more quickly.

A COMMON CRITIQUE from the left—the kind of critique, I hate to admit, that wounds me most—is that those of us who devote considerable energies to internal remedies are insufficiently suspicious of the inherent dangers of institutions, especially powerful ones like corporations and universities. The critique goes something like this: Why would we think a comically evil company like Uber— which underpays its drivers and resists basic workers' rights at every turn—could ever do good? Why would we want to have anything to do with it? At best, we are chumps. At worst, we are co-opted by institutions, manipulated to join their terrible systems in the name of reform, and in the process lend legitimacy to their abuses.

There's certainly a risk of that. I've seen organizers who fought hard to improve a school's sexual harassment policies come to feel defensive whenever the institution's process then came under criticism—as though after whatever modest concessions the movement had won, any of the school's failures were now their own. To admit that a school implemented reforms poorly would be, some feared, to admit that reform itself was wrong—which is certainly false, but can feel true. To be honest, I sometimes felt that way about Obama's Education Department: once Know Your IX had helped convince the agency to enforce Title IX more robustly, criticisms of its efforts felt personal, even where I might otherwise have been critical myself. Resisting those impulses requires work. Sara Ahmed, a British theorist who has done tremendous work on sexual harassment in academia, writes, "I think that if we as feminists are going to be involved in transforming institutions, whether we are working at them or not, 'institutional loyalty' is pretty much the first thing you need to give up (if you have it) or avoid (if you do not)." To give up, to avoid—these are active verbs. Maintaining a healthy distance from an institution you're trying to improve takes conscious effort.

Beware, Ahmed tells us. But she engages nonetheless. I strongly believe that we cannot forgo, out of fear or ideological purity, what for many survivors will be their only chance at support and something like justice. As a friend pointed out to me, a strict commitment to anti-institutionalism can serve to justify inaction in the face of others' suffering, as though radical politics require that victims "suck it up" rather than call on available support. That can hardly be the answer.

I often think of a conversation I had a few years ago at a conference at a liberal arts college. I thought I was there to talk to undergraduates about how to exercise their Title IX rights. But the moderator, a postdoc in political theory, posed a different question: Did I *like* Title IX? She listed many ways school bureaucracies can fail survivors, and especially how they can fail to recognize nuances of victims' experiences. She spoke movingly of the ways survivors must repackage a traumatic sexual encounter to be legible to a board of fact finders. All of that was true. And yet, if the question is whether I like that we have a law against sex discrimination that requires schools to handle sexual harassment, the answer is unequivocally yes. Students would not benefit if schools could again discriminate. Survivors would not be better off without the *option* of turning to their schools for help.

It's telling that activists upset with harassment policies organize to improve rather than abandon them. DSA members like Hrabar have called on the organization to amend and improve its anti-harassment efforts, not to abandon the project. Harassment isn't "going to go away overnight," Hrabar told me. "We have a duty to address it. [Anti-harassment] policies shouldn't be seen as 'Well, this is our one try. We fix it or we don't.' They should be seen as 'We are going to keep trying to make it better and better.'"

The McDonald's workers filing suit in courts across the country are demanding better reporting options, not fewer. So are CIW and other workers' coalitions that have advocated against sexual harassment. Janitorial workers, organized as the Ya Basta! coalition, successfully pushed their union to negotiate with employers to ensure companies improved their internal investigations. Such protections from sexual abuse on the job require workplace action, not simple outsourcing to cops and courts. One of the most heartening conversations I had in my research for this book was with Robyn Swirling, the founder of Works in Progress, an organization that helps progressive groups create better harassment policies. Swirling told me about her own disappointing experience reporting abuse to an employer. In the aftermath, she decided not to give up on workplace responses to sexual harassment, but rather to devote her professional life to making them better.

Survivors tell us what they want. We should listen.

PART II

TOWARD A FAIR PROCESS

6

"The Other Side"

Critiques of institutional responses to sexual harassment don't only come from concern for victims. Recent efforts to address harassment on college campuses, in the workplace, and elsewhere have also been criticized as unfair to the accused, as we've seen. And some of the accounts are genuinely troubling.

I mentioned earlier a story from Wesley College that illustrates what such unfair procedures can look like. In the spring of 2015, a student I'll call Jane told administrators that a male classmate had, without her knowledge, set up a camera in his bedroom and live-streamed their sex to other students. Jane had consented to sex, she said, but never knew she was being recorded. The same day, Wesley imposed interim suspensions on four students who had allegedly participated in the taping. One of them, "Ryan," later filed a complaint with the U.S. Department of Education—and for good reason. Wesley's own policy permitted short-term discipline while an investigation is ongoing, but made clear that students should have a chance to contest the interim suspension, an opportunity Ryan was never given. That was just the start of the procedural debacle.

According to school policy, Wesley administrators were supposed to interview parties and witnesses as part of a thorough investigation prior to any hearing and final determination. But when Ryan showed up to what he thought was a preliminary discussion with administrators, he found himself at a formal disciplinary hearing. He'd had no opportunity to see the evidence against him and, unaware of the nature of the meeting, hadn't brought any witnesses. At the hearing, an administrator presented an "incident report" prepared without Ryan's version of the events. And Ryan was never told why, exactly, the college thought he was involved. In fact, Jane didn't think he was, but he'd been named by one of the other accused men. Unaware of that testimony, Ryan was unable to rebut it. Shortly after, Wesley expelled Ryan from college altogether. In doing so, the Department of Education found, the school violated both its own policies and the law. That wasn't a onetime mistake: the government investigation determined Wesley had a pattern of violating the rights of both alleged victims and the accused.

Workers have complained of similar procedural injustices. In 2017, the investment bank Morgan Stanley fired Harold Ford Jr., a former congressman, "for conduct inconsistent with our values and in violation of our policies." A friend told the *New York Post* that the termination came within twenty-four hours of Ford denying an allegation of sexual harassment—hardly enough time for a meaningful investigation to have taken place. For his part, Ford says he was never informed why, exactly, he was being terminated. As part of a settlement, the bank later released a statement that Ford was not fired for sexual harassment but did not identify the actual reason.

Marta Tecedor Cabrero, a professor at Arizona State University, was the subject of a series of sexual harassment allegations posted on a university message board and reported to her school. Some were anonymous; others came from names she didn't recognize. None of the "complainants" were willing to talk further with ASU. In such a case, usually a school would close any investigations, perhaps leaving the reports in a file in case another victim came forward with a similar story in the future. Instead, ASU left the investigations open but on ice. The pending investigations cast a shadow over Tecedor's efforts to find a job at the University of Michigan, where her wife had been offered a dream faculty position. The two later discovered the reports had all been lodged by another professor who had been in the running for that Michigan job. It took Tecedor and her wife's own detective work to convince ASU to conduct basic fact-checking and close the investigations.

These are egregious cases. As a result, they are also, in some ways, the easiest to understand. But more subtle procedural flaws are also worthy of our concern. While writing this book, I talked to a number of people accused of sexual harassment (mostly but not exclusively men) who felt that their employer or school had treated them unfairly. The errors in their cases were less dramatic but still undermined faith in the institution's decision-making. And if we really believe in treating everyone with dignity, in pursuing justice for all, then we need to fix those problems, too.

One story that stuck with me was from a young man I will call Brandon. After graduating high school in Compton, Brandon enrolled in a junior college. To finish a four-year degree, he transferred to a public university in California, where he signed up to play football and study communications. During his first semester, Brandon told me, he had consensual sex with another student athlete, "Mary." She told friends he had raped her, and the accusation came to the school's attention. An investigation ensued.

Brandon was informed of the accusation, had the opportunity to tell his side of the story, and was allowed to respond to Mary's. In that way, he was treated far better than Ryan from Wesley. But I understand why he still feels the process was unfair. While many schools provide an adviser to help students navigate disciplinary proceedings, Brandon told me his school never assigned him one, so he was left to manage a stressful investigation on his own. When Brandon was interviewed by an investigator hired by the school, he felt she was "really nice and really helpful" and listened to his account. But she got sick, and a new investigator was assigned. This one was "an old white guy who never really looked me in my eye," said Brandon, who is Black. (Mary is a non-Black woman of color.) This investigator rushed through the interview, Brandon told me, and then asked Brandon to type up his response to Mary's account. By his own admission, Brandon did not put the requisite time and energy into his written statement. He told me he was focused on preparing for final exams instead. There was no live hearing, as is now required under California law.

After providing his responses, Brandon learned the school had decided that he did commit assault and would assign sanctions. I reviewed a copy of the investigator's report, if you could call it that, and was genuinely shocked by its lack of detail and analysis. It provided no explanation for the investigator's decision, jumping from a bare recitation of the facts to the conclusion. It included testimony provided by Mary's witnesses, but not Brandon's, without an explanation as to why. The school provided no further information. Brandon told me that when he sought out the investigator, the older man told Brandon, briefly, that he had found Mary more credible, but did not elaborate.

Brandon hired a lawyer, who helped him appeal his case to other university administrators. They "remanded" it for further investigation—a process that must have frustrated Mary, given that such a redo was not provided for by school policy. Again, the university gave no explanation for its decision, leaving both students in the dark. Ultimately, after nearly a year of investigation, the school dropped the complaint.

Soon after, Brandon graduated, his disciplinary record clean. But the process took a mental toll on him. "You can't really focus on academics, you can't really focus on sports," he told me. "I always was worried about this. Even if I was at a party having a good time, I had that in the back of my head like, all right, this could be over at any given time." Some of that stress is, unfortunately, part of any such process, even one that is carried out flawlessly. But the school's lengthy investigation exacerbated Brandon's anxiety. "I felt like I was more than a suspect the whole time," he explained. "I already felt like judgment was placed on me. So it was really hard."

STORIES LIKE THESE present big, hard questions about how to treat everyone fairly in the wake of an accusation. How, in the midst of conflict, can people do right by one another? We like to talk about these issues as matters of "due process," a legal doctrine enshrined in the U.S. Constitution. But the law, unfortunately, can't provide definitive answers here.

For one, due process is a much narrower doctrine than many imagine. It is only required (if not always achieved) when the government is taking something away from a person, whether that be their freedom, money, or a job. As a legal matter, due process doesn't apply to private organizations. So when an op-ed says, for instance, that Woody Allen's publishing house violated his due process rights by canceling his book deal, the claim is legally nonsensical. The government has taken nothing from him.

A second reason the law can't answer all our questions about fairness: due process is not a single set of rules that applies in every circumstance. Many people assume that due process always means a full criminal trial, where the accused is deemed innocent until proven guilty beyond a reasonable doubt. In my experience, that misconception is especially strong when it comes to sexual harms. In a series of focus groups, the National Center for Victims of Crime found that a significant number of men (but not women) believed that the only fair way to handle a sexual allegation is a full criminal prosecution.

In fact, though, due process is a set of flexible standards, and it applies differently to different kinds of proceedings. Whenever the government is trying to take something away from a person, due process applies—whether the deprivation happens in court or out of it. So due process is required not only in criminal trials but also in civil suits, immigration proceedings, benefits hearings, discipline of public employees and students, and so on. In each type of proceeding, due process looks different. Establishing what rules are right for different situations mostly happens through appeals: someone who thinks they were subjected to an unfair process turns to a court—or, if they were mistreated *by* a court, to a higher court—and asks the judges to weigh in. The court decides whether the procedure provided due process and, if not, what else is required. Sometimes courts disagree, and an appeals court a level higher has to resolve the issue. Together, these decisions serve as precedent, providing requirements and guidance for how similar cases should be handled in the future. In this way, judges and lawyers create due process standards for a wide range of circumstances, including many adjudications that happen out of court altogether. But there are always new situations that pose new due process questions that courts have not yet answered. And the fact that judges sometimes come to different conclusions about the same question speaks to the inherently indeterminate nature of due process. There is no perfect formula for fairness. There is just hard work, done in good faith, to try to get it right.

As a lawyer, I get frustrated when public discourse gets so much wrong about what due process actually means, especially when legalese serves as a cudgel to discourage debate. I've seen too many thoughtful Twitter conversations about the hard ethics of how to vet sexual harassment allegations cut off by a passionate but legally indefensible argument that "due process" provides a clear, legal answer—even when it does not, technically, apply at all. By disguising moral arguments about fairness in legalistic terms, such interlocutors can make it difficult for others to engage.

I recognize, though, that those underlying ethical debates are ultimately far more important than any legal ones. The law sets the floor, not the ceiling, for what processes must look like. We can, and should, demand fair policies even where those are not constitutionally required. For example, as a legal matter, most private companies can fire an employee for almost any reason (other than a few specific categories such as the worker's race or sex) without any kind of process. They can decide to terminate a worker on the spot because they do not like the color of her shirt—or because they think she may have stolen from the cash register, even if there is no proof. (Worker contracts can provide more protection than the law does, but often only unions and executives have the power to make companies agree to such conditions.) This doesn't mean, though, that arbitrary firings are permissible as a matter of *ethics*. The fact that your boss can legally fire you without warning does not mean he should. Ethically, workers deserve more.

The law, then, cannot answer all our questions about what is fair. But there is a reason why we so often use a legal term, "due process," to make moral claims: law both shapes and is shaped by our ethical intuitions. For that reason, I think a good way to establish a common agreement about the basics of fair process is to draw lessons from the law. Our ethical commitments do not need to follow bad legal precedents or get mired in the weeds of the doctrine. But we can learn from the broad principles of due process, developed through centuries of debate about what it means to be fair.

What Is Due

There are four principles of due process that, in my view, are particularly important for our debates about sexual harassment:

- Due process takes many forms.
- Due process depends on the stakes.
- Due process involves a balancing test.
- Due process does not change based on the specific allegation.

Let's look at each one in turn. (Lawyers, you'll find some more technical discussion in the notes at the back of this book.)

DUE PROCESS TAKES MANY FORMS

The first principle is one we have already encountered in the previous chapter: due process is not a single checklist but a set of standards that dictates different requirements for different kinds of proceedings.

In a criminal trial, for example, due process requires a certain set of protections for the accused. But there is a different set of due process rights for the defendant in a civil lawsuit—where the plaintiff is usually a private party suing someone for money, and prison is not on the line. Now, step outside the courtroom. If the government wants to deny or cancel an individual's welfare benefits, it also has to provide the applicant with due process, including a hearing. But that hearing is much less formal and antagonistic than a trial. I remember, as a law student, preparing for a client's benefits hearing. I expected a courtroom. Instead, I found myself sitting at a table in a conference room for a discussion with my client and a judge. The same principle goes if the government wants to discipline a public-school student or fire a public employee: instead of a jury in a courthouse, you might have a principal or boss making the call in her office.

What these widely varying situations have in common is that in each one, the affected individual is legally entitled to two things: notice of the allegation and the opportunity to be heard. My client in the benefits hearing never stood up in open court. But he knew why the government was considering taking away his benefits, and he got to tell a judge his side of the story. That's the core promise of due process.

We know intuitively from our own lives that fairness is possible outside of criminal trials and outside of court. Few people think you need to convene a jury to decide if your student cheated on an exam, or your spouse cheated on you—even if the consequences can be profound. We want fairness for all, but we also understand that not every decision we make as individuals, or as organizations, has to pass through the crucible of a lawsuit. Instead, we devise different procedures that work best for each situation. There is no one-size-fits-all model.

DUE PROCESS DEPENDS ON THE STAKES

In the mid-1990s, O. J. Simpson faced two trials back to back. First, the Los Angeles County district attorney prosecuted Simpson on charges of killing his ex-wife, Nicole Brown, and her friend Ron Goldman. The jury found Simpson not guilty. As a result, Simpson spent no time in prison for the murders. But then the victims' families filed a civil suit against Simpson. There, he lost: the jury ruled that the former football player did kill Brown and Goldman. It ordered Simpson to pay $33.5 million to the families.

Striking as they are, the different outcomes for the criminal trial and civil suit are not inconsistent—and not just because the cases were decided by two different juries. Even though the same murders were the subject of both proceedings, the two trials were held under very different rules. Most importantly, criminal prosecutions require a higher standard of proof. The jury in the first criminal trial could only have convicted Simpson if it was convinced *beyond a reasonable doubt* that he committed the murders. Clearly, it was not. But the jury in the civil suit did not have to be so sure. It only needed to believe that a smidgen more than half of the evidence—known technically as the "preponderance of the evidence"—supported the families' case. In other words, the two parties in the civil suit were on an even playing field: whoever the evidence favored, however slightly, won. The families still bore the burden of proof, as a complaining party always does (and always should) in any adjudication. But all they had to do was provide enough evidence to cross the 50 percent line. In a criminal case, on the other hand, the prosecutor's evidence must get the jury close to 100 percent certainty.

Those differences correspond to the different stakes of a civil and criminal trial. Losing a normal civil suit can certainly be devastating: the defendant can be ordered to pay a significant sum or close their business, while their reputation can be dragged through the mud in the public record. But a loss will not result in a prison sentence, as it can in a criminal prosecution. Notably, the handful of civil proceedings that do require more than the preponderance of the evidence are those with consequences much graver than money damages, like deportation or loss of child custody. In those cases, prison might not be on the line, but the potential consequences are higher than having to cut a check—and so the evidentiary standard is higher, too.

It should go without saying that not everyone actually receives all the protections that are guaranteed by law when they face criminal charges or serious civil sanctions. Police, prosecutors, and courts violate defendants' due process rights all the time. But our outrage when the rules are not followed just underscores how important these rights are. The reason we care is not that we like rules for rules' sake. We care because the consequences are dramatic.

That is probably the most important factor for deciding how much process is due: the stakes for the accused. The more serious the outcome, the more process is needed. This legal rule aligns with commonsense moral intuitions. In general, the higher the stakes, the more careful we tend to be. We proofread emails to our bosses more than texts to our friends; we add more cushioning when we pack precious family heirlooms than cheap tchotchkes. For the same reason, it makes sense that the more we threaten to take away from someone, the more protections we should put in place. The decision to not watch a new Louis C.K. special requires next to no process. He has no entitlement to your laughs, and he will be fine without you. In contrast, the decision to cut off a friend requires more care, as an ethical—though obviously not a legal—matter. If you hear that your two best friends got into a terrible fight, for example, you might want to learn the details and maybe speak to both of them before taking a side. (Still, you would never hold a trial, demand documentary evidence, or recuse yourself from the decision because of potential biases, such as a preference for one friend over another.) And the procedure for firing someone should, in turn, be more rigorous still, since someone's livelihood is at stake. At the very least, the employer should let the worker know what she is accused of doing, and give her a chance to tell her side of the story and identify witnesses who could back her up.

Whatever the law requires, our ethical commitments to fairness scale up as the stakes grow higher.

DUE PROCESS INVOLVES A BALANCING TEST

That leads me to another key principle: due process requires taking into account who else will be affected by a decision. In law, we use a balancing test to evaluate competing interests and design a process accordingly.

In the 1960s, many impoverished New York City residents received public assistance payments, often referred to as "welfare." Among those receiving support was John Kelly, a disabled man without a place to live. Kelly's welfare caseworker ordered him to move into a single room occupancy hotel, but Kelly, knowing the hotel's reputation as a hotspot for drug and alcohol abuse, decided to share an apartment with a friend instead. Because he did not have his caseworker's permission to do so, the government canceled his benefits. Alongside other New Yorkers with similar stories, Kelly sued the responsible public officials, arguing that the constitutional requirement of due process entitled him to a pretermination hearing—the chance to make his case before his benefits were taken away.

When the Supreme Court considered the case, it balanced Kelly's interest in a pretermination hearing against the government's interest in *not* providing that hearing. Kelly's reason for wanting the hearing was clear: the benefits were his only source of income. Without them, he could no longer pay for food or rent, and ended up sleeping on the streets. For the city, on the other hand, avoiding a hearing meant saving money, time, and effort. Those are valid considerations. But as we have seen, an administrative hearing can be relatively simple and informal. It does not need to drain the public coffers or place too much strain on the system. The court ruled in Kelly's favor.

Once again, I think the law here lines up with our moral intuitions. Both within legal systems and outside them, any attempt to resolve conflict requires understanding and balancing different interests. We want to know who will be affected by the decision and what's at stake for each side. This kind of approach is very useful in the context of sexual harassment allegations because it gives us a framework for promoting fairness to the accused without forgetting about the people they are alleged to have harmed. Rather than asking us to choose between protections for the accused and protections against harassment, we can develop procedures that incorporate both commitments.

In Kelly's case, the primary conflict was between an individual's interests and the interests of the government. But courts use similar reasoning when it comes to due process questions where two individuals have a direct stake in the outcome of a proceeding. For example, in 2011, the Supreme Court considered the case of a parent accused of failing to pay child support. If that parent could not afford a lawyer, was the government obliged to provide one? In weighing the different interests, the court considered not only how such a right to counsel would help the parent who allegedly owed support (the noncustodial parent) but also how it might affect the other (custodial) parent, the one who was supposed to receive the child support. Ultimately, the court decided that if the custodial parent did not have a lawyer, the government wouldn't have to provide one to the noncustodial parent. Otherwise, the court reasoned, it would risk creating an "asymmetry of representation" that "could make the proceedings less fair overall, increasing the risk of a decision that would erroneously deprive a family of the support it is entitled to receive."

Along the same lines, when designing institutional procedures to vet sexual harassment allegations, victims' interests need to be part of the equation. In a criminal prosecution for sexual assault, the state seeks to punish an individual on its own behalf. In that scenario, extra protections for the defendant make a lot of sense: when an individual is struggling against an all-powerful government that seeks to literally cage him, the state does not need any more help. But in almost all other contexts—civil suits, workplaces, schools, political clubs—alleged victims bring complaints directly against the respondent. They are now part of the calculus, and they seek concrete remedies they need for their own lives. Thinking of sexual harassment as a civil rights issue reminds us that their futures are at stake, too.

For these reasons, many advocates—myself included—think that a guiding principle for designing sexual harassment adjudication systems should be a certain symmetry. Both sides matter equally. Both should have equal rights throughout the adjudication. The scale should be evenly balanced, like in a civil suit, rather than tilted toward either party. That way we can promote equality in each case, and in society more broadly.

When critics suggest ways that a school or workplace disciplinary system could be, in their eyes, made fairer, the balancing test reminds us to consider who bears the burden of building out procedural protections. Some measures would have their cost borne by the institution: a school might offer an appeal process, for example, allowing students to seek an extra review of the decision. Or it might provide free legal services to both parties, as some very wealthy universities already do. Both students benefit; the school pays up. But other disciplinary reforms would protect the accused by burdening the alleged victim and making it harder for her to prove her allegations. In this category I would place calls to increase the weight of evidence needed to find a student responsible, as well as demands that a complainant be directly cross-examined by her alleged assailant—an experience that can be traumatizing and discourage many from coming forward. Those procedures would offer benefits to one student at the cost of the other. Such arrangements are, to me, always less desirable, and a particularly poor fit for issues that implicate the victim's equality, including sexual harassment.

DUE PROCESS DOES NOT CHANGE BASED ON THE SPECIFIC ALLEGATION

This last principle is one that I'll be repeating again and again: the level of process does not depend on the specific type of harm alleged. In criminal prosecutions, there is not one kind of trial for a defendant charged with kidnapping, another for burglary, and a third for tax fraud. Regardless of what crime is alleged, every one of these trials uses the same process because the stakes are the same: each defendant faces incarceration.

The same principle applies to civil trials. The Federal Rules of Civil Procedure govern every civil case brought in federal court, regardless of what the accusation is. And the situation is similar when it comes to discipline in public employment and schools: any offenses that could result in the same sanction—say, termination, or demotion, or suspension—are supposed to be subject to the same rules.

Such consistency is part of what gives us confidence that processes are unbiased. Universal rules are less susceptible to assumptions and prejudices about different defendants and different harms. For example, we would not want courts to have different procedures for drug offenses and white-collar crime. We might reasonably fear that the courts would be prone to provide fewer rights to defendants in the drug cases because the financiers are more likely to look like the judges. By the same token, we would not want judges to be less protective of defendants accused of sexual assault due to their personal disgust for the crime. Nor, conversely, would we want courts to provide *extra* protections for those defendants, based on a belief that the alleged victims are always scorned, vengeful women. In more technical terms, we want trans-substantive processes—processes that apply regardless of the substance of the allegations.

As before, O. J. Simpson's trials illustrate the point. In his criminal trial, Simpson received the same process as someone accused of either a less grave offense or of an even more shocking one. And in his civil trial, he was, again, subject to the same process as someone who was sued in civil court for a "better" or "worse" offense. Note, also, that Simpson's civil trial did not need to look like a criminal trial, even though the underlying conduct he was accused of also constituted a crime. In general, what matters for due process is the actual type of punishment at issue, not the punishment that *could*, theoretically, result from an entirely separate prosecution. In other words, just because your employer is trying to fire you for something that is also a crime—embezzlement, physical assault, rape, you name it—doesn't mean they have to put on a criminal trial.

Misunderstandings about this point crop up all the time in the debate about sexual assault adjudications. Some critics apparently believe that any accusation of conduct that could be criminal, like sexual assault, must be vetted by criminal-trial procedures—even if the stakes are lower, as in a civil lawsuit or employment dispute. And some seem to believe that allegations of sexual harm should be especially hard to prove because they are particularly prone to damage the accused's reputation.

But do people accused of sexual wrongs really face greater stigma than those accused of other kinds of serious wrongdoing? One answer is that this is true except where it is remarkably false. People accused of sexual harm are ostracized, except when they are celebrated and protected. Certainly, some people accused of harassment—often those whom society is not invested in defending, perhaps because of their race or class—do face significant social costs. I spoke to one student, accused of assaulting his classmate, who seemed more shaken by the social opprobrium he faced than by the academic sanction. A California professor accused of harassing one of her students spoke to me of how rumors stick to someone accused of sexual harms, even after they are cleared. And yet Donald Trump was elected president after openly bragging about how he would "grab [women] by the pussy" and get away with it because he's a "star." Clarence Thomas and Brett Kavanaugh were both confirmed to the Supreme Court despite allegations of sexual harassment. A college classmate of mine was accused of sexual assault our senior year; the allegation made its way into the papers, and a few years later he wrote in the *Boston Globe* about how it had "nearly ruined" his life. He was, at the time, a student at Harvard Law School.

Even if we do accept that being punished for sexual harassment sometimes comes with a particularly significant stigma, that does not mean we should erect extra barriers that make it uniquely hard for harassment victims to prove their case. For all the reasons I discussed above, procedural protections are based on the severity of the legal consequence at risk, not the nature of the specific conduct alleged.

Of course, adjudications outside the law need not limit themselves to the rules of our courts. But even putting the law aside, scaling process to stigma would be unfair and counterproductive. Imagine what would happen if we did adopt that approach. First, we would have to come up with some kind of agreement about what are the worst things to be accused of, and which are not so bad. Then, the worse society thought a certain kind of harm was, the *harder* we would make it for the wronged to be believed and supported. After all, outside of criminal trials, adjudications determine not only whether a wrongdoer gets labeled as such and perhaps punished, but also whether a victim can receive the support and protection they need. An employer may determine whether or not a victim will have to share a workplace with his rapist. A church may decide whether a parishioner is in fact being harassed by her pastor, and so whether an intervention is necessary for her to be able to worship safely. Does it really make sense to tilt the scales against the alleged victim precisely in proportion to how bad we think the underlying allegation is? That would mean, in essence, choosing to deny help exactly when it might be most needed.

An Incomplete Blueprint

From the law, we've distilled several key ethical principles: due process takes many forms, depends on the stakes, requires a balancing of interests, and does not change based on the content of the allegation. How should we put these broad principles into practice for handling sexual harassment allegations? What would a fair procedure built on them look like? Alas, I cannot offer a single policy, down to the nitty-gritty details, that would work for every school and workplace, synagogue and social club. While that would certainly be a satisfying payoff for the many pages that got us here, a one-size-fits-all model would be a betrayal of a central tenet of fair process: context matters. Different organizations and institutions will always need to adjust the particulars based on their unique combination of resources, capacity, goals, and values.

Still, some basic features of due process, drawn from centuries of court opinions and practical experimentation, should be a part of any institutional procedure that responds to an accusation of harm by one person against another—including sexual harassment—and could result in substantial sanctions like termination or expulsion. (Less significant sanctions and temporary interventions, like an interim suspension pending investigation, don't require the same level of careful evaluation.) These features include the following:

- Rules governing the conduct expected from members of the institution should be clear and understandable.
- A harmed person should have the opportunity to lodge a complaint, and the other person should be informed of the allegation.
- Both people should be told how the process will work, and, if possible, assigned someone to help them navigate it.
- Each should be given the opportunity, with sufficient time, to present their side of the story and any supporting evidence, including witnesses.
- Each should be able to review the other's relevant evidence (with appropriate protections for privacy) and to rebut the account the other side gave. As part of that, they should both have the opportunity to present questions to the other so as to solicit answers that might undermine the other side's story.
- The complainant, not the accused, should bear the burden of proving the allegation.
- Unbiased decision-makers should consider the evidence and explain their decision to the parties.
- Whenever possible, a party unsatisfied with the outcome should be able to appeal the decision if a procedural flaw has occurred or the result is not supported by evidence.
- When institutions have the resources and capacities to build out these protections, they should do so in ways that place the extra burden on the decision-makers, not on the complainant or the accused.

These core ideas provide the foundation for fair adjudication procedures that every institution can build on. Beyond these basics, though, no one can offer a perfect universal process. And there is legitimate debate to be had about the specific form some of these requirements should take.

ONE TOPIC THAT has attracted particular attention in the debate about how schools should handle sexual harassment is whether the institution should provide a live hearing to test an accusation against a student—and if so, what that should look like.

Some legal background: in its 1975 opinion *Goss v. Lopez*, the Supreme Court addressed the rights of students facing school discipline. The court was sensitive both to the importance of the students' access to education and to the special context of the schoolhouse, where discipline can serve an instructive purpose and resources are limited. Its decision invoked the basic principles of due process: a student facing a ten-day suspension "must be given some kind of notice and afforded some kind of hearing." This hearing did not need to look like a trial—with cross-examination and the opportunity to present witnesses—because, as the justices saw it, "even truncated trial-type procedures might well overwhelm administrative facilities in many places and, by diverting resources, cost more than it would save in educational effectiveness." The court, however, left open the question of whether stronger protections might be necessary for a longer suspension or an expulsion. For the last half-century, lower courts have been slowly filling the gap, but their rulings sometimes conflict. So there is currently no neat legal answer for what school disciplinary procedures should look like when they may lead to the most serious sanctions.

The first step toward answering this question is to identify what's at stake. An accused student doesn't face incarceration, but he might be suspended or expelled. So, while we know the process doesn't have to look like a criminal trial, the stakes are significant. Then we should identify the broader interests. The accused has an interest in staying in school; so does his alleged victim, whose education may be stalled if she cannot safely attend class and participate in campus life because she fears further harassment. The school and broader campus community have an interest in the outcome, too: they want to promote equality on campus, protect other students, and make sure neither student is unjustly deprived of an education. And, as a final step, we should reframe the question as applying to all complaints that implicate similar stakes and interests, rather than considering sexual harassment as a singular kind of accusation. The same process should apply to hazing, physical assaults, harassment based on race or disability, and other kinds of harms students inflict on each other that may result in long-term suspensions or expulsion.

With those principles in mind, we can look at the options. At many schools, as at most workplaces, no live, adversarial hearing is provided. Rather, an investigator or set of investigators—perhaps external hires or HR employees—gather evidence, interview witnesses, consider each side's account and refutations of the other's story, and prepare a written report. The investigators, or a separate board of decision-makers, then come to a conclusion about what they think happened and what the consequences will be.

This approach has its benefits and has been endorsed by the American Bar Association's Commission on Domestic & Sexual Violence. From a school perspective, an investigatory model may be less onerous than setting up a full hearing. It's less formal and more easily administered by nonlawyers. And it's less likely to intimidate the participants, some of whom might have just experienced a serious trauma. A process that is comfortable for witnesses is good in itself: no one wants to further traumatize a student, and many victims will refuse to report altogether if the process is too daunting. But intimidation also matters because some of what we take as physical or verbal signs that a witness is lying, like stumbling testimony, may instead simply be evidence that she is nervous. A decision-maker may wrongly disbelieve a truthful witness simply because she was anxious about an adversarial hearing, and come to the wrong decision as a result. Robyn Swirling, who helps organizations develop their sexual harassment policies, is confident that investigators can figure out all they need from thorough interviews with involved parties and witnesses. "Abusive people," she warns, can manipulate the process and use a hearing "as part of their abuse." She believes meetings attended by both parties are only productive at the point where the facts are established and a conversation might be useful for establishing a remedy—not to hash out what happened.

Still, there are good reasons you might choose a hearing. Hearing boards are frequently staffed by multiple people, while investigations are more often conducted by just one, which provides more room for a single person's biases to shape the outcome. Most importantly, some attorneys feel that the opportunity to challenge a witness's testimony in real time is irreplaceable. Sure, in an investigator model, each side should have an opportunity to review the other's statement and evidence and point out any holes or errors. But that's much less effective, many feel, than the opportunity to pose questions to a witness during a live hearing and follow up to clarify answers or advance a particular theory.

That, in turn, raises questions about how cross-examination should occur at a hearing. With only a few exceptions, a defendant in a lawsuit almost always has the opportunity for his attorney to question witnesses, including his victim. But many institutions are skeptical of importing this courtroom model into their own disciplinary procedures. For one thing, students in disciplinary hearings do not have a federal right to a free attorney (there's nothing akin to a public defender requirement), and few schools can afford to provide such services. Sometimes, as a result, neither student has a lawyer; sometimes only one party can afford an attorney, which can put them at a large and unfair advantage if the lawyer plays an active role in questioning. So schools have to figure out who will conduct any cross-examination.

Almost all are reluctant to allow parties to directly question each other, and for good reason. Such inquisitions are a recipe for trouble. As Swirling warns, wrongdoers can use a process to further their abuse. Imagine a rapist questioning his victim about what she wore the night of the assault, what he did to her, and whether she cried afterward. Some schools instead permit parties to choose a nonprofessional representative, like a professor, friend, or parent, to conduct the questioning. But these nonprofessionals, too, can promote disorder. An accused student's frat brother may be an intimidating examiner for a victim and may not know (or care about) the school hearing rules. In all of these different options, some administrators worry that a questioner will misbehave to bully the other side, and the school will have little recourse to constrain them. Unlike a trial judge, a school cannot threaten unruly participants with "contempt of court" in the form of fines or jail time.

Plus, there isn't much reason to think cross-examination will actually be an effective truth-seeking tool when in untrained hands. A nineteen-year-old won't have the training or experience to know, for example, how to phrase a question clearly, or how to get a witness to answer a line of inquiry they're trying to evade. And because we confuse nervousness with lack of credibility, the panic an unprofessional questioner induces in a witness may promote inaccuracy in the decision-making.

For these reasons, among others, almost all federal appellate courts to weigh in on the matter have said that schools do not need to permit direct cross-examination. Rather, a board of administrators can collect lists of questions from the student accused of misconduct and from the complainant. After screening out inappropriate inquiries ("why are you such a slut?"), the administrators can pose each side's questions to witnesses and the parties. That, the courts say, adequately protects the serious interests of the accused while also recognizing the unique context of student discipline. Many institutions and advocates prefer this approach, too.

Personally, I think full-fledged live hearings are unwise in K-12 schools where children are involved. But for adult students, I do think universities should provide some kind of hearing, which, when done right, can promote truth-seeking and help ensure that everyone involved feels heard. Some wealthier schools have considered the trade-offs and—wisely, in my view—designed hybrid models that incorporate the best parts of each approach. (At the time of my writing, these models are mostly forbidden by Trump administration rules, which I'll discuss shortly, and which I expect President Biden will replace.) For example, an investigator might collect evidence and testimony for a report, which a board would read. That board would then speak directly to the parties at a hearing, which would occur via videoconference so the students are physically separated. The hearing would still permit only indirect cross-examination by the parties through questions submitted to the panel, so that the students would not interrogate each other directly. My concerns about direct cross-examination would diminish, though not disappear, if both students were provided a trained attorney, whose employment depends on good behavior. But such a guarantee is impractical for most institutions.

In short, there's no perfect, all-purpose answer, on this or other nuanced procedural matters. But I hope that the four ethical principles I've identified, culled from a long legal tradition, offer a starting point for thinking about these kinds of hard questions about how to treat each other fairly.

A QUICK NOTE: readers might notice that a disproportionate number of my examples of fair process controversies, in this chapter and others, concern schools. From my experience and research, that is the site of our most developed, detailed debate about what fair process outside of courts should look like. It's no surprise that the conversation would focus on formal institutions with which almost all of us are familiar. That doesn't explain, though, why the conversation about school discipline for sexual harassment is so much more detailed and extensive than the debate about workplaces. To be sure, there are plenty of think pieces decrying, in a general sense, the supposed transformation of the American workplace into a witch-hunting ground. But the public discussion about workplace harassment and fairness rarely touches on the actual procedures used by employers. There is no heated debate, for example, about whether private companies should permit employees to cross-examine their alleged victims.

The primary reason for this, I think, is that unfair workplace discipline overwhelmingly hurts workers who do not have access to wealth, media, and lawyers—exactly the workers who are least likely to inspire widespread public concern. I suspect we would have a better conversation about unfairness in the workplace if senior managers were the ones regularly fired after shoddy investigations. Those executives have access to attorneys and PR teams; they could sue their former companies and generate big newspaper headlines. The fallout might spark a detailed national debate, in legislatures, on op-ed pages, and around dinner tables, about the procedures that employers use to investigate and discipline workers.

Indeed, one reason why we have such a spirited conversation about procedures in schools is that rich white kids *are* sometimes the subject of discipline there. A single set of rules applies to all students, at least on paper. When these children of privilege are occasionally punished, they are natural objects of empathy in elite society. And they have the financial and social resources to fight back in lawsuits and in the court of opinion. Often, they hire from a growing cottage industry of lawyers and consultants who help students rehabilitate their images and get back into school after being suspended or expelled for sexual assault. With these resources, the young men win legal cases. Newspapers tell their stories in shocked tones.

But while school discipline—in theory, if not always in practice—imposes the same rules on the wealthy and powerful as on the poor and dispossessed, inequality is built into employment law. In private workplaces without unions, employees have few legal rights and can generally be fired for almost any reason. The exception is top-dollar corporate officers, who are often able to negotiate, as part of their contract, a range of privileges that includes protection from unfair termination. The cost of violating those agreements is so significant—and so much greater than the cost of a lawsuit by a harassment victim—that companies tread extremely carefully in disciplining top executives. Were top executives subject to the same procedures as their employees, they might insist on better protections for workers. But as it is, those with the most power to create change, at least in nonunionized workplaces, have little reason to complain. And so, as a public, we have much less to say about fairness at work than fairness at school. This book reflects that imbalance—but I hope that acknowledging its origins might help, in small part, to spur a corrective.

9

Why Process Matters for All

Caring about two things at once is hard. It's certainly harder than caring only about one. But it's important to say as plainly as possible that there is no conflict between caring about harassment and caring about fair treatment of those on both sides of an accusation. Both sets of concerns, when genuine, are animated by commitments to individual dignity, equality, and giving people opportunities to flourish in public life.

Years ago, Know Your IX organized a teach-in about fair process for all, including the accused. The presentation, held for student organizers around the country, many of them victims themselves, explained why fair procedures should matter to all of us and what a good process should look like. Soon after, a student survivor reached out to complain about our decision to spend time discussing the rights of accused students. Her objection was not trivial. In a world in which the well-being of sexual abusers is so regularly prioritized over that of their victims, why would we, an organization dedicated to survivors, focus considerable energy on the rights of alleged harassers? More fundamentally, the world is still marked by undeniable gender inequality. Why would we encourage a movement primarily made up of women to care about a problem that primarily hurts men?

Those questions came to mind when I read Kate Manne's perceptive diagnosis of "himpathy" as a key component of misogyny. In the context of harassment, Manne explains, "himpathy" rears its ugly head as "excessive sympathy sometimes shown toward male perpetrators of sexual violence. It is frequently extended in contemporary America to men who are white, nondisabled, and otherwise privileged 'golden boys.' . . . There is a subsequent reluctance to believe the women who testify against these men, or even to punish the golden boys whose guilt has been firmly established." To Manne, Stanford student Brock Turner is a classic case. Turner assaulted a campus visitor, Chanel Miller, while she was unconscious, and he was convicted of felony sexual assault—a rare occurrence, given the low rates at which these crimes are prosecuted, and the even lower rates at which they result in a finding of guilt. The prosecutors asked for a sentence of six years in prison. Yet the judge, Aaron Persky, sentenced Turner to just six months, shocking many.

Most disturbing to me (and, I think, to Manne) was not the length of the sentence—we Americans lock people up for far too long—but instead Persky's justification for it. As he saw it, Turner was, despite everything, a good guy at heart, and for a young Stanford athlete with a bright future even a short prison term would be devastating. He had raped someone, sure, but he wasn't a *rapist*. In a letter to the court, Turner's father wrote that the whole matter had already been very difficult for his son, who had lost his appetite even for "a big ribeye steak." Of this, Manne writes: "The excessive sympathy that flows to perpetrators like Brock Turner both owes and contributes to insufficient concern for the harm, humiliation, and (more or less lasting) trauma they may bring to their victims. . . . In the case of male dominance, we sympathize with him first, effectively making him into the victim of his own crimes."

Given the pervasiveness of himpathy, it's easy to understand why some might look askance at Know Your IX when it devotes energy and resources to protecting accused students' rights. An onlooker might charge us with seeing these accused students—most of whom are male, and most of whom, statistically, *probably did it*—first and foremost as victims. That's a fair diagnosis when it comes to many critics of university efforts to address sexual harassment, who consistently care *only* for the accused, never for survivors, and who use "due process" rhetoric as a cover for their bias. As I discuss in the last part of this book, bad-faith actors regularly use procedural objections to ensure male impunity. Anti-harassment advocates are well aware of that. As a result, some are primed to view any call for due process as a sexist effort to elevate, once again, men over women, the needs of abusers over those of their victims.

But however understandable it is, the view that attention to the procedural rights of alleged harassers is inherently anti-survivor is wrong. To begin with, one can decline to feel sorry for the accused but still recognize that fair procedures are practically and politically necessary, even helpful, for victims. And I'll go a step further: measured compassion for alleged harassers facing the threat of punishment makes for better policy. After all, what Manne criticizes is not concern for the accused in any form, especially when an allegation is not yet proven. Hers is a critique of excessive empathy, misused— empathy that crowds out concern for other worthy subjects, empathy that is impervious to fact. What doesn't need to be laid aside is the basic empathy (or at least sympathy) that ought to exist among all of us as fellow humans. Just because some critics abuse the principles of due process in their quest for male impunity does not mean that we, as feminists, should reject the truer, better version of those same principles. To do so would be ethically wrong and an abandonment of the commitments—to justice, freedom, equality, human dignity—that drive us to care about harassment in the first place.

This is especially clear when we remember that not all who are accused of sexual harassment are privileged "golden boys," as Manne herself repeatedly reminds us. Concern for alleged abusers is particularly difficult and uncomfortable because so many of the best-known ones are men insulated by power or status. Harvey Weinstein and Brock Turner do not exactly tug at the heartstrings. And sexual abuse often goes hand in hand with privilege: those who feel most entitled in general often feel entitled to the bodies of others. But it's also true that there are plenty of sexual harassment allegations that occur outside the spotlight of media attention precisely because those involved, including the accused, are *not* famous, are *not* powerful, are too poor or Black or queer to make headlines.

Let me be clear: I'd never expect a survivor to sit around empathizing with the plight of someone accused of doing what was done to them. That burden does not fall on victims' shoulders. But for those of us who have taken on the task of grappling with tough policy questions, we should take to heart that we can honor both our commitment to survivors and our commitment to procedural fairness.

PART OF WHY fair procedures matter—in harassment cases and all others, both in and out of legal settings—is that they help decision-makers come to more accurate conclusions, untainted by bias or other forms of irrationality. That's why it is so important for each side to be able to review the other's evidence and present their own version of the story. As a general matter, procedures that allow both parties the opportunity to provide full information—the opportunity to be heard, in the language of due process—will facilitate truth-seeking.

But accuracy is only part of why fair procedures are so important. After all, many of the fundamentals of legal due process purposefully stand in the way of accurate decision-making. Courts toss confessions given without a Miranda warning and ignore evidence collected without a proper warrant. Ryan, the Wesley college student I mentioned earlier, might have been forthcoming with university administrators precisely *because* he did not know, walking into his interview, exactly who had accused him of doing what. That the ambush served a truth-seeking function does not mean that depriving him of notice was fair. Because fairness is about more than the outcome.

We deliberately embrace rules that sometimes get in our way because procedure, at its best, affirms the dignity of the people who must travel through it—on *both* sides of an allegation. Some of the most powerful writing on due process and dignity comes from Jerry Mashaw, a pioneering scholar in the normally dry and technical field of administrative law. An unfair process, Mashaw writes, "defines the participants as objects, subject to infinite manipulation by 'the system.' To avoid contributing to this sense of alienation, terror, and ultimately self-hatred, a decisional process must give participants adequate notice of the issues to be decided, of the evidence that is relevant to those issues, and of how the decisional process itself works." To be treated fairly is to be treated as a human who matters.

Some of the dignity-affirming features of proper process are obvious, like the right to present your side of the story. But some can be quite subtle. For example, Dan Roth, a Berkeley lawyer who represents students accused of sexual harassment, told me he wishes that schools would sign emails to his clients with a person's name rather than simply "The Office of Student Affairs." That way, accused students would know whom to contact with questions about the process—and would feel like people interacting with other people, rather than widgets on a conveyer belt headed who knows where.

The ways that process promotes or undermines dignity may sound airy and theoretical. But the effects are concrete. People notice how a procedure makes them feel, and how they feel affects how well that procedure works. A voluminous empirical literature shows that participants are more likely to buy into the result of a process when they feel it's fair—even when they do not like the outcome. And such "procedural justice" isn't just an individual matter. Research has found that people are more likely to comply with police and court orders when they perceive the system as procedurally just, a perception that is often based not only on people's personal experiences but the experiences of those around them. The flip side is that without consistent fair processes for individuals, the perceived legitimacy of an authority deteriorates system-wide.

These lessons extend to other kinds of decision-making and adjudication, including those outside the legal system. One study, for example, looked at how employees react to bosses' decisions about pay raises, examining how the process by which those decisions were reached affected how people felt about the results. The researchers found that a company's use of certain elements of fair process—such as providing reasoning based in evidence and allowing the employee an opportunity to offer input about their performance—contributed to greater pay satisfaction. It also increased employees' trust in their supervisors and overall commitment to the organization. Crucially, that was true regardless of the size of the worker's raise. A similar dynamic plays out when employees are fired: if they feel they were treated fairly in the process, they respond less negatively to the outcome. And in the wake of layoffs, the *remaining* staff are more committed to the organization, and more cooperative, if their departed colleagues were treated well.

Such procedural justice research shows that for feminists engaged in the fight against sexual harassment, attention to fairness for the accused is strategically wise. To put it bluntly, we as a movement are always on thin ice, for all the same reasons victims are disbelieved. Many people believe our cause is made up, or at least exaggerated; some believe that what we allege is real but just not worth ruining the future of a nice young man. The legitimacy derived from procedural justice can buffer against historical skepticism that there ought to be any consequences for sexual abuses at all. And this, in turn, will benefit survivors.

To put it another way: because we as a society collectively decided that sexual harassment is a problem only a few decades ago—and some people are still not so convinced—there is a built-in assumption of illegitimacy to any endeavors to address those harms, especially outside a courtroom. Consider the backlash to campus efforts to address sexual assault—efforts that some believe ushered in unfairness against the accused. The backlash's central mantra is *Get schools out of this business altogether*. As we'll see later in this book, the perception that school discipline procedures were unjust spurred state and national campaigns to limit the ability of colleges to address sexual harms at all. If these efforts succeed—and the story of the Title IX backlash is far from over—student survivors will lose access to significant remedies and will more likely be forced to choose between remaining with their abusers on campus or dropping out.

ANOTHER BENEFIT TO fair procedures: processes that engender community trust—that victims see as legitimate authorities to resolve conflicts—also reduce the likelihood of the wronged turning to vigilante options that put everyone at risk. In an essay titled "Folktales of International Justice," law professor David Luban writes about Soghomon Tehlirian, a survivor of the 1915 Armenian genocide. In the aftermath of World War I, the Allies initially hoped to prosecute the genocide's perpetrators for violating "the laws of humanity." But the Americans objected that those laws were too vague for criminal culpability, and the effort failed. A few years later, Tehlirian—then only seventeen—shot and killed the genocide's primary mastermind. Today, a monument to Tehlirian stands in Fresno, California, where he is buried. "This monument has been erected by the Armenian people in memory of Soghomon Tehlirian, the national hero who on March 15, 1921, brought justice upon Talaat Pasha, a principal Turkish perpetrator of the Armenian genocide of 1915," it reads. Luban interprets the monument as declaring: "If the law will not bring justice . . . then justice will fall to vigilantes like Tehlirian."

History provides too many instances where, as one book on the subject puts it, "the government fails to protect and to do justice," and so "victimized citizens are left with little option but to do these things for themselves." Certainly, some of the community-based approaches that arise in the vacuum left by a broken system are transformative and deeply productive. But voluntary, collective accountability and reconciliation are not always possible, and that is when the Tehlirians emerge. Such vigilantism puts ordinary citizens at tremendous risk, embroiling them in extralegal violence, transforming them into targets for the government, and putting them in danger from their victims' defenders, who might take vigilante action themselves. And vigilante efforts at justice outside the law also put suspects—not all of whom, of course, are guilty—at risk of both inaccurate and overly harsh punishment.

All this rings true to me based on my own exposure to vigilantism in far less dramatic form. When I was in college, my roommate Kate and I often spoke admiringly of Brown University students who, decades earlier, had written the names of classmates known to be sexually violent on bathroom stall doors as a warning to others. They had devised a solution to a problem we saw on our own campus. Our social circles shared news in hushed tones of who had raped whose friend, who should be avoided at parties, who seemed charming but got aggressive when drunk. My friend Miranda, bless her, would whisper words of caution into the ears of girls she saw dancing with these men. And yet the flow of information was stymied, limited by the contingencies of friendships and cliques. I could have told you who on the weekly newspaper to avoid, but had no clue who on the swim team or in the debate society had a bad reputation. Whisper networks left those least plugged into any given scene, and indeed those most isolated from their classmates as a whole, most vulnerable to serial wrongdoers.

And our college, the proper authority to handle these allegations, did nothing. None of us could trust the school to act; we rarely turned to it for help, and when we did so, the administration generally confirmed our fears about its ineffectuality. Much of this was about substance, not procedure. The school was simply unwilling to sanction students for sexual assault. But plenty of our concern was procedural, too. Multiple boards were tasked with investigating sexual harassment, covering different jurisdictions, with different powers and responsibilities. None of this was clear to harassment victims: the school's website directed students to various resources on various pages with no explanation, and did not list a Title IX coordinator, a position that federal law requires schools to have and make known. To whom a student first reported could determine the whole path of a complaint, like a labyrinth of water slides that might drop you into a pool of sludge. Even after we filed a Title IX complaint with the Department of Education, and the federal investigation brought on significant reforms, the school still attracted scandal when it empowered a single provost to reduce sanctions against faculty members. In one instance, that provost refused to remove a harassing professor with whom he had close ties.

No wonder, then, that lists on bathroom walls seemed relatively appealing to Kate and me. We knew the men who had hurt us, collectively and individually, but we had no fair process by which to hold them accountable. Why not take justice into our own hands?

We never worked up the courage—a failing for which I am now grateful, as I look back on the proposal with far less moral certainty. But in the years following our graduation, students at other schools made headlines when they did follow through on similar ideas. At the University of Chicago, students made a website listing "people known to commit varying levels of gender-based violence." At Brown, students resurrected the bathroom-stall tradition from a quarter-century before. Columbia students also scribbled names on bathroom stalls, which the university repeatedly cordoned off and scrubbed clean. Among the men on the Columbia list was a student who had admitted to raping a classmate but returned to campus after one semester. "We needed some way to warn people that these people are violent," one of the students who wrote the list told the *Guardian*. Yet because the university's confidentiality rules prohibited students from speaking about their own reports, even to friends, activists could not share such warnings except anonymously. At a

high school in the East Bay, students' bathroom lists were removed
by administrators, so a girl created an Instagram account naming
classmates and teachers accused of harassment; students at other
local high schools soon followed suit. One young woman told me
she'd started such an account for her small Catholic school because
administrators had been largely unresponsive to her report months
earlier that a student had sexually assaulted her at a party. If adults
wouldn't protect her classmates, she would.

In October 2017, a friend sent me a link via the secure messaging
app Signal. It took me to a spreadsheet titled "Shitty Media Men."
The men on the list were mostly affiliated with the New York writing scene; I'd heard of some of them and knew a few personally. Their
offenses were detailed and ranged in severity from inappropriate
texting to rape. Men accused of physical violence against multiple
women were highlighted in red. I was exhilarated by the idea that
some men might finally get what was coming to them. I feared the
messiness of the project. And I was also, I admit, scared—given my
familiarity with some of these men, my reputation as an anti-rape
firebrand, and perhaps some narcissistic paranoia—that they might
come after me, thinking I had contributed to the list.

I never edited the spreadsheet. I was too conflicted about its ethics and, now a lawyer rather than a radical college student, firm in
my desire to avoid any attendant liability. As it turned out, even
had I been inclined, my window to do so was short. Hours after I
first received the link, it went dead. *BuzzFeed* had run an article on
the list's existence—a violation of the rules announced at the top of
the spreadsheet, but probably inevitable, as the list's creator later
conceded. That woman, Moira Donegan, identified herself months
later in a thoughtful essay. (She feared the alternative was that she
might be outed by famed rape apologist Katie Roiphe in a forthcoming piece in *Harper's*.) Donegan wrote that she had created the
list because of the failings, including procedural failings, of the
other available options. "Too often, for someone looking to report an
incident or to make habitual behavior stop, all the available options

are bad ones," she explained. "The police are notoriously inept at handling sexual-assault cases. Human-resources departments, in offices that have them, are tasked not with protecting employees but with shielding the company from liability—meaning that in the frequent occasion that the offender is a member of management and the victim is not, HR's priorities lie with the accused." In other words, those processes were biased. Unfair.

I'm confident about only two things when it comes to the Shitty Media Men list. First, vigilante efforts, whether on bathroom walls or Google spreadsheets, are a dangerous method of accountability for all involved. The risk of false accusations is heightened when all reports are anonymous and there is no mechanism to vet claims. Any attempt to present an alternative account is frustrated by the lack of full detail: How does a truly innocent man defend himself from an accusation when he does not know the who, what, when, or where of it? The risks are also tremendous for the participants. After engaging in campus vigilantism, at least one University of Chicago student suspected of being involved in the website faced online retribution and intimidation. A school administrator reported an Instagram list of alleged harassers to the police—not to investigate the alleged harassment but to identify and punish the account's managers. Donegan was sued by one of the named men, who sought information about everyone who edited the document. I still fear retaliation from the Shitty men I know.

But the second thing I'm sure of is that those methods are *still* sometimes the best option available right now. "In the risk-reward calculation of 'protect myself and my friends from serial rapists in our midst' versus 'avail ourselves of processes that are demeaning, biased, and ineffective,' it's to be expected that the former will reliably, and recurrently, outweigh the latter, particularly for the young and radical," my college roommate Kate wrote to me recently. No one, I think, wants to live in a world where the Shitty Media Men list or bathroom scrawling is plausibly a top choice. The obvious solution, then, both to the sexual violence and to the dangers of vigilantism, is to provide a better alternative so victims know they can safely report through more structured paths.

CONVERSATIONS ABOUT PROCESS often make it seem like fair procedures are a concern only for the accused. But victims also need procedural protections and aren't always provided them. The HR offices that Donegan criticized, which frequently side with management over lower-ranking employees, provide an example of anti-victim structural bias. So does a case from the University of Wisconsin–Madison, which gave a student accused of rape the right to decide who would be on the disciplinary panel judging the allegation. That's why advocates for survivors, just like advocates for the accused, know a right to a fair process is paramount.

Reviewing lawsuits and stories from both student complainants and accused students, I've been struck by how often they ask for many of the same things. A clear explanation of the process and their rights. An advocate to help them navigate the system. The opportunity to present evidence and witnesses, to review what the other side submitted, and to respond. An unbiased decision-maker.

I'm not naively optimistic. Some of the procedural reforms that critics demand genuinely benefit one party and hurt the other. But when it comes to the low-hanging fruit—the basic, foundational elements of fair process—everyone wins. That's part of why I bristle when critics write about changes in sexual harassment procedures as a swinging "pendulum" or "overcorrection," as though every gain for one side is a loss for the other.

And this is to say nothing of the importance of fair procedures for victims if they end up facing their own disciplinary charges as a result of their report, like the BYU students suspended for being out after curfew when they were assaulted, or my client suspended for participating in sexual conduct at school—that is, her own rape. Other survivors face bogus counterclaims from their harassers. These are often filed to spook a victim into dropping the original complaint or to style the abuser as the "real" victim, and so protect him from consequences. A 2020 survey by Know Your IX found not only that nearly 10 percent of student survivors faced such retaliatory complaints, but that the practice has become increasingly common over just the last few years.

During my research, I spoke to a few women whose abusers reported them to university officials for sexual misconduct. Grace had been abused by her boyfriend, "Tom," a classmate. When campus security intervened in an altercation, he claimed victimhood first, much like an abuser who learns to call the cops. Afterward, Grace was subject to strict rules, designed by Tom, about where she could travel on their small campus. When she asked the school to investigate his allegations and reconsider the restrictions, it refused. Another woman, an English professor named Jennifer Doyle, reported a student, "Amelia," for stalking her. Amelia then filed a convoluted countercomplaint against Doyle, which said the English professor had propositioned her via "Morse code." Doyle told me she did not fully know the allegations against her until her interview with university administrators. She was cleared, but believes the countercomplaint explains in large part why a hearing panel ultimately dismissed her original stalking complaint against Amelia, even though the school's initial investigation substantiated Doyle's account.

Aside from all the other ethical and practical reasons to support proper procedures for those accused of wrongdoing, therefore, fair process is helpful for victims because often they *are* the accused. Of course, we should work toward a better world where survivors do not risk punishment when they come forward. But as long as the line between complainant and respondent is porous, concern for one requires concern for the other.

Chapter 10

The Limits of Process

Over the course of the twentieth century, the Supreme Court was repeatedly called upon to address race discrimination in the selection of jurors. Lawyers in a jury trial generally are allowed a handful of "peremptory challenges," which let them kick a potential juror out of the jury pool without explanation. In theory, such challenges allow attorneys to remove potentially biased jurors. Predictably, though, lawyers instead used this freedom to exclude those who they thought would vote unfavorably for their side, often based on the juror's race. In its seminal 1986 opinion *Batson v. Kentucky*, the Supreme Court condemned the use of race-based peremptory challenges and outlined, in rough form, the process by which a judge could suss out such discrimination.

The court was right to provide this procedural protection. But it's not clear that *Batson* has had much practical effect. Justice Thurgood Marshall, while concurring with the ruling, predicted that lawyers would simply come up with ostensibly race-neutral reasons to cover up their real motivation. And so they have, with judges all too eager to accept ridiculous explanations. In one case that came after *Batson*, the prosecution dismissed all six potential Hispanic jurors. In justifying his exclusion of one, the attorney explained he did not like that this prospective juror, a pipeline operator, had a job title that began with the letter "P." Even the conservative U.S. Court of Appeals for the Fifth Circuit saw this "reason" as insufficient. But the prosecutor then "remembered" that he had also heard that pipeline workers like smoking weed, which he thought might be an issue given that the case concerned possession of marijuana and heroin. The court found this post hoc justification reasonable. *Batson* didn't get rid of prejudice. It just made it operate under an alias.

In other words, process is not magic. It matters—it matters enough that I've written a book about it—but it will not solve all our ills. The procedural protections that the American legal system holds so dear do not deserve our absolute faith.

Cross-examination, for example, is often touted as a hallmark of due process. Judges and advocates regularly quote an early twentieth-century treatise on the rules of evidence, which called the ability to directly question one's adversary "the greatest legal engine ever invented for the discovery of truth." But contemporary research suggests that this might be wrong. I noted earlier that some of what we perceive as evidence of lying may instead be signs of unease about the cross-examination process. As Columbia law professor Suzanne Goldberg writes, studies show that "a witness's nervous or stumbling response to adversarial questioning is more likely an ordinary human reaction to stress than an indicator of false testimony." For that reason, among others, "many scholars say that aggressive, adversarial questioning is more likely to distort reality than enable truth-telling."

The unreliability of cross-examination casts doubt on the very American notion that an antagonistic struggle between two parties, with a judge standing in as impartial referee, is the best way to find the truth. Many other countries instead use what is called an inquisitorial model, where the judge takes the lead in investigating the case, working together with the parties to gather evidence and question witnesses. There is little evidence that one system is more accurate than the other. It's perhaps odd, then, that the question of whether and how students should cross-examine each other has become such a prominent part of the debate over school sexual harassment policies. The demand for such an adversarial system may be rooted as much in the symbolic meaning of that process as in its actual usefulness.

Another limitation worth noting: good procedures can only do so much when the rules themselves are bad, or when decision-makers are incompetent and malicious. In these cases, touting procedural safeguards as the answer is akin to saying, as law professor Craig Haney facetiously declared, "let them eat due process." Some scholars and advocates have worried—correctly, in my view—that procedural justice can serve as the lipstick on the pig of an overly punitive system. Local activists were rightly skeptical, for instance, when the notoriously violent and corrupt Chicago Police Department rolled out procedural justice training in response to protests of their brutality against Black civilians. The main problem with the Chicago PD was not the process but the substance.

In situations like this, investments in procedure can appear at best ineffective, at worst downright manipulative. After all, why is promoting police legitimacy in the eyes of the community a laudable goal if the department's actions are not, in fact, legitimate? We should not, as the theorist Dennis Fox puts it, automatically "accept the dominant assumption that legitimacy should be enhanced in order to gain greater compliance with the demands of legal authorities."

FAIR PROCESS ALSO can't entirely overcome people's investment in the end result of the adjudication. Some of the people accused of sexual harassment that I spoke to for this book complained of specific procedural errors. But for most, their dominant complaint was simply that they had lost: their boss or their school had sided with their alleged victim. Some said this was unfair because the allegation against them was false. Others conceded that it was true but still felt that they didn't deserve punishment.

One man, for instance, felt deeply that he had been treated unfairly when a fellow graduate student told their school that he had sexually assaulted her. Without a doubt, the proceedings against him did take too long, spanning over a year, and did not include protections courts have since mandated. But his primary objection was one of definitions, not process—that is, he disagreed about what constitutes sexual harm, not how the school handled the investigation. The alleged victim had reported two forms of unwanted sexual contact. The man admitted to the less severe of the two, and according to the university's report he was found responsible only for that one. In our conversation, he told me he thought this contact was not bad enough to merit sanctions. If he is right about that, he has reason to be angry. But that objection is not something process could ameliorate.

The man's story reminded me of another case, a very famous one, where I believe public complaints about process were really, at heart, about substance: the resignation of Al Franken. When a number of women accused the Democratic Minnesota senator of inappropriate sexual conduct, he acknowledged that he was sometimes too physically familiar when meeting people. And he admitted to the pantomimed groping of a sleeping talk-radio host, which had been photographed. Otherwise, he disputed the allegations. Franken called for an investigation by the Senate Ethics Committee, which he felt would clear him. Chuck Schumer, the Democratic minority leader, agreed: a full investigation would proceed. The committee would have the power to subpoena witnesses and weigh the evidence Franken and his alleged victims provided. As more women came forward, though, a number of other Democratic senators, led by New York's Kirsten Gillibrand, called for Franken to resign. "Enough is enough," she said. Schumer joined their calls and, according to Franken, threatened to encourage the rest of the caucus to do the same. (Schumer confirmed he told Franken to resign but denies the threat.) Perhaps Schumer hoped to heighten the contrast between his party and the Republicans, whose president bragged about sexual assault and whose Senate candidate from Alabama, Roy Moore, was accused of sexually abusing underage girls. Whatever Schumer's motives were, his move worked. Franken quit.

To many—wealthy Democratic donors, op-ed writers, and Franken himself—the senator's ouster was a travesty of due process. "I couldn't believe it," Franken told Jane Mayer of the *New Yorker* for a 2019 article she wrote in his defense. "I asked [Schumer] for due process and he said no." But that's not quite right. When Franken asked Schumer for an actual process, for an investigation, he had said yes. Franken could have waited out the disparagement and tried to prove the allegations false, but he chose not to do so. Franken was "entitled to whichever process he wants," Gillibrand later explained. "But he wasn't entitled to me carrying his water, and defending him with my silence."

If I had been a senator, I don't think I would have joined Gillibrand's and Schumer's calls for Franken to resign. I would have preferred to see the results of the investigation before weighing in. The photo, of course, needed no inquiry, and some sanction was likely due for that alone. But my view on whether Franken should have left the Senate would probably have depended on whether other, more serious allegations were true. Yet regardless of whether his colleagues made the right choice as a matter of solidarity or politics, they did not deprive him of *process*. As congressman Jerry Nadler put it a few years later, in calling on New York governor Andrew Cuomo to resign after multiple allegations of sexual harassment, a public official is owed due process in any government investigation that may end in formal consequences—but "political judgments" about "confidence in our political leadership" are not bound by the same constraints. You can implore a man to step down before you could convict or impeach him.

I think the real reason Franken's resignation troubled so many is the nature of his alleged behavior. He stood accused of inappropriate touching and kissing, but not, his defenders stressed, anything like the allegations of rape levied against other famous men during the same period. Mayer's article dwells on the debate about whether Franken's alleged transgressions, if true, would be enough to remove a person from office. Most of the allegations, she notes, didn't rise to the level "of grotesque misconduct that has often been exposed in the #MeToo era." In other words, it could have been worse. "This isn't Kavanaugh," Franken's friend Sarah Silverman, the comedian, told Mayer. "It isn't Roy Moore." Franken is "a warm, tactile person," explained Andy Barr, Franken's former assistant. "There's a difference between molesting someone and being friendly. But there may not be a difference between feeling molested and feeling that someone's being friendly."

There is room for disagreement about which of the allegations against Franken would have warranted removal if proven. But if a defender's answer is that few or none would, that's a claim about substance, not process. It's a messy argument to make, and I wouldn't be eager to take it up on an evening political show, explaining to viewers exactly how many gropes is too many. "Denied due process" sounds better as a complaint. But it's simply inaccurate.

ANOTHER ISSUE THAT process cannot solve is the airing of allegations in the first place. I, of course, think it's a good thing that more people are now able to come forward when they experience sexual harassment. But false allegations, however rare, obviously do occur. And I have no doubt that these can have devastating and unjust consequences for the accused. Nonetheless, there can be no process to vet an allegation before it is made. After all, it's the levying of the allegation that triggers the vetting in the first place. You can't require a victim to prove her case before requesting the investigation that would do exactly that. And I don't think most of us want to live in a world where people can't freely express their own experiences without getting sign-off from a judge first.

Yet some critics take procedural umbrage with exactly that when it comes to sexual harassment allegations. Bret Stephens, the *New York Times*' most prominent right-wing columnist, has repeatedly insisted that putative victims should not come forward publicly with allegations about high-profile men unless they have "abundant evidence"—whatever that means; presumably more than a preponderance—to prove the allegations. Without that volume of hard proof, he says, any allegation is "odious," a "smear." It is, in his words, a failure of "moral obligation." Here, Stephens's objection is not to punishment without lots of evidence, or even to newspapers publishing a story without due diligence. He objects, instead, to people airing allegations about their own lives. That, to him, is the moral failure.

Of course, plenty of real abuse simply does not result in "abundant evidence" beyond the victims' own testimony. But by Stephens's logic, survivors should not share *true* accounts of violence unless they have the paperwork to back it up. For him, whether the accusation is a "smear" turns not on its actual veracity, or lack thereof, but on the amount of documentation. One might ask why we shouldn't instead adopt the obvious, preferable rule: people should only make true allegations. What's "odious" is making a false accusation, not making a true accusation that lacks abundant proof.

Media ethics are outside my expertise. But I can't help noticing the obvious repercussions Stephens's argument holds for the press as well. If a complaint unaccompanied by abundant documentation is a "smear" out of the complainant's mouth, it's presumably also a smear when it appears in print. That's an odd position for a newspaperman to take. The question of what accusations are fit for print is not a matter of due process but of journalistic standards, libel, and defamation. In the United States, generous laws give newspapers significant leeway to print allegations of wrongdoing by public figures, so long as the publishers do not act with "actual malice." Such flexibility is frustrating to some famous people, who would prefer that fewer negative stories about their alleged misdeeds were published. (President Trump certainly would have liked to restrict the press in this way.) But the flexibility of our regime is motivated by a legal and ethical commitment just as precious as due process: free speech. It's strange to see a newspaper columnist want to import strict procedural requirements into his field, which flourishes precisely because it is not bound by them.

PROCEDURES OF THE type discussed in this book also don't provide much help in deciding how to respond to allegations that we come across as individuals—when we might judge them not on behalf of an institution, but as humans making decisions about our personal lives. Perhaps a friend says another friend raped him. Should we still invite both to our next party? Or maybe we read that the star of an upcoming film abused his coworkers. Should we skip the movie? In neither instance do we have the power, as ordinary people, to collect all the relevant evidence and convene a hearing. Your friend's alleged rapist is not likely to turn over all his text messages to you. Neither is Kevin Spacey.

Celebrities make for an easier case because we can know so much about them without affecting them in any way. Some allegations are the subject of extensive reporting. Even before Harvey Weinstein was convicted, I felt pretty confident he'd assaulted women. To form that opinion, I didn't need to run the allegations through a formal process, any more than I need a minitrial to vet any article in the *Times*. But I also don't feel obliged to conduct my own monthslong investigation of celebrity rumors that haven't been reported out. My inability to come to a fully informed judgment has no real impact on them or their lives. I'm not going to lose sleep over whether I've been fair to a multimillionaire who doesn't know I exist.

When we hear about abuse in our personal lives, on the other hand, whom we believe can of course have grave effects on people we care about. But a legalistic approach is both inappropriate and impossible there. Not least, it can be cruel. Responding to a disclosure with skepticism or hostile questioning can further isolate victims in need of help. Imagine confiding in a loved one about abuse, only to be told they couldn't offer comfort and support until they interviewed the person who hurt you. Pretending to serve as an impartial judge of our friends and family is not only a fool's errand, given our inevitable biases, but an abdication of our other more important roles as a sibling or roommate or confidant. Let me put it this way: a complainant should always bear the burden of proof in any courtroom or disciplinary action. But if your sister tells you her boyfriend raped her, your first instinct should be to believe her. Your job is to be on her side.

Some allegations fall between celebrity gossip and intimate disclosures. We may hear, for example, that an acquaintance raped another acquaintance. We may see the name of a college friend on the Shitty Media Men list and not know how to approach him at a reunion. If you worked in film before 2017, you might have heard vague gossip about Weinstein and had to decide whether to avoid working on his projects. These are not dilemmas for which I can offer a single easy solution. But they also aren't unique to sexual harassment. We hear bad things about people in our orbits all the time—that they are mean to their kids, or use racial epithets when drunk, or secretly voted for a despicable candidate. We make judgments based on our relationships and what we know about them already. I'd happily read a book about the practical ethics of dealing with rumors. But that's not a matter of fair process.

11

Straw Feminists

My favorite comic is a piece by Kate Beaton. After two parents put their children to bed and turn off the light, a pair of "straw feminists" emerge like monsters from the closet. These snake-tongued women proceed to torment the kids with ostensibly "feminist" positions that the right wing insists we sincerely believe. "Equality is shit!" one declares. "I won't stop until women have it *better* than men." The parents bravely come to the rescue, explaining that these nightmarish figments are not real. "They don't just haunt children, they haunt a lot of things," Mom explains. Before disappearing, hissing, the straw feminists lob one last remark: "Someone needed a quote for the paper so I told them all men were rapists."

Despite public misperceptions to the contrary, the vast majority of the feminists I've worked with know that process matters. When we sit down together to hash out the tough details of a sexual harassment policy, the importance of fairness is considered a given by organizers and policymakers. Many of us have backgrounds in criminal defense work. Many of us also work on race discrimination, including in workplace and school discipline, and so are acutely aware of racial inequalities in those contexts. Plenty of our survivor clients have also faced serious disciplinary action as a result of their complaints. As mentioned earlier, a shocking number of student victims are punished for rule breaking, such as underage drinking, that comes to light as a result of their reports. The organizations I have worked at since law school take on cases concerning both sexual harassment and discriminatory student discipline, and often a single client will come to us for both issues.

I confess I'm often frustrated by how quick critics are to assume we are ready to burn every man at the stake at the mere suggestion of impropriety. My friend Sam Huber put it well in articulating a shared "pet peeve": "smug pundits / naive critics raising concerns about feminist projects (Me Too, campus assault, etc.) that feminists at work on those projects are already robustly discussing (usually for years, always better)." On a number of occasions, advocates for accused students expressed surprise and delight to learn of Know Your IX's work on fair process, including a sample bill of rights for students that it drafted and pushed states to adopt. (This was after my time at the organization, so I can brag.) I was glad to know that these advocates agreed with the policy. But I was annoyed that they had previously railed against us in public based on their assumptions about our values—one lawyer called us the Death Star to his Luke Skywalker—all while ignoring our actual, publicly available work.

Know Your IX's experience is representative of a broader trend. After the Kavanaugh hearings, columnist Emily Yoffe posed a question in the *Atlantic*: "Does anyone still take both sexual assault and due process seriously?" If she had cared to look around, she might have been heartened by the number of feminists who absolutely do. Likewise, a lawyer who advises expelled college students expounded in the *New York Times* that schools should not expel someone based only on an uninvestigated allegation—as though anyone were actually advocating for that position. She offered no specific recommendations relevant to the live debates of the day, such as how to structure cross-examination in student hearings. Instead, she offered platitudes: schools should "seek the truth without bias and evaluate all the evidence." Of course. The question is *how* to do so. And in the wake of the Weinstein allegations, opinion page pundits who hadn't thought about harassment since Anita Hill offered their takes on why feminists shouldn't advocate for men to be fired based on accusations alone. No shit. We were busy writing white papers on the merits of different investigatory methods; it was not exactly news to us that employers should have a process to vet complaints. Everywhere, women were having smart, measured conversations about Me Too, while oblivious critics worked themselves into a tizzy about feminists' inability to comprehend exactly the nuances we'd been the first to parse.

The dynamic was never more pronounced than when a little-known website called Babe published a woman's account of her negative sexual experience with the self-proclaimed feminist comedian Aziz Ansari. To put it mildly, the article would have benefited significantly from a lawyer, a better editor, and some basic fact-checking. The woman, Grace, called her experience sexual assault, but it was hard to tell what, exactly, had happened—not only as an ethical or legal matter, but as a question of facts. Had Ansari chased Grace around a room in an attempt to force her to have sex with him? Had he repeatedly tried to initiate sex in different parts of his apartment, and failed to read her cues that she was not interested? Neither reading was flattering to Ansari, but the difference between them mattered. And that was exactly the conversation many of us engaged in, online and in person.

We talked about negative sexual experiences, and their range from the violent and sanctionable to the disrespectful but perfectly legal. We talked about how the allegations should be evaluated in a way that was fair to Ansari, and what consequences, if any, would be appropriate. On Twitter and in my office, feminists acknowledged that Ansari's alleged behavior might very well not rise to the level of assault, but reflected an inequitable script that too many men of his (and my) generation follow: to take every "no" as a "maybe," to push and push and push until you get a "yes." That might be legal, but it certainly isn't ethical or kind. We discussed what to do about that class of allegations, in and out of the public spotlight. One point on which nearly everyone agreed: the Babe article was a mess and had done a disservice to both Grace and the cause. Yet in major publications, critics like Bari Weiss and Caitlin Flanagan denounced the feminist movement for failing to recognize exactly the distinctions, gradations, and complications on which we were—as any quick Twitter search would have shown—completely fixated.

SOMETIMES IT SEEMS like the media is not merely ignorant but willfully misrepresenting the facts, because it *wants* sexual harassment advocates to be engaged in witch hunts. I saw this constantly in coverage of the Obama administration's work on campus sexual assault and student discipline.

A little legal background: government agencies regularly publish "policy guidance" documents to help the public understand various laws. These documents don't change the rules, but they explain how the courts and civil servants interpret them. Starting in 1994, the Department of Education began publishing guidance documents that detailed schools' obligations under civil rights laws to address harassment based on race, sex, and disability. Many schools, though, failed to live up to their responsibilities. In 2011, President Obama's Department of Education wrote yet another guidance, this one known as the "Dear Colleague Letter"—the "colleagues" being schools that receive federal funding and so are subject to Title IX. The letter again laid out schools' responsibilities to address sexual harassment under Title IX, focusing mostly on sexual assault on college campuses. Schools had been falling down on the job. They needed a legal refresher and a kick in the pants to change their ways.

Other than identifying the correct standard of evidence (which I'll discuss more later), the Dear Colleague Letter, like previous guidance documents, talked a lot about how schools must help victims but did not say much about the specific mechanics of disciplining the wrongdoers. Whatever you think of the wisdom of that choice, it was not particularly surprising. Disciplinary remedies are only one part of a school's duty to victims under Title IX, and the Supreme Court and the Department of Education have historically given educators considerable discretion in designing their disciplinary procedures. If a school did pursue disciplinary charges, it would, of course, have to respect the rights of the accused, as the department noted. But accused students' procedural rights arose from the Constitution and state laws, not Title IX, the statute that the Dear Colleague Letter was sent to explain. Accordingly, the letter discussed process only in connection with protections required by sex discrimination law, rather than laying out all the rights an accused student might derive from every legal source. The closest the letter got to requiring specific procedures was in explaining the department's view that, per Title IX's equality mandate, schools must use an equitable standard of evidence and offer each side of an accusation the same rights and opportunities—whatever those were under the school's specific policy. For example, if the school allowed one side to appeal a decision, it must allow the other side to do so, too.

In the wake of the letter, many schools changed their policies and, for the first time, began suspending or expelling students for sexual harms. Some critics believe that in doing so, schools treated accused students unfairly. I don't doubt this was sometimes true. Schools regularly mishandle discipline for all kinds of offenses; it's not a problem specific to sexual harassment. And as law professor Samuel Bagenstos points out, the Department of Education might have foreseen that, after years of ignoring their Title IX responsibilities, some schools might implement sloppy, unfair policies in their rush to comply. That threat could have been addressed through more guidance and technical assistance. The Dear Colleague Letter should have better emphasized that the department took fair discipline very seriously and expected schools to do the same. To provide some helpful clarity, perhaps the department could have sketched out a few different models for disciplinary procedures that it believed were fair to everyone involved.

All that being said, the schools' procedural errors were absolutely not required by the Dear Colleague Letter. Many, in fact, were *counter* to it. And the letter in no way removed existing legal protections for accused students; there was no federal right an accused student had the day before the letter was published that he didn't have the day after. In short, a school could follow all the rules and recommendations in the letter while also treating accused students fairly. There was no conflict.

But you wouldn't have known that from the press. Many opinion writers and journalists were quick to attribute schools' alleged procedural failures to the Dear Colleague Letter. To fit their narrative, many made claims that were simply inaccurate on their face. For example, they often claimed that the Department of Education had forbidden schools from providing hearings or cross-examination, though it never had. (How so many of these errors got by fact-checkers in reputable papers I will never understand.) The accounts also left out the fact that the department actively investigated schools for violating the rights of accused students. And they failed to mention that under the Obama administration, the same department had done groundbreaking work *promoting* fair discipline, by using race and disability discrimination laws.

A casual observer reading the press coverage could be forgiven for thinking that the Obama administration cared only for victims, with no concern for due process. They could be excused for taking home the message that Title IX required schools to treat accused students unfairly. But none of that is true.

Conflict, I suppose, makes for a better story. In the wake of the Weinstein allegations, *USA Today* approached the writer Ijeoma Oluo to solicit a piece about Me Too. The editorial board was planning to write a column extolling the importance of due process in sexual harassment proceedings. They were looking for a counter-point article from someone who did not "believe in due process" and thought "that if a few innocent men lose their jobs it's worth it to protect women." Oluo refused. She *did* believe in due process. She tried to pitch a more nuanced account about how victims were denied basic opportunities to be heard, and how the singular focus on the careers of accused men served to recenter the conversation on the abusers, not the abused—a similar point to Manne's himpathy objection. But *USA Today* was not interested. They wanted a hyper-bolic screed by a caricature of a feminist, not a thoughtful take on a complicated issue.

A media narrative of straw woman zealots, incapable of balanc-ing different interests, isn't just unfair to the feminist movement. It hurts our collective ability to find common ground. It discourages advocates for fair process from engaging with us. (Think again of all the groups that were pleasantly surprised to discover Know Your IX had developed policies that they would have discovered earlier if they had not tuned us out.) Misrepresentations like these also feed the idea that the fight around sexual harassment is an intractable battle. On one side, we have the victims' people; on the other, the process people. They disagree on everything. Their interests are, tragically, irreconcilable. And we have to choose which team to join.

That dichotomy is false, thank goodness. But most people are only exposed to this debate through the media. So it's no wonder that many are inclined to throw up their hands and abandon the whole enterprise altogether. *Just leave it to the police! Anything else is too com-plicated!* I would probably think the same if all I knew of advocates was their caricatures.

I think of a conversation I had a few years ago with a journalist who was then writing for the *Atlantic*. She asked to talk about a story she was working on about why campus sexual assault is not a bipartisan issue. By her telling, the Republicans had chosen to care about the accused, and Democrats had chosen the victims. That notion was superficially appealing, I told the journalist, but it overlooked two obvious data points: the two major campus sexual assault bills considered by the Senate over the past decade. The Campus Accountability and Safety Act, championed by Claire McCaskill and Kirsten Gillibrand, both Democrats, was cosponsored in 2015 by a number of heavy-hitting Republicans, including Orrin Hatch of Utah and Lindsey Graham of South Carolina. And the Campus SaVE Act, which provided additional rights to all students involved in sexual assault allegations on campuses, was sponsored successfully by Bob Casey, a Democrat from Pennsylvania. The bill, eventually passed as part of the reauthorization of the Violence Against Women Act, enjoyed bipartisan support.

The journalist included none of this. Instead, she wrote that "policy recommendations remain largely divided along party lines." Nowhere did she so much as mention the two biggest policy efforts undertaken by the Senate, both of which undermined her thesis. A story of warring factions, it seems, was a more appealing one to tell, even if it was wrong.

SUFFICE IT TO say, I'm tired of the assumption that feminists are bulls in a china shop of men's futures. Nevertheless, some of our movement's strategies and messaging obscure our commitment to do right by all involved. Consider the activist rallying cry of "believe women" or, alternatively, "believe survivors." The slogans are ubiquitous at marches, in opinion pieces, and in social media declarations of solidarity. I understand why that phrase is important to many victims. It's a call to resist what is, for so many, a knee-jerk distrust of people who disclose sexual victimization, whether in close confidence or on the public stage. When the widespread default is to disbelieve survivors, a corrective is necessary. "Believe women" means "don't assume women as a gender are especially deceptive or vindictive, and recognize that false allegations are less common than real ones," says the feminist author Jude Ellison S. Doyle. "Treat women seriously, and don't automatically just believe the man," writes columnist Monica

Hesse. These lessons apply well to the situation where our response to a disclosure of victimization matters most: when someone close to us turns to us for support. "I believe you" is a great response if a friend tells you he was harassed by his boss or abused by an ex. Your job is to comfort, not to adjudicate. "Where's your proof?" would be cruel.

When we're considering public allegations, "believe women" can be a helpful reminder to check any instinct to immediately side with the accused. And it makes for a better Women's March sign than "respond with compassion, rather than skepticism, when people confide in you about traumatic experiences of sexual violence," or "we should combat undeserved skepticism—rooted in age-old misogyny!—of people who publicly report sexual harassment." As a matter of political strategy, though, I still have my concerns about the phrase. It is, I fear, particularly subject to misinterpretation—specifically, that "believe women" means "believe all women, all the time." The latter just can't be right. To embrace that view, even as a corrective to history, would inappropriately abandon two central tenets of fairness: that the decision-maker should be unbiased and that the complainant bears the burden of proving her case. If some people use the phrase to demand absolute, automatic acceptance of any allegation, regardless of context, I profoundly disagree.

I don't think anyone really believes that, though. From what I can tell, those who encourage us to "believe survivors" or "believe women" have a broader meaning in mind. They may fairly accuse me of critiquing a straw man, just as I accuse others above. Susan Faludi, the journalist and expert on anti-feminist backlash, has traced the use of two hashtags on Twitter, #BelieveWomen and #BelieveAllWomen. The latter, she found, is used almost exclusively by Me Too critics. Feminists don't actually think "believe women" means "believe every single woman about everything she says." That's just how the right wing has caricatured us.

But part of the reason the phrase is so ripe for misrepresentation is that it doesn't effectively communicate the more nuanced stance.

I have only anecdotal evidence, but a couple of friends and Twitter netizens have asked me—I believe in good faith—if the rallying cry calls on them to automatically believe everyone who says they were assaulted, without question and regardless of the evidence. Of course, the answer is no. But you can see how they might have gotten there. And as Hesse noted in her assessment of the slogan, "If you're explaining, you're losing."

At the least, people who use the phrase should understand when and where it is useful and when it isn't. When I was at Know Your IX, I was asked to review a policy guide, meant for college administrators, that had been drafted by an established anti-violence nonprofit. The guide urged schools to adopt "believe survivors" as an underlying principle motivating their policy design. What did that mean? I would hope the nonprofit meant that schools should respond to allegations with empathy and design adjudications that resist our built-in skepticism of harassment claims. That schools should offer supportive services to students regardless of whether they pursue disciplinary charges, based on an understanding that, statistically, most who come forward are telling the truth. Anti-violence professionals likely understand all those nuanced meanings within the short phrase. But a recently promoted associate dean of student life, new to the issue and public debate, could reasonably interpret "believe survivors" to mean just what it says: a school should abandon its appropriate neutral role and presume the truth of every claim. If that's not what the nonprofit meant, it should have explained more clearly. (I suggested as much. My edits were not accepted.)

MISUSE OF THE "believe survivors" slogan is sloppiness at best. But I've also seen what might be considered the opposite error: an inappropriate commitment to legal precision. In discussions about what process is due, it's disappointing to see some feminists understate the stakes for a worker threatened with termination, or a student facing suspension. And to be honest, I have sometimes fallen into the same trap.

Often, the conversation goes something like this: A critic says that a workplace should adopt some policy right out of the criminal justice system—for example, that employers should only sanction workers if they find responsibility "beyond a reasonable doubt." The anti-harassment advocates note that such a high standard is not required when the threatened punishment is less severe than incarceration. "It's not prison!" we say. "It's *only* firing." Legally, that's correct. But firing is a weighty punishment, as is suspension from school or expulsion from a beloved community group. Our legalistic rejoinder is unresponsive at best, and insensitive at worst, to the underlying accurate ethical claim that these sanctions matter. A better tack is to point out why criminal-style procedures are inappropriate in the workplace, while also acknowledging how terrible it might be for someone to be fired—for their economic stability, their future, and their self-worth.

I felt a similar frustration about the response from some feminists to Al Franken's resignation from the Senate over sexual harassment allegations. As I explained in the previous chapter, the controversy over Franken was really more about the substance of his offenses than the process by which they were handled. But it should be uncontroversial that, had Franken decided to stick it out and try to clear his name rather than resigning, he was absolutely entitled to a fair investigation. A certain corner of the internet, however, had a legally and ethically wrong response: Franken, they said, had no inherent right to be a United States senator and so could be fired on a whim. That notion is incorrect as a matter of law. Under the Constitution, a member of Congress may only be expelled with the vote of two-thirds of their chamber. But more fundamentally, the fact that Franken did not have a birthright to his Senate seat does not diminish the simple moral fact that it would have been unfair to kick him out without a chance to defend himself.

A minority of feminists, it seems, have been sucked into the narrative that justice for survivors is incompatible with concerns for fair process. "Here's an unpopular opinion: I'm actually not at all concerned about innocent men losing their jobs over false sexual assault/harassment allegations," one wrote in a widely criticized Twitter thread. "First, false allegations VERY rarely happen, so even bringing it up borders on a derailment tactic. It's a microscopic risk in comparison to the issue at hand (worldwide, systemic oppression of half the population). And more importantly: The benefit of all of us getting to finally tell the truth + the impact on victims FAR outweigh the loss of any one man's reputation."

Maybe this is condescending of me, or unduly sunny, but I can't help but think that this tweeter—like everyone else—would have been better served by a media that doesn't consistently pit due process and feminism against each other. Maybe then she wouldn't have felt like she had to pick one side over the other in such an absolute way. She is right, of course, that false accusations are far rarer than sexual harassment, and that overblown concern for the former can suck attention away from the latter. But her calculus is just not necessary: we don't have to choose between stopping "innocent men [from] losing their jobs" and "all of us getting to finally tell the truth." Rather, we can develop ways for victims to come forward, and for their claims to be vetted fairly before anyone is fired. We can have both. We must.

PART III

EXCEPTIONALISM

An "Exceptional" Harm

In December 2018—over a year after the Me Too deluge began, and shortly after Brett Kavanaugh's confirmation to the Supreme Court—Kathleen Parker wrote in the *Washington Post* of a worrying trend. Many men in finance and other industries, she said, were adopting the "Pence Rule," the vice president's insistence that he avoid time alone with any women besides his wife. These men feared, or purported to fear, a false accusation of sexual harassment. According to Parker, this development was an "inevitable" consequence of Me Too. And the reason for it was not sexism, paranoia, or sensationalist reporting. It was, instead, the "erosion of due process" for accusations of sexual harassment, rendering men afraid that their innocence would not protect them. "In many ways," she wrote, "this is all new terrain for us societally: How do we balance the right of every individual to be believed innocent until proven otherwise, while also giving accusers a platform to be heard?"

Perhaps issues of fair process were new to Parker's column. But the question itself is very old. How to balance the rights of the accused and those who say they have been harmed is, quite literally, an ancient problem, one that has shaped the development of our legal systems from the beginning.

And here's the key: *it isn't a question unique to sexual harassment.* Governments, workplaces, schools, political organizations, and social clubs all get called upon to investigate misconduct of all varieties. Employees get into fights, steal company property, and call each other racial slurs. Members of the local charity board embezzle funds. Political organizers punch each other in the face over strategic disagreements or romantic entanglements. Students beat each other up, vandalize campus landmarks, and taunt classmates with disabilities. In 2007, a student at my alma mater repeatedly threatened to kill his roommate, leaving messages in fake blood on their shared dorm wall.

In short, people hurt each other. Their communities are then tasked with figuring out what happened and what to do next. Every one of these examples demands we answer Parker's challenge: How do we respect fair process while giving victims the chance to come forward? None of this is unique to Me Too. The reasons I've given for why process matters for sexual harassment apply to every other kind of misconduct as well. Fair process is important for sexual harassment allegations because it is important for *all* allegations.

Indeed, many of the concerns that have been raised about the treatment of alleged harassers speak to systemic issues that aren't specific to harassment at all. Chief among these is the precarious nature of employment in the United States. Critics like Parker assume that accused harassers are often fired without any fair investigation. I have no sense of whether that's true. But if it is, that's only possible because most workers are utterly unprotected from arbitrary termination, thanks to the shrinking membership of labor unions over the last half-century and the "at-will" employment arrangements for almost all nonunion employees. That's not a story about Me Too. That's a story about work in America.

The same goes for anxieties about student discipline. Many critics express shock at how few protections students accused of sexual harassment have—or at least had, until Betsy DeVos stepped in (more on her in a moment). But these students were no less legally protected than any of their classmates accused of other forms of serious student discipline. In some cases, even before DeVos, they had *more* legal rights. The real problem is with the paucity of law governing student discipline in general, not student discipline for one particular offense.

Yet our national conversation about harassment so often forgets this. Critics talk about protecting workers accused of sexual harassment rather than advocating to end at-will employment or revitalize the labor movement. Policymakers demand new school disciplinary procedures for sexual harassment, when they should be overhauling school disciplinary procedures for all misconduct, period. And, almost always, they demand that these new procedures make it *uniquely difficult* to report and prove allegations of sexual harm. They advocate for extra obstacles, like higher standards of evidence and more intrusive methods of questioning, beyond those faced by victims reporting other forms of misconduct. I refer to this as "exceptionalism"—an assumption that sexual harassment allegations should be subject to different, and usually more demanding, procedures than all other forms of misconduct.

This approach flies directly in the face of a core principle of due process: proper procedures do not depend on the specific allegation. We scale procedural protections to account for what's at stake for the accused and other interested parties. We do not adjust them based on what specific kind of wrongdoing the accusation concerns. And as I'll explain in the next chapter, all the common reasons given to break that rule for sexual harms—for example, a belief that these claims are uniquely hard to prove—don't hold water.

Exceptionalism also makes the job of figuring out a fair process much more difficult. When we pose the question as "What procedures are appropriate specifically for sexual harassment?" we have to create an entire system out of whole cloth. If, instead, we ask, "What procedures are appropriate for interpersonal harms?" we have an easy place to start: the systems our institutions already use to deal with misconduct in general. If your group has an existing process for dealing with allegations of other kinds, you can build from there. You might need to add special training, or a couple of tweaks, to make sure that the process works for sexual harassment and other sensitive matters. But there's no need to start from scratch.

What's more, when we design a procedure that's meant to address sexual harassment allegations alone, it's too easy for sexist biases to determine our choices. All of us, even avowed feminists, bring a specific set of myths and assumptions to conversations about sexual harms. As a culture, we often believe (wrongly) that such allegations are particularly unlikely to be true, that women are vengeful liars, that men are frequently the hapless victims of false allegations. We think rape is a crime, and only a crime. So if we create a process just for allegations of this one particular kind, all those myths and biases will infect our design. We may decide we should make it uniquely hard to prove sexual harassment allegations because—consciously or not—we think sexual harassment allegations are uniquely deserving of skepticism. We may make choices that, if we knew *all* allegations would be vetted in the same way, would seem obviously wrong.

And thinking about process in the context of sexual harassment alone makes it harder for us to recognize these bad policies when we see them. Over the years that I've worked on these issues, I've seen many proposed procedural "reforms" aimed exclusively at sexual harassment allegations, changes that would tilt the scales dramatically in one direction: protecting the accused by disadvantaging victims. That policymakers and critics do not insist on the same reforms for other kinds of accusations should be a tell. But if those points of comparison are outside our frame of reference, the exceptional nature of these proposals is harder to recognize.

THERE IS PERHAPS no better example of exceptionalism than the Title IX regulations that Trump's Department of Education issued in 2020. As

I write, litigation about these regulations (including a suit for which I serve as counsel) is still ongoing; by the time this book is published, I hope they will be overturned in court or rescinded by the Biden administration. But at the moment, they are the law of the land. And even if they go away in the near future, they are worth looking at, since they illustrate so clearly the many problems that exceptionalism creates.

The new regulations make it harder for student victims to hold schools liable for mishandling sexual harassment. With a few exceptions, they excuse schools from addressing sexual harassment unless it is both "severe and pervasive"—that is, both very bad and very frequent. They allow schools to ignore sexual harassment that was not formally reported to the correct official. They also limit the geographic scope of school responsibilities, restricting them just to incidents that occurred on school grounds or on an official school trip. If a student was raped by her teacher or classmate across the street from the school, for instance, and now had to share a classroom with her rapist, the Department of Education no longer requires any action from the school. And if a school does investigate a report, the new regulations require special protections for students and staff accused of sexual harassment. In large part, the burden of those new protections falls on victims, with rules that make it uniquely hard to make and then to prove an allegation of sexual harassment.

The rules were published by Education Secretary Betsy DeVos, the right-wing billionaire whose résumé was startlingly devoid of relevant experience when she became the most important education official in the country. DeVos had never worked for a school and was unable to answer basic questions about education policy in her hearing. The closest she had to qualifications were her large donations to right-wing groups that champion privatizing education and rolling back civil rights. After alienating Republican senators with her opposition to public schooling and ignorant remarks about disability rights, DeVos was the first cabinet member in history confirmed not by the Senate itself but instead by the vice president's tie-breaking vote. At the start of her tenure, she hired as her top civil rights official Candice Jackson, an anti–affirmative action advocate who (incorrectly) told a *New York Times* reporter that "90 percent" of campus rape allegations were illegitimate, brought by women who, after a breakup, "just decided that [previous drunk sex] was not quite right."

DeVos and Jackson styled their Title IX rules as a response to the Obama administration's 2011 Dear Colleague Letter, which they said inadequately protected the rights of the accused. As noted earlier, this diagnosis was off. The Dear Colleague Letter did not disturb any student discipline rights guaranteed by the Constitution or state law. If advocates believed that those protections were insufficient—as I generally do—that was a problem with student discipline law in general, not with a policy guidance about sex discrimination. There was, after all, no reason to grant extra rights to students accused only of one particular kind of misconduct.

Yet when Trump came into office, that's exactly what his Department of Education set out to do. The new Title IX rules force schools to treat sexual harassment allegations in a different way from all other student discipline. For example, the regulations require schools to ignore any statements made by the respondent if he refuses to participate in a hearing—which he can do while retaining the right to cross-examine the complainant and witnesses. That means a student who admitted to raping a classmate in a text to a friend, or even on video, can block the school from considering that evidence simply by refusing to answer its questions. This is simply not how evidence ever works in America. Indeed, the nonsensical rule goes well beyond protections for criminal defendants facing incarceration, whose own past statements are admissible regardless of whether they testify. And it certainly goes beyond any right afforded elsewhere in student discipline. As a result, a student who was sexually harassed has a much harder time proving her claim than a student hurt in any other way. That is exceptionalism at work: a process built only to handle allegations we collectively regard as suspect is prone to adopt bizarre and novel protections for the accused. It is difficult for me to imagine that if the rule were applicable to anything other than sexual harms, anyone would think it was a good idea.

The new regulations also require schools to hold hearings where the victim can be cross-examined directly by a representative of the accused student. Schools are forbidden from using a common model approved by nearly all courts and preferred by many institutions: a hearing at which students would submit questions to one another through a presiding panel, rather than directly. Such a model, apparently, is good enough for students facing other disciplinary charges—but not for those accused of sexual harassment.

Thanks to advocates' efforts, one particularly egregious provision was abandoned before the regulations were finalized. Under it, a school couldn't use a lower standard of evidence for sexual harassment than it did for any other conduct violation that might result in the same sanction (e.g., suspension). But even if the school used a low standard of evidence for *all other* student conduct, it was still allowed to use a higher standard for sexual harassment alone. That is, inconsistency was allowed only if it resulted in a higher standard for sexual harassment, not a lower one. As a result, many victims of sexual harassment would have been required to provide more proof than a classmate who reported any other kind of wrongdoing, including closely analogous harms like nonsexual assault and racial harassment.

The proposed rule ignored the good reasons why schools sometimes used different standards of evidence in different contexts. Most schools use one of two standards for student discipline: "the preponderance of the evidence" or "clear and convincing evidence." Preponderance is the lower standard of proof; as we have seen, it is the one used in virtually all civil trials, ranging from slip-and-fall lawsuits to the wrongful death suit against O. J. Simpson. It puts the two parties on a level playing field: the decision-maker adopts whatever conclusion is supported by most of the evidence. School professionals prefer this preponderance standard for student-versus-student cases because it equally values both students' educations.

After all, a decision *not* to suspend one student, or restrict their movement through campus, might force the other to drop out. When some schools do use the higher "clear and convincing evidence" standard of proof, they might reserve it for harms like cheating and vandalism, offenses that are primarily "against" the school rather than another student. The administration can afford to tilt the scales against itself and carry a heavier burden; if it loses, it will suffer far less than a student victim who could not prove their case. The inconsistency is purposeful, rational.

But under DeVos's proposed rule, if a school used "clear and convincing evidence" as the standard for *any* disciplinary issue with similar consequences, for either students or staff, it would have to use the same standard for sexual harassment. DeVos's explanation for forcing this onto schools? The supposed "heightened stigma" that attaches to allegations of sexual harassment. As readers will recall, no matter whether or not such stigma is real, it is legally irrelevant. Tellingly, DeVos expressed no concern for societal biases against victims of sexual harassment, or existing barriers to reporting sexual violence, which would only be further entrenched by the new policy.

This is another crucial problem with exceptionalism: it stigmatizes sexual harassment victims. When policymakers implement heightened procedural protections only for people accused of sexual harassment, or when critics demand the same, they send a clear message: *Sexual harassment allegations are uniquely dubious. People who come forward as survivors are uniquely deserving of our suspicion.* And communities absorb these lessons. Those views make it harder for survivors to seek the support they need, including from friends and family, and to pursue justice how they see fit. The result is a vicious cycle: rape myths promote exceptionalism, which promotes rape myths, which promote exceptionalism yet again.

Imagine a student with two friends who are both brought up on disciplinary charges. One is alleged to have bullied a classmate; the other is accused of similar conduct that includes sexual comments, and so constitutes sexual harassment. The first goes through the school's normal disciplinary procedure. The second is provided an array of additional rights and protections in a more formal, drawn-out process that requires more convincing evidence from the victim. Watching those two separate tracks, the student may internalize the lesson that sexual harassment allegations and those who make them (mostly women) should be treated with particular skepticism—the kind of stereotype that a discrimination law should combat, not promote.

AT THE SAME time DeVos was drafting her final regulations, Missouri Republicans pushed legislation that would have granted additional rights to college students facing disciplinary measures—but only if they were accused of sexual assault. As originally drafted, the bill would have allowed those students to introduce into the proceedings any and all information about their alleged victims, including their sexual history and preferences. Schools would be powerless to exclude these or other potentially prejudicial and irrelevant details. What's more, students accused of sexual assault would have the right to appeal a college's disciplinary decision directly to an outside judge. The school would be forbidden to institute sanctions until that appeal was complete. (The original complainant would not be allowed any appeal; nor would students accused of any other type of wrongdoing.) And after all that, students accused of sexual assault would have a special right to sue not only their schools for any procedural errors, but their alleged victims for filing a report in the first place.

The bill was bad policy, period, for any kind of discipline. Courts and tribunals of all kinds exclude certain evidence to make sure decision-makers aren't influenced by information that may appeal to their biases but has no relevance to the question at hand. And the threat of a retaliatory lawsuit would surely discourage many victims from coming forward. Think about it: Would you ever report if you knew that, should a court decide you lacked enough evidence, you would have to pay your rapist? That's the reason why the law tries to protect victims from those risks. For example, you cannot be sued for reporting a crime to the police, even if they decide not to move forward with the case or a jury acquits, unless the accused can prove you did so maliciously.

I also think that setting up a direct appeal to a judge probably would be unwise. There are good reasons why college discipline is not generally subject to this kind of immediate external oversight. (Students can usually sue if the school broke a law in the course of its discipline—for example, if it didn't use the correct procedures—but not simply because they disagree with the result.) Direct judicial appeals would further lengthen the timeline of what is supposed to be an internal adjudication, possibly until well after both students had graduated. That would frustrate the whole purpose of student discipline. And that's to say nothing of the inequality of providing an appeal to the respondent but not the alleged victim.

But even if someone could make the case for the proposed law's provisions, there was no reason to make them available to *only* students accused of sexual harassment. Students accused of other kinds of misconduct should have shared all the bill's protections as well. If a particular procedure is necessary for people accused of sexual harassment, it's also necessary for people facing other allegations that can carry serious consequences. Either a protection should be available in all cases, or, as with this law, it is not actually necessary to begin with.

As it turned out, the legislation was developed by a lobbyist who started a dark money group devoted to changing school harassment policies after his son was expelled from Washington University in St. Louis for sexually assaulting a classmate. If the original bill had succeeded, the young man's case would have been appealed to an administrative commission where his mother was a presiding judge. It's hard to see the family's lobbying as anything more than an attempt to buy their kid's way back into college. In that light, it's telling that they did not try to "reform" student discipline writ large. They decided that legislators would be more likely to vote for these reforms if they applied only to sexual assault, rather than to other forms of discipline as well. That is, the family assumed legislators would agree that students accused of sexual harassment deserved special protections. They banked on exceptionalism.

ONE LAST PROBLEM with exceptionalism: it ensures that advocacy and policy change leave out the vast majority of people who need greater reforms and protections. Intense national interest in people accused of sexual harms has not translated into concern for their colleagues, classmates, and neighbors facing unfairness related to allegations of other kinds. Why hasn't concern about men being fired for sexual harassment without an investigation translated into support for general "just cause" laws, which forbid employers from firing a worker without a good reason and evidence to back it up? And why hasn't concern about student discipline for sexual assault extended to students who face discipline for other kinds of misconduct? If advocates for the bad Missouri bill had been right that their proposals were necessary, why only offer these rights to students accused of one particular kind of harm? Why deny them to students who face equally serious disciplinary consequences for a fistfight or for setting their dorm on fire?

An obvious rejoinder to this objection is that it's better to promote good policy selectively than not at all. I'm sensitive to the charge of "whataboutism," a common strategy debaters use to deflect criticism. "You don't like *this*? Well, what about that other problem?" Usually the answer is simply that, as a matter of practicality, we must be allowed to work on specific issues, or particular parts of an issue, because we cannot save the world in one fell swoop. And it's true that consistency is only one of many virtues. If DeVos had written Title IX rules that ensured a smart disciplinary process for sexual harassment, fair to both victims and the accused, I think I would have begrudgingly accepted them. I would have

greatly preferred a law or regulation that guaranteed the same procedural rights to all students, regardless of their alleged offense, and
avoided promoting stereotypes of sexual harassment victims. But if
that weren't an option, I can't imagine battling to overturn a narrow
but otherwise well-designed regulation.

That doesn't mean that exceptionalism is wise, though. And it
doesn't only hurt victims. The way exceptionalism restricts the benefits of increased interest in fair procedures only to people accused of
sexual harms is damaging to others, too.

DeVos, again, provides an infuriating illustration. As we have
seen, her Department of Education revoked Obama's Title IX policy
guidance—the Dear Colleague Letter—on the basis that it supposedly didn't provide enough protections to the accused. In 2018, she
also revoked a different Obama-era policy letter, known as the "Discipline Guidance." That guidance document explained the kinds of
racially discriminatory discipline practices that the Department of
Education and Department of Justice saw as violating Title VI, a
civil rights law that prohibits a wide range of discrimination, including racial bias in schools. The guidance also provided suggestions for
policies and practices schools could adopt to avoid discriminating
against students of color in their student discipline. These included
establishing clear rules and procedures, limiting the role of school
police officers in routine student discipline, and collecting data about
who the school was punishing for what, to identify any troubling
patterns.

Without question, the Discipline Guidance was sorely needed.
The academic year before DeVos revoked the guidance, Black students in DC's public schools—in her backyard—were more than
five times as likely to receive out-of-school suspensions as their white
peers. Before the Discipline Guidance, the rates had been even worse.
So, why would DeVos's Department of Education—which claimed,
in the context of Title IX, to care deeply about fair discipline—
rescind the Title VI policy guidance?

The answer is easy: DeVos and her colleagues cared about fair process when they imagined a white college man accused of sexual assault—falsely, of course—but not when it came to a young Black kid suspended for violating the dress code or being late to school. And their hypocrisy on student discipline wasn't subtle. For instance, Hans Bader, who'd worked for DeVos as a senior official at the department, published a letter in the *New York Times* claiming that the new Title IX regulations were necessary to protect Black students from disproportionate punishment. Yet he had long waged war against the Title VI Discipline Guidance, publicly insisting that Black kids were punished more often not because of racism but because they misbehaved more often—which is decidedly not true. In other words, Bader was only concerned about disproportionate discipline of Black students when he could use those concerns to roll back the rights of sexual assault survivors. It is hard not to conclude that DeVos's department only valued fair process if it benefited white people. That attitude was shared throughout the Trump administration as a whole, which was staffed by ideologues deeply committed to protecting white men's dominance and impunity. The same month DeVos published the new Title IX regulations, Trump himself threatened anti-racism protesters in Minneapolis with extrajudicial killing—perhaps the most profound violation of due process imaginable.

Given these leanings, the hypocrisy of some conservatives regarding DeVos's abandonment of the Discipline Guidance document was not surprising. I was distressed, though, not to hear more outcry about it from the (mostly white) prominent critics on the *left* who had worried about Obama's Title IX efforts. They had loudly critiqued the sloppy sexual harassment procedures that some schools adopted after the Title IX Dear Colleague Letter, denouncing them as ripe for racially disparate outcomes. But they were silent when DeVos revoked the Title VI Discipline Guidance. Where were their op-eds expressing grave concern? Did they think discriminatory discipline only mattered if it was for sexual harassment? I had expected that from Bader, but not from liberal professors and lawyers. After all, racial disparities are certainly not a problem unique to sexual allegations. Although we don't have particularly reliable national data on discipline rates for these offenses, what we do have suggests that racial disparities are *less* pronounced in connection with sex-based harassment and bullying than other offenses. According to the Department of Education's data, during the 2013–14 school year, Black boys nationwide were one and a half times more likely to be disciplined for sex-based offenses but three times more likely than their white male peers to be disciplined in general.

We obviously should care about any racial disparities in student discipline. The data just shows there is no reason, as a matter of racial justice, to focus on sexual harassment discipline alone. But somehow, that's just what those liberal critics had done, decrying potential racism in sexual harassment proceedings while ignoring DeVos's decision to unambiguously permit racism in student discipline broadly. And we needed their voices. Had they spoken out in defense of the Discipline Guidance, perhaps their objections would have registered with national media—which mostly ignored the story as it unfolded, stymieing advocacy efforts. The liberal critics' silence shows how exceptionalism hurts not only the victims of sexual harassment but everyone who would benefit from fair process.

13

The Roots of Exceptionalism

Why this view that sexual harassment allegations should be treated as their own roped-off category? I think the mistake can be attributed, in part, to our quick association between rape and criminal law—the incorrect assumption that sexual harms are inherently criminal and therefore that every adjudication must look like a criminal trial. An article in the *Atlantic*, for instance, complained that a certain university's sexual harassment policies were "inconsistent with due process for accused sex criminals," as though that were the relevant standard. If a criminal trial is the expectation, every institutional process will seem inadequate by comparison, no matter if it is fair and consistent with the institution's policies for handling other misconduct.

The civil libertarian critic Judith Levine made a similar error when discussing how schools have responded to pressure from Know Your IX and related groups. "Colleges and universities," she lamented, "have instituted codes of sexual conduct and quasi-judicial tribunals that ignore the constitutional protections afforded defendants in the criminal justice system." But of course university disciplinary systems will not mirror criminal prosecution. That is not what they are called to do—legally, practically, or ethically. And the same goes for workplaces. When Minnesota Public Radio fired Garrison Keillor, the longtime host of *A Prairie Home Companion*, because of his alleged repeated sexual harassment of a former employee, a fan wrote in to protest that "Keillor was convicted without a trial." Another MPR listener ended her membership because, in her view, the radio network was "turning [Keillor] into a criminal." I have no idea if MPR's process for investigating the harassment complaints was sufficient. But a trial, certainly, was not required. In firing Keillor, MPR did not "convict" him of a crime.

A similar set of assumptions came to the fore in the uproar over the Obama administration's Dear Colleague Letter and its guidance on evidentiary standards. Even before the 2011 letter, most schools were already using "preponderance of the evidence"—the lower of the two common standards. The Dear Colleague Letter made that standard an official requirement for sexual harassment investigations into students. Personally, I think the preponderance is the right choice. It best balances the interests of both people whose educations or careers will be deeply affected by the outcome, promotes accuracy, and is used in comparable proceedings in and out of schools. That said, I do understand the objection that discipline can come with serious stakes, which perhaps suggests a higher standard. But regardless of what you might think about it as a matter of policy, there's no question that long before the Dear Colleague Letter, the preponderance standard was used every single day in schools and civil trials for a wide range of harms, including sexual assault. Courts have confirmed that its use in student discipline is constitutional. Even the Trump administration required schools to use the preponderance standard when investigating harassment based on race or disability.

Yet from the response to the Dear Colleague Letter, you might have thought that preponderance of the evidence was a special kind of torture device. In an article titled "When Does a Watershed Become a Sex Panic?" Masha Gessen presented the preponderance standard as an example on the wrong side of that divide and decried that it would contribute to a reduction in consensual sex. (Never mind that someone could be sued for the same conduct under the same standard in a civil proceeding.) A professional organization representing professors wrote that the preponderance "conflicts with due-process protections." In the *Wall Street Journal*, conservative political scientist Peter Berkowitz decried the preponderance as an "egregiously" low standard and bemoaned that schools now imposed "a presumption of male guilt." (Regardless of the standard of evidence, a complainant always has the burden of proving her case.) Perhaps Berkowitz had forgotten that, when he had unsuccessfully sued Harvard for denying him tenure, his claim was subject to that same standard.

In a public statement, the libertarian Foundation for Individual Rights in Education, known as FIRE, wrote: "The preponderance of the evidence standard does not sufficiently protect an accused person's right to due process. While this standard is acceptable for lawsuits regarding money, allegations of sexual violence or sexual harassment are far more serious than disputes that can be resolved by transferring money from one individual to another." Accordingly, it urged, schools should use a higher standard of evidence, closer to that used in criminal trials. Note this: FIRE's argument was not that the preponderance was the wrong standard for student discipline in general. It said that the preponderance was inappropriate *for sexual assault*.

The basis for FIRE's argument is patently incorrect. The preponderance standard is not only used for suits for money damages. But even if that were our metric, lots of sexual harassment disputes *are* resolved through the transfer of money! That might come in the form of a jury verdict at the end of a civil lawsuit, or as a settlement to avoid litigation. Indeed, financial damages are often the only remedy available when a survivor brings a civil case against a perpetrator or institution. (And that payment might be more useful to her than her assailant's incarceration.) Clearly, the seriousness of a sexual assault allegation does not foreclose a monetary remedy, any more than the seriousness of murder foreclosed the civil suit seeking money from O. J. Simpson. Here is the clincher: a civil suit for sexual assault will go through the same procedure as any other civil suit. This means that, like nearly all civil cases, it will be subject to the preponderance of the evidence standard. The gravity of the underlying harm does not dictate a higher standard of proof.

Clearly, FIRE was only thinking about sexual assault as a crime, ignoring the various other contexts in which those same claims may be adjudicated. It should have known better. But FIRE's flawed assumptions are widely shared. That's the rub: FIRE's exceptionalist argument persuades many not in spite of its mistaken focus on rape as a crime and crime alone, but because of it.

SCRAPE THE SURFACE of exceptionalism and you'll usually find misogyny beneath. Our collective fear of scorned, lying, irrational women who falsely "cry rape" has been ingrained in our culture and law for centuries, no matter the baselessness of the archetype. It serves as the unified, animating force behind the casual rape apologias, explicit doubts, and flawed policies that stand in the way of justice for survivors and an end to the violence. If we look at how rape victims have been treated historically, especially in criminal law, we can recognize contemporary exceptionalism as just the latest iteration of a long, terrible tradition. We believe we need special protections from sexual harassment allegations because we think that these accusations are particularly likely to be untrue.

The seventeenth-century English jurist Sir Matthew Hale did not invent this exceptionalism. But through his influential writings, he gave it form and force that shaped centuries of Anglo-American law for the worse. Rape, he said, "is an accusation easily to be made and hard to be proved, and harder to be defended by the party accused, tho never so innocent." For this reason, Hale insisted, "we may be the more cautious upon trials of offenses of this nature, wherein the court and the jury may with so much ease be imposed upon without great care and vigilance." As anthropologist Peggy Reeves Sanday has written, Hale's views were animated by the idea that many women accused men of rape in order to extort blackmail. That fear of women as manipulative liars was a common one during Hale's time and shaped rape law from the ground up. Women victims, for example, were expected to defer to the judgment of their husband or father as to whether to levy charges. A woman who instead came forward on her own behalf "conjured the image of the aggressive Eve, whose complicity with the serpent made all mortal women susceptible to the wiles of the devil: they were prone to be sexually voracious and enticing, spiritually weaker, and less rational," writes Sanday of seventeenth-century British attitudes. "More likely than not, a woman bringing rape charges on her own was either a scorned woman or one out to blackmail the man who seduced her."

Hale's biases were not limited to theories about lying accusers. He did not believe a woman had the right to deny her husband sex, and thought men should lock up wives who spent too much money. Presiding over a 1662 witchcraft trial, Hale dismissed evidence that proved the innocence of the two accused women, and then sentenced them to death. "Contrary to Hale's well-known concern to give rape defendants the benefit of the doubt," Sanday notes, he showed "no evidence of giving defendants in witchcraft trials the same benefit."

Hale's warning about rape accusations was also empirically incorrect. "Rape is not, and never has been, an easy charge to make and a difficult one to rebut," writes criminologist Gilbert Geis. "It certainly was not so before or in Hale's time." Although British law prescribed harsh penalties for rape, including capital punishment, convictions were so unheard of that one judge "entertained friends with jokes about it." In Hale's seventeenth century, far more women were executed for witchcraft than men were executed for rape. In eighteenth-century London, the 17 percent conviction rate for rape was the lowest of any capital crime, less than a third of the 56 percent conviction rate for burglary.

Nonetheless, Hale's warning was adopted into British common law, which deeply shaped the law of its American colonies. Many U.S. courts instructed jurors in rape cases accordingly, telling them to be unusually suspicious of the charges before them, and continued to do so well into the second half of the twentieth century. To this day, the Model Penal Code—an authoritative source, originally published in 1962, to which states look in drafting their own laws—encourages the use of a Lord Hale instruction. It recommends that "in any prosecution before a jury [for sexual offenses], the jury shall be instructed to evaluate the testimony of a victim or complaining witness with special care in view of the emotional involvement of the witness and the difficulty of determining the truth with respect to alleged sexual activities carried out in private." Extensive amendments to the Model Penal Code's treatment of sexual assault were officially proposed by a formal committee of experts in 2019, but at the time of my writing, the American Law Institute has not adopted them.

Fortunately, on this point the Model Penal Code's impact on law has diminished with time. Over the last decades of the twentieth century, anti-rape advocates and scholars successfully pushed states to stop requiring judges to echo Lord Hale's words. In 1975, a defendant convicted of rape appealed to the California Supreme Court, arguing that the trial judge had improperly refused to read a Lord Hale instruction. In response, California's highest court not only overturned its previous rule that the warning was required, but decided it was, in all circumstances, inappropriate. "Criminal charges involving sexual conduct are no more easily made or harder to defend against than many other classes of charges, and those who make such accusations should be deemed no more suspect in credibility than any other class of complainants," the court wrote. "When such prosecutions present close evidentiary questions, they do so not because a victim—generally a woman—claims to have been sexually assaulted or abused, but because the alleged crime took place in evanescent circumstances difficult to reconstruct in court, a happenstance . . . which is indeed a typical occurrence in such non-sexual crimes as fraud and narcotics transactions." In other words, the challenges that sometimes arise in sex crimes prosecutions arise in plenty of other prosecutions, too.

ADJUDICATING SEXUAL OFFENSES may indeed be harder than parsing *some* other kinds of wrongdoing. If a defendant goes on a videotaped shooting spree, or a student prints out a Wikipedia article and presents it as his own essay, those offenses will be easy to prove. The evidence there is clearer than, say, in a sexual assault investigation where the accused says that the alleged victim consented. In such a case, the distinction between sex and rape may turn on what was said and done behind closed doors without a witness. But the common instinct that sexual accusations are somehow uniquely unknowable overlooks two vital points.

First, there's often much more evidence in a sexual harassment case than one might assume. Sometimes a coworker hears the "jokes" about an underling's skirt that a boss makes at a meeting. Sometimes a college roommate hears the assault. And often the two parties create their own evidentiary trail. In some cases, the assailant directly admits to the misconduct, sometimes in the form of an apology and sometimes a boast. (Soon after my client Darbi's rape, her assailant told classmates, "That's just what I do"—"that" being sexual assault.) In other instances, a victim might seek medical care and a "rape kit," or might tell his friends. He might suddenly stop going to work, class, or church—signals that *something* happened.

Second, even where there isn't much evidence beyond the two parties' stories, *many* adjudications that have nothing to do with sex or violence are effectively "he said, she said" situations, where the decision turns entirely on the credibility of the people involved. Take a fender bender with no video footage or witnesses, for example. I say I stopped at the stop sign before you barreled into me; you say I didn't, so you had no chance to brake as I zoomed past. Either way, there are dents in both our cars. A judge, or an insurance agent, will have to decide which one of us seems more likely to be telling the truth. To do so, they will consider factors like the consistency of our stories and our apparent trustworthiness.

The same dynamic plays out, with much higher stakes, in self-defense cases. You say I came at you outside the bar in a drunken rage and shot you in the foot; you barely had time to draw the knife from your pocket. I say you charged at me with your knife drawn, threatening to kill me; I shot your foot to save my own life. If no one witnessed the altercation, the jury will be left to consider our testimony and weigh how credible we each seem.

And it's not only courts that have to deal with such "evanescent circumstances," as the California Supreme Court put it. Institutions handle them all the time. What if a school catches us with identical answers on a test? We sat next to each other during the exam. Did I peek at your papers or did you cheat off me? If neither of us was the clear academic superstar beforehand, the discipline board will have to make a decision based on, well, which one of us seems more likely to be the liar.

It is telling, then, that "he said, she said" has become shorthand for an unsolvable case. When it's "he said, he said," we are perfectly comfortable adjudicating. Add in a woman, and add in sex, and suddenly the waters are impossibly muddy.

What's more, in a hypothetical case where there is truly no evidence beyond the parties' testimony, and no basis at all for finding either person more credible than the other, the decision-makers have a clear mandate to follow: they have to find in the accused's favor. In any conflict and any context, it is the complainant (or the prosecuting state or institution) who always carries the burden of proof, by whatever standard of evidence governs the proceeding. If there is no way to determine whether the harassment probably occurred, it is the alleged victim who will lose.

So why, then, the insistence on special warnings about "easily made" rape allegations? Hale and his legacy make clear that the logic of exceptionalism is that sexual assault allegations must be so specially guarded against because they are uniquely likely to be false. But we have no actual evidence that sexual violence is misreported at especially high rates. As I mentioned earlier, it's impossible to know exactly what percentage of reports are false, because there is no failproof method of distinguishing the real from the fake. Rarely do fraudsters fess up, and any outside observers' guesses at whether a report is true or not will be based on incomplete information and filtered through their own biases. To reach an informative estimate, researchers have to scrutinize police classifications of false reports according to consistent criteria. At the least, they must apply a clear definition of a false report that doesn't lump untrue complaints together with credible complaints that were never prosecuted. Studies that follow these guidelines converge on rates between 2 and 8 percent, consistent with rates of false reporting for other crimes. To put this in perspective, by any of these counts a man is significantly more likely to be sexually assaulted than to be falsely accused of sexual assault.

No matter how many studies confirm low rates of false rape reporting, men's rights activists—anti-feminists who believe that men, not women, are the disadvantaged sex—insist the number is far higher. These critics often point to a 1994 study by Eugene Kanin, which reported that 41 percent of the 109 sexual assault reports made to a police agency were false. But the determination of whether reports were true or not was made by the detectives, and not reevaluated by Kanin—or anyone else. Given what we know about law enforcement biases, there's good reason to double-check their classifications. Sexual assault researcher David Lisak explains that Kanin's approach "violates a cardinal rule of science, a rule designed to ensure that observations are not simply the reflection of the bias of the observer." As Lisak notes, "the greater the scrutiny applied to police classifications, the lower the rate of false reporting detected."

Another common error in statistical analyses is eliding the difference between people who lie and victims who lack sufficient evidence to confirm their account. During Brett Kavanaugh's confirmation process, for example, some of his defenders latched on to a then recent Pentagon study showing that the military dismissed nearly a quarter of the rape complaints it received for lack of proof. But, of course, a lack of proof does not mean an assault did not occur—it just means a decision-maker concluded that the complainant did not have the evidence necessary to pursue the case.

HALE WAS NOT the only English jurist to shape U.S. rape law for the worse. For centuries, English common law required victims of violent crimes to "hue and cry"—basically, to immediately call out to their neighbors to get the assailant. Over time, courts largely abandoned that requirement, noticing that it was not, in fact, a particularly helpful way to catch criminals. They long retained it, though, for sexual violence alone. In the nineteenth century, U.S. courts adopted a modified approach: a rape case was allowed to proceed if the victim had not "hued and cried," but her failure to come forward quickly could be used against her by the defense.

The idea behind what is known as the "prompt complaint requirement" comes from what judges thought rape victims would always do, not from how actual victims often act. In 1900, for example, the all-male Utah Supreme Court postulated that "the natural instinct of a female thus outraged and injured prompts her to disclose the occurrence, at the earliest opportunity, to the relative or friend who naturally has the deepest interest in her welfare." A woman who delayed her report, then, was unnatural—a liar. Ninety-one years later, the Supreme Court of Illinois reinforced the rule, writing that "it is entirely natural that the victim of forcible rape would have spoken out regarding it, and the fact that she did not do so would in effect be evidence of the fact that nothing violent had occurred."

We now know the many reasons a victim might not report to

the police at all, let alone promptly. But the Model Penal Code still contains a uniquely short statute of limitations of only *three months* for sexual offenses. Its statute of limitations for other first-degree felonies, meanwhile, is six years—except for murder, which has none. The code's justification for this choice, as formally memorialized in 1980, explicitly invokes the myth of widespread false rape accusations by scorned women: "The requirement of prompt complaint springs in part from a fear that unwanted pregnancy or bitterness at a relationship gone sour might convert a willing participant in sexual relations into a vindictive complainant." In a critique, early rape law scholar Susan Estrich noted that the Model Penal Code commentary "is startlingly attentive to the problem of the vindictive, spurned woman, but silent about the woman who legitimately worries about the receptiveness of police, prosecutors, juries and even friends or employers to a report that she was raped." Luckily, the states have outpaced the Model Penal Code in abandoning the prompt complaint requirement.

We cannot blame the Brits for everything. One of the exceptional features of American rape law is very much of our own making: the requirement of corroborating evidence—that is, evidence other than a victim's testimony—to support a conviction. The first law to require corroborating evidence for sexual abuse convictions was passed by the New York legislature in 1886. The result, yet again, was a unique burden placed on allegations of rape. In one bizarre 1960s case, a defendant was convicted of attempting to rape a woman and stealing her coin purse. He appealed the conviction, pointing out that the victim had no corroborating evidence for either of the claims. The rape verdict was overturned, but the state's highest court held that the theft verdict could stand; the opinion explained that corroboration was required only for the rape itself, not for other, nonsexual crimes committed at the same time. An article published the next year in the prestigious *University of Pennsylvania Law Review* explained that the corroboration requirement was necessary because "women often falsely accuse men of sexual attacks to extort money, to force marriage, to satisfy a childish desire for notoriety, or to attain personal revenge. Their motives include hatred, a sense of shame after consenting to illicit intercourse, especially when pregnancy results, and delusion." The author cited one psychiatrist's assertion that "most women" have rape fantasies, and that "neurotic individuals" are unable to distinguish those fantasies from reality.

Over the course of the twentieth century, New York's corroboration rule spread. In 1904, the Supreme Court of Georgia declared that a corroboration requirement was legally necessary. Without such a requirement, the court explained, "every man is in danger of being prosecuted and convicted on the testimony of a base woman in whose testimony there's no truth." Absent such a protection, the court continued, "the man is powerless." Interestingly, the court cited Lord Hale for support—even though he had never endorsed such a rule requiring corroborating evidence. In fact, in a rare moment of insight, Hale had explained that an alleged rape victim's own testimony does constitute evidence on its own; whether it is credible is a question for the jury. But the Georgia justices could perhaps be forgiven for forgetting the particulars: the big takeaway from Hale, after all, is that women lie and men must be protected.

In 1965, the Supreme Court of Minnesota explained in clear terms why it, too, required corroboration for sex crimes. In an opinion overturning the conviction of a man accused of sexually abusing his daughter, the court quoted at length from Dean John Henry Wigmore's treatise on evidence, the most influential work on the subject in American jurisprudence for most of the twentieth century. Special rules were required in rape trials, the court said, because, according to Wigmore, the "psychic complexes" of "errant young girls and women . . . are multifarious, distorted partly by inherent defects. . . . One form taken by these complexes is that of contriving false charges of sexual offences by men. The unchaste (let us call it) mentality finds incidental but direct expression in the narration of imaginary sex-incidents of which the narrator is the heroine or the victim. . . . The real victim, however, too often in such cases is the innocent man."

The U.S. Court of Appeals for the D.C. Circuit, the country's most powerful tribunal after the Supreme Court, agreed in a 1973 opinion. "It is established law in this jurisdiction that a person may not be convicted of a 'sex offense' on the uncorroborated testimony of the alleged victim," the court wrote. "Complainants all too frequently have an urge to fantasize or even a motive to fabricate." As with the other exceptional rules for sexual assault, the corroboration requirement is still recommended by the Model Penal Code, though only a handful of states today include it in their statutes.

These three exceptionalist rules—the Lord Hale Instruction, the prompt complaint requirement, and a requirement of corroborating evidence—were obvious targets for feminist legal reformers in the late twentieth century. But even as states revised their rape laws, the biases and myths upon which they relied continued to circulate in our culture. As the feminist legal theorist Michelle Anderson puts it: "After scrubbing down the foul Model Penal Code and tidying up a dozen or so state codes on the bookshelf, one might toss these relics— prompt complaint, corroboration, and cautionary instructions—into the dustbin of historical misogyny, declare a victory for the second wave of feminism, and go home. But the cultural dirt from the criminal law has drifted into an adjacent room previously assumed to be uncontaminated."

That adjacent room includes institutional responses to sexual harassment and public debates about what fair process should look like. Today, as throughout history, exceptionalist policies treat allegations of sexual harassment as uniquely suspect. We see the continuation of this long tradition in the demands that students accused of sexual harassment must receive extra protections, in the special rights for such students that DeVos guaranteed and Missouri legislators drafted, and in the vilification of a perfectly common standard of evidence simply because it was applied to accusations of sexual assault. We see it, unsubtly, in the "justifications" that some critics provide for their preferred policies, sweeping declarations that the truth of sexual assault allegations is uniquely unknowable and the risk of wrongful blame uniquely high. Invariably, these assertions are accompanied by no citation, as though they are self-evident—as though we should base national policy on these writers' instincts, which might be another word for biases. There isn't much distance between ancient misogynists and some of today's critics, such as Berkowitz, for example, who insisted in his attack on the Dear Colleague Letter that rape investigations are particularly prone to erroneous outcomes because "where erotic desire is involved, intentions can be obscure, passions conflicting, the heart murky and the soul divided." In other words, women fling around rape allegations because they don't know what they want.

It is easy to see the ghost of Potiphar's wife—the lying, scorned woman who cries rape—in those sweeping, inaccurate, age-old generalizations. And the impact of long-standing legal traditions on contemporary policy means that misogyny has an even broader effect than one might initially realize. In Lord Hale's time, rape was generally defined as a crime against a woman; there's no question that his warnings about "an accusation easily to be made and hard to be proved" had women in mind. In recent decades, rules against sexual harms have expanded to encompass victims of all genders, but the exceptionalism persists. As a result, those ancient sexist myths now haunt every allegation, not only those brought by women. Stereotypes about one sex have become stereotypes about all survivors.

14

Exceptions to Exceptionalism

Exceptionalism usually results in exceptionally bad treatment of victims of sexual harms. Occasionally, though, exceptionalism works the other way, treating these victims particularly well. Those anomalies may seem like victories in the short term. But advocates should be wary.

Before my classmates and I filed our Title IX complaint with the Department of Education, our college had used a single disciplinary process for all misconduct, including sexual harassment. Other schools within the university had their own disciplinary systems, which likewise handled every form of misconduct. Shortly after the Department of Education opened its investigation, the school created a separate, centralized board, known as the University-Wide Committee, to address only disciplinary charges related to sexual harm—an exceptional process. Other schools have done the same. As concern for student survivors started to garner federal attention, these colleges and universities looked to use best practices to reduce opportunities for re-traumatization and conflict—for instance, by hiring professional, external investigators to interview witnesses and collect evidence. But rather than incorporating those practices into their usual discipline systems, the schools set up separate and generally less antagonistic disciplinary protocols just for sexual harassment.

I get the schools' logic. Their old systems had been terrible. And they were right that adjudicating a sexual harassment allegation requires more sensitivity, knowledge, and training than presiding over a student disciplinary charge for, say, plagiarism. Why not create a separate track?

One answer is that sexual harassment is not the only kind of sensitive allegation schools must address. They receive reports of other forms of discrimination, including harassment on the basis of race, religion, or disability. Sometimes, a victim is harassed based on multiple identities, and so unable to separate out what abuse is "sexual" from, say, what is race-based. Schools also hear from students who have been targeted in equally traumatic ways even if their experiences do not implicate civil rights. The student a year above me in college whose roommate repeatedly vandalized their room and threatened to murder him for getting a better part in a play was, without a doubt, upset and afraid. School administrators should have been trained to question him with care. He, too, would have benefited from an investigation process that avoids unnecessary re-traumatization.

I also fear that even when exceptionalism appears beneficial for survivors of sexual harassment at a given moment, it invariably hurts them in the long run. Nothing illustrates this better than the recent history of sexual harassment at Harvard Law School and its impact on national politics.

Harvard had long come under fire for its mistreatment of sexual harassment survivors. As Michelle Anderson has extensively documented, the university's policies drew from many of the old, sexist traditions of criminal law, including prompt complaint and corroboration requirements. Administrators were explicit that these rules were designed to help the school quickly dispose of sexual assault allegations, which administrators felt should be handled by criminal law. Unsurprisingly, such policies and attitudes led to terrible outcomes for victims. One undergraduate student reported a rape and submitted a list of fifteen witnesses; the university nevertheless decided it was a "he said, she said" situation that they were powerless to address.

In 2014, the Department of Education announced that an investigation into Harvard had turned up Title IX violations. The government's focus was the law school, which had its own separate disciplinary procedures, distinct from the rest of the university. In designing its unique system, the law school had made some baffling choices. For example, it permitted a student found responsible for misconduct, including sexual harassment, to appeal the disciplinary finding if the sanction included dismissal or expulsion. No such appellate right was available to the student who had filed the complaint. At that extra hearing, the accused student could call witnesses and present their case, but the complainant could not. That bears repeating: students found responsible were given an additional hearing to challenge the decision, where complainants—the classmates the school believed they had sexually harassed—weren't allowed to tell their side of the story at all.

During the course of the Title IX investigation, Harvard administrators designed a new university-wide disciplinary system for sexual harassment allegations alone. The new procedures looked much like the processes that Harvard's college and academic graduate schools already used to investigate other forms of student misconduct. Those general protocols include interviews of the parties but no live, adversarial hearing with cross-examination. Decisions are made based on a unique and ambiguously worded standard—that the disciplinary board be "sufficiently persuaded"—that Harvard's lawyers have said is equivalent to the preponderance of the evidence.

The new university-wide sexual harassment procedures, however, were a dramatic departure from how Harvard Law School approached student discipline. Unlike the rest of the university, the law school used live hearings with cross-examination and required "clear and convincing" evidence, a higher standard than the preponderance. As a result, when sexual harassment cases were moved into the separate university-wide system, the law school ended up in an unusual position: its students who reported sexual harassment would now face a lower standard of proof than students who reported other misconduct. The new policy also meant that Harvard Law students would now face live, adversarial cross-examination for all complaints other than those related to sexual harassment. Contrary to the usual trend, sexual harassment victims would be treated, at least on paper, exceptionally well.

A group of twenty-eight Harvard Law professors—including many leading voices of the academic left—were displeased, both that they had not been consulted and that the new university-wide policy was, in their view, deeply flawed. In a 2014 public letter in the *Boston Globe*, the professors laid out their specific procedural concerns with the new system, saying that it was "inconsistent with many of the most basic principles we teach."

Whether the letter was itself an example of exceptionalism depends on whether your focus is Harvard as a whole or its law school specifically. Anderson, the rape law scholar, notes that much of the professors' critique—for instance, their insistence that the process had to include a live "adversary hearing"—was equally applicable to the university's long-standing procedures for other forms of misconduct. Outside the law school, the usual disciplinary process at Harvard did not include such a hearing, regardless of the type of conduct alleged. Where was the professors' letter objecting to that process? Just a few years before, Harvard College had mass-suspended students accused of cheating on a political science exam. The legal theorist Katharine Baker points out that the same law professors issued no comparable coordinated critique about that incident, even though the suspended students were not given the rights the professors' letter extolled. Did the signatories only care about ensuring heightened protections when it came to allegations of sexual harassment?

That diagnosis seems less clear if you zoom in on the law professors' corner of the university. Maybe the scope of their attention wasn't defined by the topic of sexual harassment but instead by the boundaries of the law school, where they taught, spoke to students, and had power to shape policy. There, regardless of university-wide trends, the process for sexual harassment now looked very different from the process for all other misconduct. One signatory, Jeannie Suk Gersen, told me that she and other professors were in fact motivated by a *rejection* of sex exceptionalism, insofar as the new policy required a different standard for sex-based harassment than the law school used for race-based harassment. Most of their critique called on the law school to treat sexual harassment more like it treated other harms; it was, in that way, anti-exceptional. A few months after the letter, the university allowed the law school to design its own sexual harassment procedure that looked much more like its usual discipline process, including a live hearing where students could submit questions for the board to pose to the other party and witnesses.

No matter what your view, it's clear that the discrepancy between the law school's general disciplinary policy and the new process for sexual harassment made the latter vulnerable to critique. Then, because the professors' criticism concerned only sexual harassment procedures, their letter created fertile ground for reactionary exceptionalism in line with the historical, misogynist trend: extra skepticism for sexual harassment allegations. When DeVos was pushing to roll back Title IX protections for survivors and impose exceptional procedural requirements on their allegations, the Department of Education and its allies cited the Harvard Law episode to defend DeVos's proposals. Here were mostly lefty academics agreeing with them—or at least so it seemed at first glance—that schools needed to provide unique protections to students accused of sexual harassment. At an oral argument in a lawsuit challenging DeVos's treatment of Title IX guidance, for which I served as cocounsel, the judge brought up the Harvard professors. How could DeVos's actions be illegal sex discrimination if *they* agreed with her?

In the short run, an exceptionalist policy like the separate university-wide system that Harvard administrators had instituted in 2014—the one law professors criticized—may help victims of sexual harassment. The lower standard of proof obviously increases their chance of a finding of responsibility, for example. But in the long term, practices that treat sexual harassment differently from all other harms will ultimately hurt victims most of all—even if those practices were motivated by unique concerns for survivors. Exceptionalism breeds exceptionalism. Once we start down the road of special procedures, we're more likely to bring along our cultural baggage about sex and gender, and invite others to do the same. It's much easier to make the criminal rape trial the yardstick for sexual harassment when school policy separates out discipline for sexual harms from discipline for everything else. Suddenly, the preponderance of the evidence standard, for example, might feel inappropriate for sexual harms even if a school uses that standard for all other student misconduct.

By refusing to treat sexual harassment as a wholly separate issue, we keep our eyes on the right comparison for sexual harassment procedures: other discipline by the same institution with the same stakes and a similar balance of interests. With that context, it becomes clearer which critics want to make it especially hard to prove sexual abuses, and what misogyny drives them to do that.

CRUCIALLY, DE-EXCEPTIONALIZING SEXUAL harassment as a matter of *process* does not require advocates to minimize the injuries it causes or the special role it plays in reinforcing inequalities. A few years ago, I shared my argument about exceptionalism at a conference. A feminist scholar told me she worried that my position suggested that sexual assault is no different than any other injury, such as, say, being punched. The message then might become that rape victims should just get over it, ignoring the unique forms of trauma sexual victimization carries. Perhaps some might read my push to de-exceptionalize to mean that there is no need for special civil rights protections for victims of sexual harassment.

But we can distinguish substance from process. I obviously think sexual harassment is hugely important; I have devoted most of my adult life to ending it. Not all victims find it life-changing, but many do. And I do think harassment's ramifications for individuals and society are more sweeping than is typical of the conflicts that institutions are often called on to resolve. We passed vital antidiscrimination civil rights laws precisely because these kinds of offenses really, really matter.

Yet none of the ways in which these offenses matter *substantively* require entirely separate *procedures*, so long as the "standard" process is thoughtful, sensitive, and fair. After all, race- and disability-based discrimination really matter, too, and their victims are guaranteed distinct civil rights protections. But those violations are not channeled into single-issue processes. Instead, institutions figure out how to protect race and disability civil rights within the same general procedure used for other interpersonal allegations. Courts, of course, do the same. Prosecutions for lethal hate crimes and for victimless fraud use the same process. So we as feminists can recognize the ways in which sexual harassment is a unique harm for victims and the world, while also deciding it's wiser not to have it adjudicated through unique procedures.

None of this is to say that, as they stand today, all general disciplinary proceedings in schools and workplaces are well-equipped to respect the rights of victims. But there is no reason those proceedings can't be improved for everyone's sake. Similarly, while responses to sexual harassment certainly require more sensitivity than a dispute over a drunken fistfight might, this doesn't mean that they need an entirely separate process. Rather than set up one thoughtful process and one obnoxious one, why not just create a single good track? There's no reason, for example, to ever make a complainant submit to direct questioning by someone he has reported, regardless of the specific allegation. And plenty of disciplinary matters that are common in settings like schools and workplaces require sensitivity, training, and expertise. Without a doubt, I would want an HR professional who is investigating a groping allegation to have training to avoid re-traumatizing complainants and check her own biases. But the same goes for an investigator looking into racial harassment. Why not make sure every decision-maker is trained to address whatever set of allegations come before her?

We might take inspiration, too, from the special sex crimes units in police departments and prosecutors' offices. From experience, law enforcement has learned they need specially trained staff to work with sexual assault victims. They might provide these victims extra forms of support. But then they prosecute sex crimes using standard, trans-substantive procedures.

In retrospect, I wish that rather than creating such a different, separate process, Harvard Law and the Department of Education had figured out a way to improve the school's broader disciplinary framework so it would be appropriate for allegations of sexual harassment. Perhaps with some small adjustments the law school could have largely preserved the procedures its faculty had endorsed for other disciplinary matters while still protecting the Title IX rights of victims. It might have done so while keeping its "clear and convincing" standard of evidence for all alleged misconduct, except that which threatened another student's education—including different forms of harassment, bullying, and physical assaults. Maybe those reforms would have sat better with professors, who then wouldn't have written their letter, which then wouldn't have provided fodder for Betsy DeVos. I'm not well versed enough in Harvard's internal politics to know whether such an arrangement would have been feasible. All I know for sure is that when the backlash comes—and it always comes—victims lose when sexual harassment is an island of its own.

15

Ugly Histories

In 1973, a renowned progressive jurist, Chief Judge David L. Bazelon, was called upon to decide whether his court should maintain the corroboration requirement for allegations of rape and rape alone. He recognized that some of the justifications for this rule were archaic, and might be motivated by sexism. But he nonetheless endorsed the requirement, based in part on what he saw as the heightened threat of racism against the accused in rape cases. "There has been an enormous danger of injustice when a black man accused of raping a white woman is tried before a white jury," he wrote. "There is still racism in our society and that racism may be particularly likely to surface in a case involving alleged sexual violations."

Half a century later, this same notion often emerges in endorsements of exceptionalist policies, most notably (though not exclusively) from those on the left. Some advocates I've met explicitly put forward reasoning that mirrors Chief Judge Bazelon's. Others don't expressly endorse exceptionalism, but I suspect a similar instinct is at play when they invoke Black men's unique vulnerability to such accusations while promoting policies that are unquestionably exceptionalist—as was done by influential defenders of DeVos's rules. Because this justification for exceptionalism, unlike those discussed earlier, is rooted in a genuine and critical problem, it deserves particular attention.

I understand why, on first glance, the logic might make sense. False rape allegations have long played an outsize role in the oppression of Black men. (Allegations of sexual violence also play a significant role in the policing of queer people and non-Black people of color; remember Trump invoking fears of Mexican immigrants as rapists to launch his campaign. But critics' primary focus, and so mine here, is anti-Blackness.) While available data these days suggests that conviction and discipline rates for sexual harms are less racially disparate than for other forms of misconduct, that research is limited, especially regarding sanctioning outside the courts. History, on its own, might suggest that tilting the scale more fully toward the accused specifically for sexual abuse allegations is a good way to promote racial justice.

But that position ignores the pressing need for racial justice for victims. As a long history stretching back to slavery shows, sexual abuse is often used as a tool of white supremacy, especially against Black women. And to this day, survivors of color face unconscionable obstacles to support and justice because of their race. In short, concerns about racial justice weigh on both sides of the scale. To the extent, then, that racism is exceptionally present in adjudications of sexual harms, we are pulled equally in both directions—to make it both exceptionally hard and exceptionally easy to prove. As I see it, the answer must be to follow the general rule, what might be called this book's mantra: subject these accusations to the same procedures used for all other misconduct that implicates similar interests and similar stakes.

TO FULLY UNDERSTAND sexual harassment and exceptionalism today, we have to recognize the ways the history of anti-Black racism is inextricably tied to sexual violence. Much of that history takes place outside the courts—in extrajudicial lynchings, in Black victims' stories that no judge would hear.

During and after Reconstruction, white communities latched on to the myth that Black men were unrestrainable rapists with animalistic sexual appetites, especially for white women. Investigating 728 lynchings of the 1880s and '90s, the advocate and journalist Ida B. Wells highlighted the role that rape accusations played as an excuse for those murders. Nearly a third of the men lynched were accused of sexual assault. But the motivating force for the lynchings, Wells explained, was a desire to maintain racial hierarchy, not genuine concern about violence against white women. "Lynching was merely an excuse to get rid of Negroes who were acquiring wealth and property and thus keep the race terrorized," she observed. The sociologist E. Franklin Frazier captured a similar sentiment: "The closer a Negro got to the ballot box, the more he looked like a rapist."

Lynchings for alleged rapes were specially targeted to maintain a central component of the racial order: the prohibition on consensual interracial sex and romance between Black men and white women. After the Civil War, Southern states began to outlaw interracial marriage. Many Black men accused of rape during this time were likely partners in consensual, but illicit, relationships with their white putative victims. In an 1899 decision, the Supreme Court of Georgia explained how judges should handle a case where a Black man accused of raping a white woman testifies in his defense that in fact they'd had consensual sex. "The vital question . . . to be considered, is whether, under the circumstances of the particular case, a negro could reasonably be presumed to have thought that a white woman would consent to his lustful embraces," the court wrote. And "no such inference will ever arise in his favor unless the circumstances are such that no other inference can be possibly drawn." Put another way, sex between Black men and white women was presumptively criminal.

Even the most minor suggestions of sex were used to justify white violence. In late 1943, fifteen-year-old Willie James Howard of Live

Oak, Florida, gave a Christmas card to his crush, a white girl with whom he worked. "I love your name. I love your voice. For a S.H. [sweetheart] you are my choice," he wrote in rhyme to Cynthia Goff. After Goff showed the note to her father, he, along with two other men, abducted Willie and his father, James. The white men bound Willie's hands and feet at the banks of the Suwannee River and told the teenager to choose: they could shoot him, or he could jump into the water. James, restrained by the men, watched his son drown. The NAACP took on the case to no avail. A grand jury refused to indict the murderers. The field secretary who led the NAACP's campaign for Willie was killed, along with his wife, when the KKK bombed their home. A little over a decade after Willie's death came the vicious mob murder of fourteen-year-old Emmett Till for allegedly grabbing and whistling at a white woman, Carolyn Bryant Donham. Donham would later tell a historian that her claim was "not true."

Brandon, the California football player who told me about his experience of being investigated by his school, saw his own story as one more example of a Black man falsely accused of sexual assault but assumed guilty by white authorities. He got the sense that the investigator who handled his case assumed that because Brandon is Black, "I'm automatically aggressive and hyper-masculine," and, as a result, found his account less credible than that of the non-Black complainant. Undoubtedly, those stereotypes still carry dangerous force today. Even though conviction patterns for sex offenses are less racially disparate than for other crimes, Black people are still overrepresented on sex offender registries. And Black defendants are wrongfully convicted of rape at a disproportionately high rate. In 1989, Trump spent $83,000 on ads calling for New York to "bring back the death penalty" as a direct response to allegations that a group of teenagers had raped a woman in Central Park. Four of the boys were Black, and one was Latino; the woman was white. With no inside information or unique insight, Trump was convinced of the teens' guilt. We now know that the woman had indeed been brutally raped, but not by the boys the police zeroed in on, all of whom were convicted and served long sentences despite their innocence. "The Central Park Five," as they came to be known, were cleared in 2002 by DNA evidence and the actual rapist's confession. Now they go by "The Exonerated Five." Nonetheless, as of 2019, Trump remained unshaken in his conviction that the men were guilty.

WE'RE RIGHT TO worry that unfounded stereotypes of Black men as hypersexual rapists may influence responses to sexual harassment reports against them. We're right to be careful that our own efforts to address sexual harassment do not continue that racism. Yet the use of false accusations to justify violence against Black men is only one terrible part of the role of sexual violence in the perpetuation of white supremacy. Another is white people's rampant sexual terrorization of Black people, particularly Black women, before and after emancipation—and the widespread white tolerance of this abuse. Wells observed that as with the lynching of Black men, the rape of Black women by white men served both to enact and enforce racial hierarchies. Often, she said, the very same white men who lynched Black men in the name of white women's honor also raped Black women. The KKK used the gang rape of Black women as one of its tools of terror.

Legal sanctions for these sexual abuses were "practically unheard of," writes the historian Sharon Block. "No rape conviction against a white man, let alone a victim's owner, for raping an enslaved woman has been found between at least 1700 and the Civil War." Before 1861, a Black woman in the American South was not legally permitted to even file a rape charge against a white man.

White impunity derived from the very nature of slavery. Because enslaved women were understood by law and white society as property rather than actual humans, explains historian Peter Bardaglio, "the law treated the rape of one man's slave by another white man as a trespass against the slave woman's master rather than a crime against the woman herself." White tolerance for sexual abuse of enslaved people also rested on stereotypes about Black sexuality. In 1859, a Mississippi appeals court overturned the conviction of an enslaved man who had been convicted of raping an enslaved child. "The crime of rape does not exist in this State between African slaves," the court explained. "The regulations of law, as to the white race, on the subject of sexual intercourse, do not and cannot, for obvious reasons, apply to slaves; their intercourse is promiscuous, and the violation of a female slave by a male slave would be a mere assault and battery." The following year, the legislature forbade Black men from raping Black girls under the age of twelve. It declined to place any restrictions on white men's legal right to rape Black girls and women.

Without legal protection, Black women were also unable to physically protect themselves, at least not without risking an even worse fate. In 1855, a Black woman named Celia killed the man who enslaved her when he attempted to rape her. Under Missouri law at the time, a woman was allowed to use force to resist the "imminent danger of forced sexual intercourse." But Celia was charged, convicted of murder, and hanged for her crime. The judge held that a "master" had an absolute right to sex with his slave, who thus had no right to protect herself. Some other victims who defended themselves from white rapists were lynched by mobs.

The racist and sexist ideologies that left Black women unprotected by law outlasted slavery. In 1897, the governor of Florida commuted the sentence of a man convicted of raping eight-year-old Hattie Dargan, after his white defenders argued the Black child was a "hoar" who "traded sex for candy." Cole Blease, who served as the governor of South Carolina from 1911 to 1915, pardoned many men, both Black and white, who had been convicted of violence against Black women and girls. He was candid as to his motivation: "I am of the opinion, as I have always been, and have very serious doubt as to whether the crime of rape can be committed upon a negro." Pardoning a white man convicted of sexual violence against a Black woman, Blease expressed skepticism that anyone would risk conviction for "what he could usually get from prices ranging from 25 cents to $1." In other words, Black women were so sexually available as to be unrapeable. Courts instructed juries that Black women were less likely to be chaste than white women, and, based on that belief, applied different legal standards to rape claims brought by victims based on their race. A 1968 study concluded that officers were less likely to pursue rapes reported by Black victims than by other complainants because they believed two stereotypes: Black people were unusually untrustworthy and unusually promiscuous.

It's easy, in discussing the sexual vulnerability of Black women before and after emancipation, to render them weak and helpless. To do so would be a grave mistake. Historians Crystal Feimster and Danielle McGuire, among others, have documented Black women's efforts to combat sexual violence—efforts that laid the groundwork for what became the civil rights movement. Crucially, even when courts were unlikely to recognize their injuries, Black women publicly bore witness to white sexual abuse.

In 1944, Recy Taylor was raped at gunpoint in Abbeville, Alabama, by six white men who abducted her on her way home from church with her family. She was twenty-four, a Black sharecropper and mother. When Taylor begged the men to let her go, Herbert Lovett, the group's leader, ordered her to "act just like you do with your husband or I'll cut your damn throat." One of the men confessed to the rape, and four admitted to having sex with her (consensually, they insisted), but two grand juries made up entirely of white men refused to issue an indictment; the case never went to trial. Rosa Parks led an NAACP investigation and then a national campaign to protest the inaction. In her book about the case, McGuire convincingly argues that the campaigns for Taylor and other Black victims abandoned by the law were direct predecessors of the Montgomery bus boycotts and racial justice fights across the country, providing structure and strategy for these later struggles. (After McGuire's book was published, in 2010, the Alabama legislature apologized to Taylor. A documentary about her assault, *The Rape of Recy Taylor*, was released in 2017, three weeks before her death at the age of ninety-seven.)

The hypocrisy of white frenzy over the mythical Black rapist while white communities and courts tolerated the rampant, unchecked rape of Black people by white men was not lost on civil rights activists. Advocates realized that these two strands of history are not conflicting narratives but part of the same story. Both were designed to maintain racial hierarchy. Both were often enacted by the very same white supremacists. Both were justified by the same stereotypes of Black people as hypersexual and untrustworthy—stereotypes that persist today.

I NEVER LEARNED those histories of sexual violence, and of Black women's central role in social change, until I met Feimster in my final year of college. For so many of us, our knowledge of white racist violence and Black resistance leaves out half the story—the female half, specifically. And our erasure of Black women's history shapes how we understand sexual violence today. So often, in conversations about sexual violence and race, we ignore how racism affects victims, too. We leave out how white supremacy renders people of color, and especially Black women, vulnerable to violence, and how it shapes their access to support and justice afterward.

I recognize that I'm wading into fraught territory for a white woman like myself. Luckily, there is plenty of excellent work on the topic from those who have more skill and authority in this space than I. These include, recently, the Black women who wrote and organized to stop the entertainer R. Kelly. Allegations of sexual abuse of Black girls, backed by documentary evidence, had dogged the R & B singer for years. One video showed what appeared to be R. Kelly urinating on an underage girl, among other sex acts; a criminal case based on that evidence failed when the girl believed to be depicted refused to cooperate with prosecutors. In 2017, two Black organizers, Kenyette Barnes and Oronike Odeleye, started the #MuteRKelly campaign, urging listeners to become "financially divested from the man and his music" in response to the harm he had inflicted on Black girls. The two were angered that R. Kelly was scheduled to perform at a county-owned venue in Atlanta. "I have been hearing about R. Kelly's sexual abuse of young Black women since I was in my teens," Odeleye explained at the time. "Every few years more women come out with their stories. More images and videos surface. More Black girls are scarred for life just as they are coming into their womanhood and sexuality." Audience dollars—and tax dollars—should not be supporting the man responsible for that damage, she and Barnes thought.

The campaign simmered. Then it exploded, thanks to a 2019 documentary by the filmmaker dream hampton. First Illinois, and then New York and Minnesota, charged R. Kelly with sexual abuse and other crimes. His record label dropped him. The singer sat for an ill-advised interview with Gayle King, during which he shouted denials, cried, and, in one particularly dramatic turn, jumped out of his chair. Facing consequences for his alleged actions, after all this time, was apparently too much to bear.

The central public defense of R. Kelly was not, exactly, that he was innocent. Rather, some—primarily but not exclusively men—argued that R. Kelly was only a target because of racial animus. After all, plenty of white male predators walked free. A rival hashtag campaign proposed a different course: #FirstThem, "them" being white rapists. Until they were held accountable, the logic went, R. Kelly shouldn't be, either.

Supporters of the #MuteRKelly campaign pointed out that #FirstThem's racial politics excluded the singer's victims. R. Kelly targeted Black girls, which might explain why it had taken so long for the entertainment industry and legal authorities to concern themselves with the allegations against the singer. As Saida Grundy observed in the *Atlantic*, the justifications used to excuse the sexual abuse of Black girls are rooted in stereotypes harkening back to slavery. The idea that Black girls are "fast" parallels the notion of Black men as hypersexual rapists.

Plus, Grundy noted, R. Kelly's otherwise extraordinary alleged abuses were typical in one respect: "sexual assaults, like nearly all

other violent crimes, overwhelmingly happen *within* a racial group."
To demand a delay in consequences for Black people accused of sexual assault, then, means demanding a delay in justice for their overwhelmingly Black victims. "We know that this system is unfair to
Black people—not just Black men, but Black people," hampton
explained during an NPR interview. "We know what this system
does to us, right? So to turn to that system for justice is itself an
oxymoron. But at the same time, we have a knee-jerk reaction to
protect Black men, always at the expense of Black women." Kimberlé Crenshaw, the legal academic most famous for developing the
theory of intersectionality, diagnosed the same pattern—which, she
wrote, can be weaponized by alleged abusers: "Here anti-racism
marshals support for Black men accused of abuse, but it is absent in
the defense of the women and girls who have come forward to hold
them accountable." This she dubs the "'Save Our Brotha' ('SOB')
playbook."

I must admit I often feel anxious writing about abuse of Black
victims by other Black people because I fear I will say something
racist. Focusing on white people—"minding my own business"—
seems a lot easier. But Crenshaw denounces that route of comfortable silence, however tempting it may be. The SOB playbook, she
writes, "works primarily to reinforce white laissez-faire in matters
of intra-racial abuse, persuading non-Black allies to remain silent
as a gesture of anti-racist solidarity, and abetting the disregard of
others who write off the allegations of intra-racial abuse so long as
the predation stays confined to Black women and girls."

Crenshaw compares the defense of R. Kelly to that offered for
Clarence Thomas when he was a nominee for the Supreme Court
accused of sexually harassing Anita Hill, among others. Thomas
and his defenders insisted that the accusations against him were
racist, or what the nominee called a "high-tech lynching." Lost
in their objection was that Hill herself was Black. "Underlying
[Thomas's] comment was the idea that sexual harassment, like
the feminism that pointed it out, was a white preoccupation

incompatible with antiracism," Crenshaw writes. Hill's experience was not interchangeable with that of a Black man's, nor—as too many white feminist supporters assumed—a white woman's. Instead of acknowledging the intersections of identity that informed Hill's experience, Thomas's defenders simply erased her race, acting as if the only potential for racism lay with those who would condemn Thomas. But didn't the Senate Judiciary Committee's, and the country's, evaluation of her credibility and worth also implicate racial inequality?

We see similar dynamics in play when opponents of Title IX protections argue that efforts to address sexual assault in schools will be bad for Black students without so much as mentioning Black survivors. My friend and former colleague Nia Evans called back to Hill's mistreatment in her writing about Title IX, observing, "We're seeing the same flawed arguments today. Is it not also a matter of racial justice to support and believe Black women? We face high rates of sexual harassment and violence all over the country, and it's largely unseen. Just look at Harvard, Howard, and Spelman where Black women have been speaking out for years about the violation of their Title IX rights. Their right to learn free from sexual violence is a matter of racial and gender justice, but because they sit at the intersection—just like Anita Hill—they're slipping through the cracks."

A narrow vision of racial justice that leaves out victims "contributes to the trend of rendering Black sexual assault survivors invisible," writes Wagatwe Wanjuki, a writer and longtime anti-rape activist who was one of the original Know Your IX organizers. Often, the races of alleged victims are selectively elided to present a simplified narrative. For example, in an influential 2018 op-ed, Lara Bazelon, a lawyer and professor, presented the experience of one of her clients, a Black male student who had been accused of sexual assault by a white female classmate. The school had taken her word over his, and Bazelon suggested that this determination was the result of racism. Because of stories like his, she explained, she supported

DeVos's rules as a matter of racial justice. But as a letter to the editor later revealed, Bazelon had left out a key detail: a second woman who had also reported her client, but whom the school hadn't believed—a student Bazelon mentioned only in a parenthetical without any racial identifier—was a woman of color. There were two stories here about race. One was of a white woman's word taken over a Black man's, the other of a woman of color deemed less credible than her white classmate. Apparently only one of these factored into Bazelon's assessment of DeVos's policies. Only one was worth telling.

Law professor Nancy Chi Cantalupo notes that "discussions of campus sexual violence tend to omit race in the discussions of accusers." As a result, writes fellow law professor Deborah Brake, they allow critics to pit "a racially diverse group of accused students, with black men featured prominently among them, against a race-less (and implicitly white) group of accusers." The blame lies at the feet of journalists and commentators, yes, but student anti-violence movements also have a role in allowing this narrative to take hold: Wanjuki has spoken about how the unrepresentative whiteness of our public-facing advocates rendered us ill-prepared to counter the erasure of survivors of color.

An erroneously simple story of rape and race—in which only Black men are (alleged) rapists and only white women are (supposed) victims—also ignores Black men's own sexual victimization. In 2019, students at Morehouse, the famous all-male historically Black college, came forward as survivors of sexual harassment by the same staff member. The school, by their account, knew about the predation but took no action to protect its students. Not only do Black men face stereotypes that they are prone to commit sexual violence, but they are also confronted with myths and biases that make it harder for them to protect themselves and to be believed when they are abused. "Overshadowed by the specter of violence and deviance and death, many people do not believe Black men can be victims of rape," writes the scholar Tommy Curry. Among the contributing stereotypes: "Black men are insatiable. They want sex;

if they did not want it, they are (or should be) capable of fending off an attacker." Yet self-defense comes with costs, too. Terry Crews, the actor and former NFL star, spoke publicly in 2017 about a high-level Hollywood executive who had grabbed Crews's genitals at a party. Crews didn't react in the moment, he explains, because, as he puts it, "'240 lbs. Black Man stomps out Hollywood Honcho' would be the headline the next day."

I THINK OFTEN of a conversation I had with a white lawyer who had published a critique of some proposed protections for student victims. "All I want to do is whatever will help poor Black and brown kids," she told me in explanation. I pointed out that Black and brown kids, not just white students, get sexually victimized. "I hadn't thought of that," she said. The comment startled me, because it put so starkly the racial assumptions that underlie conversations about sexual violence, and also because it was unquestionably racist. This lawyer, who understood her mission as promoting racial justice, was only able to see young people of color as alleged abusers, not as victims. They can, of course, be both, and face racism in both positions. (Although my focus here has been anti-Blackness, a similar tension can arise in connection with queer rights: while some worry that institutional efforts to address sexual harassment may end up targeting queer people disproportionately, queer people are also at tremendous risk for sexual victimization, and thus particularly need institutional protections.)

Supporters of policies like DeVos's fail to realize—or fail to care—that by making it exceptionally hard for anyone to prove allegations of sexual harassment, they are making it exceptionally hard for survivors of color, too. Worse yet, some of those policies could exacerbate the effect of racist stereotypes that survived the end of slavery and Jim Crow. The scholar Jessica Harris notes that even on contemporary college campuses, "Black women are described as promiscuous" and "Latinas are seen as sexy and feisty." White women, on the other hand, are historically "constructed as pure and virginal." As a result, "acts of sexual violence against white women are more believable but also more tragic and compelling because they, unlike the stereotypes of women of color, have never asked for sex." Against that backdrop, exceptionalist procedures like DeVos's may guarantee that only white victims have a real chance of success. For example, as Wanjuki and Brake have argued, a heightened standard of evidence may devastate survivors of color, who, in the eyes of administrators, may never be "clear and convincing" victims. And the civil rights stakes for these survivors are immense: the consequence of disbelief is not only impunity for their assailants but loss of access to much-needed institutional support and a profound frustration of their ability to learn, work, live full lives. Our task, then, must be to root out stereotypes and prejudices that hurt those on both sides of a sexual harassment accusation—a goal that cannot be achieved by creating more obstacles for one side in favor of the other.

Of course, people of color find themselves on both sides of every kind of adjudication, in and out of the courts. How to design policies and procedures that ensure racial justice for both victims and the accused is a tremendous task, one that has been the subject of considerable debate among scholars and activists, especially with respect to criminal prosecution. I do not pretend to offer a comprehensive answer on how to weigh these interests across different adjudications with different stakes. My point here is far narrower: whatever balance we strike in general for allegations vetted through a given system, we should use for sexual harms, too. Because even if these cases implicate unique stereotypes and histories, that weight pulls in two directions.

The exceptionalist "fix" is attractive because it's simple, concrete. In rejecting it, I wish I could point toward a single perfect solution that addressed racism on both sides of the ledger. Our project, however, is of course far more complicated. But the good news is that we already have tools at our disposal. Looking beyond the particular context of sexual harassment, we can learn from the broad strategies recommended by advocates and civil rights leaders for combating discrimination in organizations and communities—including their advice regarding discipline for nonsexual harms. Rules should be precise and specific to reduce discriminatory enforcement; if it's clear from the written policy what conduct is prohibited, there's less room to enforce it selectively. Good procedures can help both sides without tipping the scales—for example, by giving everyone the opportunity to tell their story, present evidence, and rebut the other side's account. Institutions should train a diverse group of decision-makers on how to resist their personal biases. And, to hold themselves accountable, they should track outcomes for all investigations based on the identities of the people on both sides of the accusation and publish anonymized data. These are smart practices regardless of the alleged offense.

Rooting out prejudices is easier said than done. Yet taking the simpler, one-sided way out is not an option. Nor is giving up on addressing sexual harassment altogether once we are faced with thorny complexity. The only way to the other side of this mountain is over it. We cannot throw up our hands and settle on the side of violence.

PART IV

CO-OPTATION

16

Of Men's Rights and Famous Men

Sometime in the middle of law school, when Know Your IX was gaining real national traction, I started finding photos of myself on Twitter. In each, my face was photoshopped into depictions of the Salem witch trials. Witch trials, of course, were persecutions of women, often because of the women's defiance of male authority or their deviant sexualities. But in these doctored photos, I was the inquisitor; the persecuted witches were college boys. Sometimes my face was accompanied by those of other anti-rape organizers. Tracking the photos, I found screeds against Title IX, supposedly the instrument of contemporary witch hunters. Sometimes the screeds sent other Twitter accounts my way, to remind me that I was the enemy of due process, an idiot, a man-hater, a liar.

That was my personal introduction to so-called men's rights activism, a reactionary anti-feminist movement that has long flourished on message boards in dark corners of the internet and is now making its way into the light.

Plenty of decent people hold bad ideas about sexual violence.

We're all raised on myths and biases; no wonder we end up believing some. With many critics, even when I deeply disagree with them, and even when I think their advocacy is rooted in some internalized sexism, I have no doubt they genuinely care about fairness and equality. They're trying to do good, as best they can.

This isn't true of everyone, however. With every action comes an equal and opposite reaction, and as women and other survivors have gained legal and social standing, the extremist men's rights movement gains strength and numbers. Men's rights activists, or MRAs, insist on a funhouse version of gender inequality: men, not women, they insist, are the subordinate sex in the contemporary United States.

MRAs identify some rigid stereotypes that certainly do hurt men and must be addressed as part of any campaign for gender justice. For example, assumptions about men and women's proper roles within a family can pose challenges to men seeking custody of their children. Domestic violence programming is not always responsive to male victims' needs. Men die by suicide at higher rates than women, perhaps because men are expected to be "strong," and so get shamed for seeking mental health support. But MRAs do not draw the more obvious conclusion from these data points—that sexism hurts people of all genders, as feminists have long said. Instead, they wage war on what they see as overwhelming female dominance over poor, defenseless men. "We have watched our predictions of men being reduced to indentured servants to a malicious matriarchy come true, even as society continues to dismiss and humiliate us for speaking," bemoans Paul Elam, the reliably histrionic founder of the leading MRA publication, *A Voice for Men*.

The common (unfounded) complaints: Structural misogyny is a myth. The gender pay gap is nonexistent, or entirely the result of women's choices. Men do just as much domestic labor as their wives. Domestic violence is rare, and women are equal perpetrators. Post-*Roe*, women gained control over their reproduction, but men are still "slaves" because they are expected to pay child support for a baby their partner chooses not to abort. Open discussion of sexual violence demonizes men, who are never adequately celebrated for their accomplishments and contributions. Warren Farrell, known as the father of the men's rights movement, was upset, for example, that journalists were more interested in covering Mike Tyson's 1991 rape trial than the heroic deeds of male firefighters who put out a fire near the courthouse. "Two firefighters died, but men-as-saviors don't make news," he complained in his 1993 book *The Myth of Male Power: Why Men Are the Disposable Sex.* (The title alone tells you most of what you need to know about Farrell's views.) Meanwhile, institutions from courts to campuses are systemically biased against men. "There is now a second sexism and it is anti-male," says professor Miles Groth. Groth is a prominent advocate for "male studies," a right-wing discipline that, echoing Farrell, denies "the continuing myth of male power." He believes that, with proper investment, his field "would give serious attention for the first time to the unique experience and history of human beings who are male."

It's almost funny, except it's deadly serious. Roy Den Hollander, an MRA lawyer, sued Columbia University over its women's studies program, part of a yearslong and wildly unsuccessful anti-feminist litigation strategy. In 2020, he went to the home of Esther Salas, a federal judge who had presided over one of his cases, and opened fire, killing her son and wounding her husband. (As with many MRAs, Den Hollander's misogyny was inextricably tied to his racism. In his writings, Den Hollander dismissed Salas as "a lazy and incompetent Latina," while also noting his attraction to her.)

Thanks to women's liberation, MRAs warn, women can now use accusations of sexual harassment and rape as a tool of feminine control. "Sexual harassment legislation is a male-only chastity belt," Farrell writes. "With women holding the key." Rape is rare, MRAs claim, and many accusations of it are false, sending thousands of innocent men to prison each year. The "false accusation industry," Elam explains in *A Voice for Men*, perpetuates a vicious cycle: "Women lie about being raped, judicial politicians make careers off of putting away sexual offenders, and a brainwashed public cheers it all on. That so many of the men caught up in this are innocent doesn't stop the grinding wheels of all this injustice for even a moment." Never mind that false accusations are actually rare. Never mind that so little sexual abuse is reported, so few abusers convicted. Never mind that, of students found responsible for sexually assaulting a class-mate, only a third were expelled. Never mind the facts: men, the MRAs are sure, are terribly vulnerable to women's lies.

The solution, they say, is due process. In recent years, all the most visible lobbying efforts of the major MRA groups have focused on protections for students accused of sexual assault. Elam labeled the 2011 Dear Colleague Letter "hypocrisy [that] borders on treason," and further evidence that "professors and legislators acquiesce to virtually any initiative that strips males of whatever it is they may still possess, including their self-respect and especially their free-doms." Farrell later concurred, citing the preponderance standard—again, the standard of evidence used in almost all civil trials—as a violation of due process that requires correction. And MRAs do not limit their due process demands to schools: Elam claims that, when it comes to the criminal prosecution of rape (and, of course, rape alone), "the system is rigged" against men.

Perhaps unsurprisingly, though, MRAs' commitment to due process extends only so far as it serves to protect men. They are less concerned about—and even openly disdainful of—actual rules that facilitate fair adjudications. Elam calls upon jurors in rape tri-als to vote to acquit "even in the face of overwhelming evidence that the charges are true." "Your fellow jurors, who can be assumed to be living unconsciously in the misandric [anti-men] matrix, and prepared to condemn men on accusation alone, cannot be trusted," he warns. "Voting not guilty on any charge of rape is the only way to remain faithful to the concept of presumed innocence." To Elam, "presumed" apparently means "guaranteed and permanent." Those who decried the Shitty Media Men list or the students at Brown for semi-publicly naming accused harassers might be surprised to learn that the National Coalition for Men (NCFM) posts the photographs and names of women, including young students, who are "false accusers"—that is, those who NCFM believes, seemingly without any actual investigation, have lied. Apparently, only accusations against men need to be vetted. (Another MRA blog once identified me as a "suspected false accuser," before shifting to the shorter identifier "this cunt." They did not identify any accusation I had made, or note why it was not credible.)

For MRAs, due process matters only as a defense against accountability for male violence. They are not looking to treat parties fairly; they seek impunity. For them, "due process" is first and foremost a dog whistle, as Professor Cantalupo puts it. Despite the mismatch between their actual commitments and the legal label they put on them, their rhetorical strategy is effective because it evokes our Constitution and national morality, sources of legitimacy. Frequently, the MRAs cite left-leaning advocates of due process, like the Harvard Law professors critical of the school's Title IX efforts, as support. *Look, even the experts agree. Ours are mainstream views.*

But they aren't. In their own writings, MRA leadership makes clear that their criticism of anti-violence efforts is always, first and foremost, driven by a belief that women deserve to be abused and men deserve to get away with it. Speaking of the football player Ray Rice's videotaped assault on his then fiancée, NCFM president Harry Crouch explained to a reporter that "if she hadn't aggravated him, she wouldn't have been hit." Daryush Valizadeh (also known as Roosh V), a notorious "pick up artist" and publisher of the MRA site Return of Kings, has proposed decriminalizing rape on private property. Paul Elam declared October—nationally recognized as Domestic Violence Awareness Month—"Bash a Violent Bitch Month." Elam claimed satire as defense; the humor eludes me. "A lot of women . . . get pummeled and pumped because they are stupid (and often arrogant) enough to walk through life with the equivalent of a I'M A STUPID, CONNIVING BITCH—PLEASE RAPE ME neon sign glowing above their empty little narcissistic heads,"

Elam wrote in 2010. "In my opinion their 'plight' from being raped should draw about as much sympathy as a man who loses a wallet full of cash after leaving it laying around a bus station unattended."

IT'S EASY TO dismiss the men's rights movement as an offensive but ultimately harmless campaign, too fringe and ineffective to be worthy of concern. But the movement has gained real traction in the halls of power, especially since Trump's election. DeVos's Title IX regulations were the result of a "deep collaboration" between MRAs and Trump's Department of Education, a *Nation* exposé uncovered. The groups had unparalleled access to federal officials to shape the substance of the rules and, emails showed, MRAs and the department coordinated a joint public defense. Hans Bader, the senior department official who argued for DeVos's policies in the *New York Times*, was the primary funder of one of the MRA groups. (The *Nation* also uncovered that Bader had previously given $680,000 to a group that pays drug users to be sterilized. Its logic, the group's founder explained: "We campaign to neuter dogs and yet we allow women to have ten or twelve kids that they can't take care of.") Trump's most loyal attorney general, Bill Barr, blurbed a book about the supposedly precarious position of young men in higher education. In the endorsement, Barr accused the Obama administration of "fanning the false narrative of a 'rape culture' on college campuses" and promoting "kangaroo justice." Even John Hickenlooper, then a candidate for the 2020 Democratic presidential nomination, met with Farrell to discuss Farrell's proposal to devote more White House resources to men and boys.

President Trump himself echoed key MRA rhetoric about male vulnerability to false accusations, women's resulting power over men, and the need for a particular flavor of "due process." "Peoples [*sic*] lives are being shattered and destroyed by a mere allegation. Some are true and some are false. Some are old and some are new," Trump tweeted in February 2018. "There is no recovery for someone falsely accused—life and career are gone. Is there no such thing any longer as Due Process?" Later that year, he warned: "It's a very scary time for young men in America" because "somebody could accuse you of something and you're automatically guilty." When a journalist asked what message he had for girls, the president insisted that women "are doing great." Trump's language perfectly mirrored the MRA outlook: when it comes to sexual harassment, the vulnerable are the potentially accused—assumed to be men—not the potentially victimized, assumed to be women. Rightly, the MRAs recognized Trump as their own. Soon after his comments, Farrell published an article titled "Why This Is a Very Scary Time for Young Men," in which he ran through standard MRA talking points.

MRA ideology is a good fit for the contemporary GOP, and not only because of the party's hostility to women's rights. The through line of contemporary conservative identity politics is that the powerful are oppressed by the historically powerless. Race is as much a part of that story as sex: after all, punishment for sexual harms, real or imagined, is new only to white men. And their resentment is so potent it delivered Trump to the White House. For a long time, these voters had felt they could get away with anything—sexual harassment, yes, but also more than that. They had known that American society was theirs for the taking. But that privilege is (very) slowly disintegrating. White people now have to work alongside immigrants and report to women of color. They can no longer use racial slurs or sling casual homophobia without the "PC police" reminding them *we don't do that anymore*. They are, as Arlie Hochschild's book by the same name puts it, "strangers in their own land." They feel like victims even as they continue to dominate.

To be fair, the feminists and anti-racists and social justice activists have, in fact, taken something from them: small slivers of impunity. For those used to power, every inch toward equality feels like an injustice. The threat of accountability for white men's sexual harassment—a truly novel idea—is a perfect focal point for all these anxieties.

And so the message spreads. By the year after the Weinstein

allegations emerged, four in ten Americans surveyed by NPR agreed that Me Too had gone "too far." Some cited procedural concerns, including a lack of respect for the presumption of innocence, as the heart of the problem. "We have females that make false allegations and jumping on the 'me too' bandwagon. And it's ruined a lot of guys' lives," explained one respondent, Nate Jurewicz, who ran a popular anti-feminist Facebook page. When asked if *proven* allegations of sexual harassment should disqualify a political candidate, Jurewicz said no. "No one's perfect," he explained.

ATTITUDES LIKE JUREWICZ'S, still front and center in our national discourse about sexual harassment, boil down to a belief that men should not be accountable for sexual harassment. Plenty of people across the political spectrum—not only reactionary conservatives—share this goal. The lawyer Linda Hirshman cataloged a long history of left-wing apologists and enablers in her 2019 book *Reckoning*. At the height of Me Too, self-professed feminists lined up in the *Atlantic* and the *New York Times* to decry social opprobrium of serial harassers as over-punitive hysteria. Yet few outside MRA circles explicitly acknowledge that they seek to ensure male impunity. Even Trump doesn't go so far. Instead, those who seek elite liberal legitimacy borrow a page from the MRA playbook: to combat accountability for sexual harassment, they use the sanitizing language of due process.

During the deluge of accusations that followed Weinstein's downfall, bad-faith due process arguments were frequently deployed in defense of famous men. The actor Tony Denison insisted it would be unfair to credit the dozens of reports about Weinstein himself without seeing the abuse with one's own eyes. "Until somebody shows me pictures and has me outside the door, and I open the door and that is what is going on, until [that happens], it is innuendo," Denison insisted. "I can't and won't point fingers at people unless I have proof." Weinstein was, of course, eventually criminally convicted, even though jurors did not personally witness him sexually abusing any women.

I think again of the performance night Weinstein attended in New York while awaiting trial, the one where comedians compared him to Freddy Krueger and confronted him about his abuses. Their comments were critical, angry. But no one deprived Weinstein of anything. He was fine. Yet their words were, a Weinstein rep decried, "an example of how due process today is being squashed by the public." In a perfect irony, Weinstein was allowed to stay at the club while some of the critics were escorted out without any kind of process of their own. You may remember that one performer recalled, "This guy was leading me out the stairs, just repeating 'due process, due process' to me." The term had no content. It was just a buzzword excuse for male impunity.

The return of Louis C.K. provides another prime example. In the fall of 2017, just weeks after the allegations against Weinstein went public, the *New York Times* published another story on sexual abuse in the entertainment industry. In it, five women performers said Louis C.K., the edgy and purportedly feminist comedian with an eponymous show, had masturbated in front of them or while talking to them on the phone. Only sometimes did he bother to ask for permission; only sometimes did women over whom he had power feel able to say no. Rumors to this effect on gossip sites had followed Louis for years, but, the women explained, they had feared reprisal if they came forward publicly. In response to the allegations in the *Times*, Louis did something rare: he confirmed the women's accounts. "These stories are true," he wrote in a widely published statement, which many press outlets mischaracterized as an apology. (He did express remorse. He did not apologize.) "I have spent my long and lucky career talking and saying anything I want," he concluded. "I will now step back and take a long time to listen."

"A long time," apparently, meant a bit over nine months. The August after Louis stepped back, he emerged again with a surprise appearance at the Comedy Cellar, a fabled New York comedy club.

His fifteen-minute set, according to reports, did not address the reason for his absence.

For many, Louis's return was too little, too early. Comedy Cellar's owner, Noam Dworman, expected a backlash for handing over the mic so soon. But he felt his decision was just. "Bottom line, I can't compel testimony, I can't punish perjury, I don't have a forensics lab. If I'm judge and jury, I'm going to get it wrong," he wrote in a statement. "We have a civil and criminal justice system to punish people. We all respect the notions of fairness that are contained in the rules of due process. The Comedy Cellar is just not the institution to be meting out such serious punishment. I think we'll be better off as a society if we stop looking to the bottlenecks of distribution—Twitter, Netflix, Facebook, or Comedy Clubs, to filter the world for us. It will just end in one biased inconsistent mess."

There are undoubtedly hard questions to ask about the terms by which famous harassers can return to public life. What is absolutely not hard to figure out is that club owners get to decide who comes on their stage, and they do not need a police investigation or court decision to justify that choice. Dworman's position is especially absurd because here the accused *admitted* he did it. Let's repeat that. Louis told the world he had nonconsensually masturbated in front of women, and Dworman's response was: *I don't have a forensics lab, so who can really say?* This disingenuous call for due process was, blatantly, no more than a call for impunity.

And yet, judging from the online response, Dworman's statement passed the smell test for more people than it should have. I'd wager it succeeded because of exceptionalism. We're so used to talking about sexual harassment allegations as a unique procedural challenge, one that requires uniquely criminal-trial-style safeguards. So we fail to catch the flaws of arguments that, if made to excuse any other misconduct, would be obviously ridiculous. Ubiquitous exceptionalism provides a first line of defense for abusers, allowing cultures of disbelief and dismissal to disguise themselves in plain sight.

Dworman and Denison are hardly the greatest political threats of our day. It is a little too easy to dismantle these entertainers' self-interested legal reasoning. But just as Hollywood's condemnation of abuse in the wake of the Weinstein revelations shaped public views about sexual violence, so can the defense of abuse, or the shrugging away of it, in the wake of others' misconduct. And, what's more concerning, the poorly executed excuses of entertainment hacks reflect the strategies of more powerful, coordinated misogynists.

It may be obvious that Weinstein's supporters and men's rights activists are not earnestly trying to work out a system of adjudicating sexual harassment that is fair to all involved. But as we'll see in the next chapters, the project of discerning who's acting in good faith and who isn't becomes trickier as the players become more polished and more politically mainstream. Some readers may disagree with my assessment of some people's motivations. That uncertainty, though, is part of the problem. Those of us trying to get it right need partners and interlocutors who come from different perspectives. But when we know that some in the debate are acting disingenuously, pretending to care about fairness when all they care about is reducing accountability, we don't know who to trust. It's tempting, then, to just stick to our own camps.

A few years ago, I spoke with a defense attorney who often represents students facing school disciplinary charges for sexual assault. He was upset: on a panel about Me Too, a lawyer he otherwise respected had drawn connections between MRAs and advocacy for accused student harassers in a way that, to him, felt dismissive. It's certainly true that not all champions for accused students' rights are MRAs. But, the defense attorney and I both agreed, it does make it tricky that plenty of them are.

The People Who Want to
Bring You Mandatory Referral

If you had to design a perfect villain for the fight against campus sexual violence, you could not do better than Earl Ehrhart. For three decades, Ehrhart, a businessman from Cobb County, served in the Georgia House of Representatives. (He retired in 2019, and his wife, Ginny, stepped into the seat.) The Republican "made a name for himself as a lightning rod around social issues," wrote Tyler Kingkade in a 2017 exposé for *BuzzFeed News*. "He fought affirmative action for years, tried to pass laws undercutting anti-discrimination ordinances in Atlanta, and declared in 2005 that what 'militant homosexuals are seeking is special rights, not equal rights.'" He also defended long mandatory minimum sentences that "denied due process to young offenders, most of them black teens." Kingkade's article focused on Ehrhart's most recent crusade, which centered on "changing how colleges deal with sexual assault, out of concern for the treatment of accused students."

At the time of its publication, Ehrhart had just come close to passing a bill designed to do exactly that. As originally drafted, that law, known as House Bill 51, would have required a university to wait until the end of a criminal investigation and trial before taking any steps of its own to address a report of sexual assault or other felony. Even then, the law would have only allowed the university to discipline a student who had been found guilty or chose not to contest the charges. The bill offered just one narrow exception: a school could place a student on interim suspension before the end of a successful criminal prosecution if to do otherwise would pose "an immediate threat to the life, health, or safety of the student body." That is a remarkably high bar. What if you think someone is likely to rape again at some point during their time at the school, but not "immediately"? More worrisome, even that exception was available only if prosecutors brought charges. If not, the school's hands would be tied entirely.

Ehrhart insisted that such radical change in schools' approach to sexual harassment—forbidding them to respond in all but the narrowest of circumstances—was necessary to restore due process protections for accused men, though he never explained exactly how. "My advice is to shut down this office and all pending kangaroo courts until my bill passes," Ehrhart emailed administrators at the University of Georgia after a constituent contacted him, worried that her son, accused of sexual misconduct, was being treated unfairly by the state's flagship school. That kind of direct intervention into schools' disciplinary actions was commonplace for Ehrhart. Both Kingkade, in *BuzzFeed*, and Kathryn Joyce, writing in the *New York Times*, reported a series of cases in which the state representative contacted university administrators to demand that they conclude that a specific, always male, student had not committed a sexual offense.

One such instance involved a woman at Kennesaw State University, whose complaint said that a male friend had raped her after she'd consented to some sexual contact but refused to have intercourse. At first, the woman told Joyce, she was not sure how serious the breach had been, and let the man—a fellow KSU student—stay over. They ate breakfast together. But after the man blew off their later plans, she spoke to friends about the event, which they recognized as a sexual assault. (For a variety of complicated reasons, including cognitive processing of trauma, many survivors do not immediately turn against their assailants. I of course have no knowledge of the truth of these particular accusations.) An investigation commenced, during which both parties felt aggrieved. According to the complainant, administrators asked whether she only considered the incident to be rape because the man hadn't called her. The accused student's attorney, meanwhile, reported that investigators fell out of contact with her client for months. Ultimately, investigators found the man responsible for the assault and recommended he be suspended for two semesters.

That is when his attorney looped in Ehrhart. We do not know what their first conversations looked like, or how much Ehrhart knew about the case. But public records show that the attorney emailed KSU's president, Sam Olens, in December 2016, urging the school to revisit the disciplinary charges—and copying Ehrhart on the message. Ehrhart was well known to the KSU administration. A sports complex he ran sometimes partnered with the university, and he had supported Olens's candidacy for the KSU job back when Olens was Georgia's attorney general. Now Ehrhart followed up, writing to Olens: "This was the second of the absolutely ridiculous cases I was concerned about. I label this one 'Breakfast with a rapist' made for TV absurdity." Ehrhart also pointed out to Olens that prosecutors had earlier decided not to pursue a criminal case against the student. Citing that decision not to prosecute, Ehrhart told KSU's president: "How on earth a University bureaucrat can be allowed to draw a different conclusion ruining someone's life escapes me." In other words, if an assault did not result in a criminal conviction, it did not happen, period. Olens forwarded Ehrhart's email to KSU's Title IX coordinator, who told Olens the case had been reopened and that she would keep the president updated.

According to the *New York Times*, when the school told the complainant her case would be reviewed again, it also provided her with a new list of witnesses who would testify in support of the man. Among them was Ehrhart. "I had no clue who he was or what he could possibly know about somebody raping me," she said. "As soon as Ehrhart's name came up, everything went crazy, and they dropped any care they had for me." In early 2017, at the recommendation of an external reviewer, KSU reversed the previous finding of responsibility. The male student was off the hook, and now the woman who said he had raped her would need to share a campus with him. Eventually, she withdrew.

Perhaps KSU was swayed by Ehrhart's reasoning. The two prongs of his argument—that real victims immediately recognize rape as such, and that criminal prosecution is the only valid arbiter of a sexual assault claim—reflect widely held beliefs about the nature of both rape and our legal system. Perhaps the investigation actually had been mishandled on the first go-round. Or perhaps KSU was influenced by the fact that Ehrhart was the chair of the Georgia House's higher education appropriations subcommittee—that is, he held a huge amount of power over KSU and other state universities' budgets. If KSU was paying attention, they knew that Ehrhart was not afraid to use that power to make sure student disciplinary cases went as he saw fit.

In 2016, for example, Ehrhart learned of a student who wanted to transfer to Georgia State University. GSU wanted to first conduct a background check on him because the student had left his previous school during a pending investigation of his alleged sexual wrongdoing. Ehrhart emailed a GSU lobbyist to demand that an assistant dean involved in the matter be fired for her "thuggish behavior." He instructed the lobbyist to inform GSU's president that "I am tired of these issues, and I am going to inform all of my decisions on University funding by those who harbor these types of thugs on their campus." (The language is worth noting. "Thugs" are not exactly known for their commitment to background checks. Given Ehrhart's documented opposition to racial justice, it is hard not to wonder if he chose that word because the dean involved had a distinctively Black name.)

In 2015, a Black woman accused members of the Georgia Tech

chapter of Phi Delta Theta of yelling racial slurs at her from their on-campus house. Georgia Tech imposed restrictions on the frat's activities, including their partying, and mandated sensitivity training. Ehrhart thought the punishment was unfair and convened a legislative hearing on the topic. His aim was not just reinstatement of Phi Delta Theta but exposure of what he saw as a witch-hunt culture, especially with respect to sexual assault allegations. "You want to talk about 'safe space'?" Ehrhart asked, rhetorically, in an interview before the hearing. "In the vernacular of campus discussion today, there's no safe space for young men at Tech. You want to be safe? Go to class, then go run and hide in your dorm. That's where we are at Tech right now." (At the time, the school was more than two-thirds male.) During the hearing itself, Kingkade reports, Ehrhart warned university administrators in attendance: "Hear me clearly. You got a bond project? If you don't protect students of this state with due process, don't come looking to us for money." Shortly afterward, the frat was fully reinstated.

A disciplinary process in which a school like KSU or Georgia Tech may be forced to throw its own determination out the window at the whim of a powerful legislator who has heard only half the story is, to put it mildly, not fair. It lacks all the markings of fairness required by due process and our moral intuitions: Impartiality. Consistency. Predictability.

I have no direct knowledge of the fairness, or lack thereof, of Georgia universities' disciplinary responses to sexual harassment. With only public reports to go on, I cannot definitively say whether the students on whose behalf Ehrhart intervened were treated correctly by their schools. I do feel confident, though, that Earl Ehrhart is not interested in fairness. He's interested in reducing accountability for young men, especially young white men, whom he sees as endangered victims of liberal hysteria.

EHRHART'S HOUSE BILL 51 was only the most extreme version of a wave of similar bills introduced in state houses across the country and in the U.S. Congress, backed by a coalition of fraternity lobbyists, libertarian nonprofits, and conservative legislators. These bills all sought to diminish (and in some places remove) schools' responsibility and power to address sexual harassment, by mandating that law enforcement be involved in all such complaints—and often requiring schools to defer to that separate process.

Central to many of these proposals, including Ehrhart's bill, was a "mandatory referral" policy that would have forced colleges and universities to forward student reports of sexual assault to the police. Mandatory referral bills come in two basic forms. The first requires schools to pass along all such reports, regardless of the victims' wishes. (That is, once a survivor tells the school about her assault, she has no control over whether a police report is made.) The second doesn't require schools to forward reports, but prohibits them from taking disciplinary action in response to reports of sexual assault until the police are notified, and, in some cases, until there is a conviction or guilty plea. As originally drafted, HB 51 would have combined both those approaches. It would have required Georgia colleges and universities to pass along every report of an alleged felony to law enforcement, and—aside from the narrow "immediate threat" exception—the schools would have been allowed to initiate disciplinary proceedings against a student only after a criminal prosecution had been concluded successfully. In short, the law would have paralyzed the schools.

The idea that HB 51 was necessary to protect accused students' due process rights simply does not hold up to scrutiny. Forcing schools to delay their disciplinary proceedings, potentially for years, would not make them fairer in any way. It would simply make them rarer, slower, and less effective. The other version of mandatory referral legislation, requiring schools to report sexual assault to the police against victims' wishes, wouldn't have promoted due process any more effectively. Indeed, for the accused students, such bills— proposed in Delaware and Virginia, among other states—seem to place them in a *worse* position, now having to juggle both criminal and disciplinary proceedings against them at the same time.

Yet for many, policies that require police involvement in sexual assault allegations are intuitively appealing. They speak to so many widespread, if incorrect, assumptions about sexual violence. Isn't calling the police the obvious choice after a rape? Isn't criminal prosecution the best way to take rape "seriously"? If schools are doing such an awful job responding to these assaults, the logic goes, why not send the reports to the real pros in the police department? To people trying to do the right thing, mandatory referral might sound like a victim-friendly reform.

In truth, though, it would be a disaster for survivors. As we have seen, there are a million reasons why a victim might want to avoid getting involved with law enforcement. She might fear police harassment, or revealing her immigration status. She might not wish to call on the reserves needed to endure a long trial. She might not want to see her assailant in prison. At the same time, she might still need some basic support services from her school, like a dorm change or mental health services. She might feel that suspension, but not imprisonment, is the just punishment. Deciding to whom to report, if at all, is a complicated decision, and it is not an on-off switch: the fact that a survivor wants certain kinds of help does not mean she is ready to involve everyone. But mandatory referral policies narrow the range of student victims' choices. Where once they could decide to report to just their school, just the police, or both—either at the same time or in succession—now there would be fewer options on the table. Tell the police. Tell your school, which will tell the police. Or tell no one at all.

And survivors tell us this last option, in all likelihood, would be the most appealing one to many students under a mandatory referral regime. A 2015 survey by Know Your IX and the National Alliance to End Sexual Violence indicated that survivors would be less likely to report to anyone if they knew that their school reports would be forwarded to the police.

Plus, under Ehrhart's ideal regime, even if a victim did report, the school's hands would be tied unless and until the accused pleaded guilty or was convicted. Such results, we know, are rare for reasons that have nothing to do with whether the reports are truthful. And, by the time the case resolved itself, appeals and all, both students would likely have long graduated—if the survivor had not already dropped out because she was forced to share a campus with the man who assaulted her. As a result, mandatory referral policies directly aggravate the problem Title IX seeks to address: unequal access to education.

Apart from these measurable harms, there's also a unique psychic injury in depriving survivors of the opportunity to make a choice. Liz Roberts of Safe Horizon, the country's largest victims' services organization, put it well when she told the *Washington Post*: "The traumatizing nature of sexual assault is that sense of powerlessness that the victim experiences. . . . Our work is focused on restoring that sense of power and putting the survivor in the driver's seat as much as possible. Any policy that takes away choice and options from victims has the potential to do real harm." Jasmine Lester, the founder of Sun Devils Against Sexual Assault at Arizona State University, echoed these same concerns to the *Huffington Post*. "Sexual violence robs victims of power over their bodies, their minds, and their futures," she said. "Survivors need to feel like they have choices. The option not to report to police but still have schools investigate is imperative."

Despite all these flaws, bills supporting mandatory referral were popular, especially on the state level, in the mid-2010s, at the height of the backlash against advancements in Title IX. Some of the advocates and legislators who tried to pass these laws were well-meaning. In 2014, when top Democratic senators were interested in taking up the mantle of addressing sexual assault, student activists had to talk our closest allies off that path: all the interested senators were former prosecutors, so unsurprisingly their first instinct was to pull in criminal law. Luckily, they were responsive to our arguments and backed off.

But that was not true for the most determined champion of

mandatory referral, Ehrhart. For him, the threat to survivors posed by mandatory referral policies was the point. After all, Ehrhart made no secret of the disdain he felt for the student survivors who opposed his crusade. At the hearing for HB 51, he spoke not of taking rape seriously but of the terrible injustice of male accountability—what he elsewhere called "an environment of male gender bias on campuses throughout the country." Repeating one of his favorite lines, Ehrhart encouraged student opponents to "trigger somewhere else" when they snickered after a men's rights activist testified that 40 percent of rape accusations are false and that being falsely accused is a trauma equivalent to rape. "I'm not going to allow spoiled children to hoot and holler and act ridiculous," Ehrhart told Kingkade afterward. Grace Starling, who helped lead the ultimately successful campaign against HB 51 as a Georgia student, recalls that when she went to shake hands with Ehrhart after a critical vote, he angrily asked her, "Could you grow up?" Perhaps taking their lead from Ehrhart's tone and tactics, his supporters called Starling a "pretty little liar." In short, Ehrhart and his men's rights allies demonstrated they knew exactly what they were doing when they introduced a bill that would silence student victims. That seemed to be their consistent goal.

Ehrhart made clear what some other proponents of mandatory referral were perhaps too politic to say out loud: mandatory referral only promoted "due process" to the extent that it ensured no process. In Ehrhart's mind, the fact that a school could punish someone for sexual assault was the problem that needed to be fixed. "It's shocking to me that some think that you should be tried without due process, with some nonjudicial proceeding," Ehrhart told a reporter. "You don't get to do that with untrained college bureaucrats." (University decision-makers are, in fact, required by law to be trained on adjudicating sexual harassment, which juries are not.) In other words, Ehrhart based his policy on the popular but utterly incorrect conviction that due process is only available through courts. His explanation reeks of obvious exceptionalism: he did not think schools should get out of the business of student discipline altogether. The following year, he made headlines for pressuring KSU to punish cheerleaders who took a knee during the national anthem to protest racial injustice.

Ehrhart was wrong, but his argument gained legitimacy from errors in mainstream discussion of campus sexual assault. Readers and voters, even sophisticated ones, were used to seeing discipline for sexual assault discussed as an entirely separate matter from student discipline overall. And they were used to seeing sexual assault treated as an inherently criminal matter, uniquely suited for cops. Armed with these broadly shared misconceptions, Ehrhart mainstreamed MRA ideology, with its dedication to treating sexual harassment claims as distinctively suspect.

The campaign was really a call for no process. "Due process" just sounds better.

WHILE EHRHART WAS the public face of House Bill 51, the intellectual and financial groundwork for mandatory referral legislation was done by organizations like the libertarian, Koch-funded FIRE and the national fraternity lobbying group perfectly known as "Frat-PAC." These groups have long opposed campus discipline for sexual harassment and have worked alongside conservative allies to resist expanded Title IX enforcement. From the start, FIRE had led the charge against the Obama administration's efforts to ensure schools' compliance with Title IX, objecting both to the methods the Department of Education used and the standards it set. In public statements, FIRE was clear that its ultimate goal was not just to return to the state of Title IX enforcement as it had been under George W. Bush's administration. Rather, it believed schools should get out of the business of disciplining students for sexual assault altogether, despite long-standing administrative and judicial requirements to the contrary. This was no secret. The organization explained that its "position [is] that police and actual courts of law—not campus administrators—should be investigating and adjudicating these serious crimes."

Buttressing FIRE's commitment was its sense that sexual assault on college campuses was a rare event. A 2011 article reposted in part on FIRE's website declared that "Washington's push to force colleges into taking a more aggressive stance is based on a highly inflated notion of an 'epidemic' of campus rape." In 2020, during the coronavirus pandemic, a senior fellow at FIRE coauthored an article supposedly proving that sexual violence was rare on college campuses: if rape was rampant just like COVID-19, why had schools only closed down to stop the latter? (Some answers to start: the risk of sexual violence is no higher for college students than for their non-student peers, while campuses are set up for uniquely rapid spread of an airborne communicable disease. So leaving campus wouldn't protect students from sexual assault but would protect them from coronavirus. Also, death is worse than rape.)

The argument about the rarity of campus rape was echoed by one of FIRE's champions in the press, Emily Yoffe, who insisted that if sexual assault on campus was as common as research reflected, schools would sex-segregate their dorms. FIRE also heaped praise upon Northwestern professor Laura Kipnis's book on campus "sexual paranoia," which centered on a lengthy defense of one of the author's colleagues. He had been accused, among other things, of pressuring a student to drink in order to force sex. But Kipnis thought "the story just didn't add up" because "single non-hideous men with good jobs (or in this case, an international reputation and not without charm) don't have to work that hard to get women to go to bed with them in our century." That claim, made just a few months before Me Too exploded with stories of sexually violent celebrities, has aged poorly.

For FIRE's partner FratPAC, the call to action on mandatory referral came in late 2014, after a series of fraternities and sororities were suspended at a number of schools, including Johns Hopkins,

Emory, Clemson, and, in the wake of a now-debunked *Rolling Stone* article about a gang rape, the University of Virginia. Perhaps those punishments had something to do with the fact that fraternity members are three times more likely to commit sexual assault than their non-Greek peers. Regardless, by November of that year, the North American Interfraternity Conference, an umbrella organization for national frats, identified stopping organizational suspensions as a top priority. A coalition of Greek organizations developed a policy agenda that included mandatory referral and "deferral of any campus judicial proceeding until completion of criminal adjudication (investigation and trial)"—essentially House Bill 51. In other words, they would protect their members by making it harder for victims to report.

To add firepower to the effort, the groups recruited Trent Lott, the former Republican senator from Mississippi. Lott had once been Senate majority leader, but resigned that post after facing criticism for a glowing speech he gave at the hundredth birthday party of longtime South Carolina senator Strom Thurmond. In 1948, Thurmond had run for president on an explicitly white-supremacist platform, which included supporting racial segregation and using the banner of "states' rights" to resist the civil rights movement. At Thurmond's party, Lott declared to the attendees, "I want to say this about my state: When Strom Thurmond ran for president, we voted for him. We're proud of it. And if the rest of the country had followed our lead, we wouldn't have had all these problems over all these years." Now Lott was tasked with protecting frats' rights.

Like Ehrhart, FIRE and FratPAC insisted that mandatory referral was necessary to protect accused students' due process rights. Unlike him, FIRE and FratPAC kept their tone generally civil and made an effort to suggest their efforts were motivated by concerns for both the accused and the victims. To that end, they argued that rape is simply too "serious" a matter for schools to have any role. "We need to do everything possible to ensure our nation's campuses provide safe environments for learning and growth," wrote Lott and lawyer Cleta Mitchell in the *Columbia Daily Tribune*. "When a perpetrator has been found guilty by the school, the most serious punishment available is expulsion. But those who commit sexual violence should be prosecuted to the fullest extent of the law." FratPAC partner Jean Mrasek explained to the *Washington Post* that "police involvement sends a strong message that sexual assault must be treated as the heinous crime that it is. . . . I think everyone will acknowledge that sexual assault is a crime, is a felony, and really, if you step back and think about it, what other felony do we allow a victim to evade police investigation by using the college conduct process?"

Of course, colleges investigate and discipline students for all sorts of conduct that is both a crime and a violation of campus codes. I mentioned earlier that the year before I started college, my school removed a student from campus after he repeatedly threatened to kill his roommate. Would it have been better for the university to throw up its hands and wait until a trial concluded before protecting the student body from a likely violent classmate? Notice, too, that even as FratPAC attempted to cast its push for mandatory referral as rooted in concern for survivors, it still depicted victims as untrustworthy, sneaky, and manipulative. In FratPAC's telling, the victims are not choosing to pursue school remedies rather than criminal charges. They are "using" their school to "evade police investigation."

One might ask if perhaps FIRE and FratPAC's reasoning reflects misguided but genuine care about victims. But we should not be so credulous. These groups have consistently opposed policies that would aid survivors; in a series of legal briefs filed in 2020, FIRE admitted that its goal was not to balance the rights of victims and the accused but to advocate only for the latter. The more obvious explanation for these groups' advocacy for mandatory referral, then, is that they, like Ehrhart, support the policy not in spite of its major flaws but because of them. (After all, if they did not think

mandatory referral would depress reporting rates or otherwise pre-
clude schools from effectively responding, there's no reason for
them to expect that it would in any way benefit students accused
of sexual wrongdoing.) These groups likely judged that trying to
amend Title IX to remove schools' responsibility to address sexual harassment would be too heavy a lift. But a federal or state
law requiring mandatory referral—justified as a procedural protection that is also responsive to the "seriousness" of the harm—could
achieve the same result.

During the House Bill 51 debates, I wondered how these organizations, which generally have more mainstream credibility than
Ehrhart does, felt about their comrade in arms berating his young
opponents, many of whom identified as rape survivors. Perhaps they
found him despicable. Or perhaps they were grateful he was willing
to say exactly what they were thinking.

AFTER TRUMP'S ELECTION, Ehrhart was less worried about there being
"no safe space for young men" on a college campus. For much of her
time as secretary of education, Betsy DeVos was the least popular
member of Trump's cabinet, which is saying something. But the
Michigan billionaire found a fan in Earl Ehrhart. During the fight
over House Bill 51, Ehrhart and Steve Wrigley, the chancellor of
Georgia's public universities, traveled to Washington, D.C., to meet
with DeVos. The three discussed, among other issues, Ehrhart's legislative efforts to address what he saw as a lack of due process for college students accused of sexual assault. "Secretary DeVos is a breath
of fresh air," he later said. (DeVos also met with the National Coalition for Men, the group that publishes the names and photos of
supposed "false accusers.")

In truth, DeVos's much-debated changes to school discipline
procedures weren't even the most important part of her Title IX
regulations. The worst alterations were not about how investigations and hearings would proceed, but about limiting schools'

responsibilities to address sexual harassment at all. Readers will remember that the new regulations excuse schools from addressing harassment unless it is "severe and pervasive"—both the worst of the worst and repeated. Schools are no longer required to address harassment that occurred off campus, even if that means a victim has to share a classroom with their rapist. A school's responsibilities are only triggered if the victim reports to the correct senior official. And even if the harassment was bad enough and occurred in the right place and the survivor knew exactly whom to call to report, the school is still only responsible for doing the bare minimum: as long as administrators are not "deliberately indifferent" to sexual harassment, they will be in the clear. "Ms. DeVos all but abdicates her department's authority to hold schools accountable for violating students' rights," wrote Dana Bolger, my Know Your IX cofounder, shortly after the proposed rules went public. "American parents probably wouldn't be happy to learn that. No wonder, then, that Ms. DeVos presents her proposal as defending the rights of the accused, rather than shielding institutions from liability."

DeVos's supporters showed their hand in their hysterical criticisms of an ACLU lawsuit challenging the new regulations, filed on behalf of a number of organizations including Know Your IX. The *National Review*, citing the importance of live hearings and cross-examination, bemoaned that "the ACLU is suing the federal government in the hope of *weakening* its due-process standards." But the suit didn't challenge the hearing and cross-examination requirements. It focused on DeVos's substantive redefinition of what kinds of sexual harassment schools must address, and how much support they must provide victims. Aside from one provision related to evidentiary standards, the ACLU left all of DeVos's procedural requirements alone. Yet the *National Review* saw the ACLU's position as insisting that "men who are accused of rape [should be] discriminated against to the point at which their guilt is preordained." A similar op-ed by two outspoken defenders of accused college men framed the suit as "the ACLU vs. due process," even though the authors had to admit that, yes, technically, the lawsuit didn't have much to do with process at all. Their critique only made sense if "due process" actually meant "freedom from accountability."

Indelible in the Hippocampus

The most famous supposed clash between due process and the fight against sexual harassment has, in fact, little to do with process at all. The confirmation of Brett Kavanaugh to the Supreme Court says more about how we discuss due process than about how we should respond to harassment allegations.

The story will be familiar to most readers. In July 2018, Christine Blasey Ford, a psychology professor at Palo Alto University, wrote a letter to her senator, Dianne Feinstein of California. It stated that Donald Trump's nominee to the Supreme Court, federal appellate judge Brett Kavanaugh, had tried to rape her thirty-six years before, with the assistance of another young man. Blasey Ford thought the senator should know, but the professor said she was not prepared to come forward publicly. "I expect you will maintain this as confidential," she wrote. As Blasey Ford later explained, she knew the cost of coming forward would be great, and she had little faith her story would change the trajectory of Kavanaugh's nomination. "Why suffer through the annihilation if it's not going to matter?" she said.

Perhaps predictably, news of that letter eventually leaked in the lead-up to the Senate Judiciary Committee's scheduled vote on Kavanaugh's nomination. Feeling "her privacy being chipped away," Blasey Ford decided to go public in an interview with the *Washington Post*'s Emma Brown. That article put a face to the accusation, provided further details about Blasey Ford's allegations, and revealed a key piece of corroboration: therapist's notes from 2012, which recounted Blasey Ford disclosing that she had been assaulted by students "from an elitist boys' school" who were now "highly respected and high-ranking members of society in Washington." She had not named Kavanaugh, but the description fit. Some advocates and Democratic senators announced they found the accusations credible.

Republicans, however, would run the show. They controlled the Senate, which the Constitution charges with vetting and confirming Supreme Court nominees. They would decide what process, if any, Blasey Ford and Kavanaugh received to test the allegations. Blasey Ford, her lawyers, and their Democratic allies insisted that the FBI should reopen its impartial background investigation into Kavanaugh to gather evidence about the allegations—probably the most reliable investigative process available at that moment. That, they explained, would ensure that any subsequent hearing about the matter included the fullest possible record.

One might have thought that Kavanaugh and his defenders would be eager for a thorough investigation to clear the judge's name. Instead, the Republicans on the Senate Judiciary Committee insisted on rushing the proceedings. Proper process takes time, and the GOP did not want to delay a vote—the midterm elections were approaching, and the window to confirm a conservative justice before a possible switch in party control of the Senate was getting narrower. The Republicans wanted to schedule a hearing for just days after the allegations went public.

Chuck Grassley, the Republican senator from Iowa who chaired the Senate Judiciary Committee, publicly opposed any FBI investigation into Blasey Ford's accusation. The FBI's job in the confirmation process was simply to present a background check to the Senate, he said; that had already happened, and now it was the Senate's job to make a decision. The Department of Justice, under which the FBI falls, also put out a statement. A new background investigation was unnecessary, it said, because "the allegation does not involve any potential federal crime." (Unless the victim or perpetrator moves across state lines during the assault, sexual crimes are usually prosecuted by state offices.) Of course, Democrats were not asking the DOJ to start a criminal case. They simply wanted the FBI to reopen their original background check to investigate these new claims. But Grassley was firm: the "FBI investigation of Judge Kavanaugh is closed."

Grassley was joined in his opposition to an investigation by fellow Republican senator Orrin Hatch. While Blasey Ford's lawyers negotiated with Republicans behind the scenes about her possible appearance before the Senate committee, Hatch tweeted that the "FBI does not do investigations like this," adding that the "responsibility falls on us"—that is, the Senate. This echoed Grassley's position that "the job of assessing and investigating a nominee's qualifications in order to decide whether to consent to the nomination is ours, and ours alone." To be sure, the Senate is constitutionally assigned the job of giving "advice and consent" to a Supreme Court nomination. The FBI does not have a vote. But that's like a judge saying that a detective shouldn't investigate a crime because ultimately the court would hand down the verdict.

Both Grassley and Hatch understated the role the FBI plays in vetting the background of nominees in order to assist the Senate in its deliberative role. The law enforcement agency had already dug deep into Kavanaugh's background to produce a report for the Senate's benefit. That report was simply incomplete, as Blasey Ford's accusations revealed. And reopening an FBI background check under such circumstances was hardly unprecedented. In 1991, the FBI had reopened Clarence Thomas's background check at President George H. W. Bush's request after Anita Hill and other women said the then nominee had sexually harassed them. At that time, Hatch stated that further investigation was "the very right thing to do." But now, the Republican senators were proposing public testimony instead of an FBI investigation. The only alternative, they threatened, would be to proceed straight to a confirmation vote.

The Republicans' argument that the Senate Judiciary Committee did not need the FBI's help was disingenuous not only because it ignored the FBI's usual role but because the committee refused to use the other investigatory tools at its disposal. Most importantly, it rejected calls from Democrats and Blasey Ford to subpoena the putative witness to the alleged assault: Mark Judge, Kavanaugh's friend who, Blasey Ford said, had held her down during the attempted rape. As a matter of political tactics, one can understand the Republicans' reluctance: Judge was, to put it mildly, a liability for Kavanaugh. Even if he did not directly corroborate Blasey Ford's account, his earlier accounts of his time at Georgetown Prep made the assault seem more than plausible. In his 1997 memoir, *Wasted*, Judge recounted debaucherous adventures with his Catholic school classmates. Among these was a character by the name of "Bart O'Kavanaugh," whose star turn in the book comes when he vomits and passes out in a car. More than once, Judge writes about waking up from a drunken blackout worried he might have hurt a girl. Later, Judge's college girlfriend would say that Judge had told her that, during their Georgetown Prep years, he and a group of friends had taken turns having sex with a drunk woman. That sounds a lot like gang rape.

In short, if you were trying to figure out if Kavanaugh had assaulted Blasey Ford, Judge was a necessary witness—to the night in question, to the Georgetown Prep atmosphere, and to Kavanaugh's behavior in high school. But if you were trying to confirm Kavanaugh, Judge was the last person you wanted to have testify.

Ultimately, the Democrats, and Blasey Ford, relented. The professor would testify publicly, as would Kavanaugh, without any preceding investigation. None of the other women who lodged additional allegations of sexual harassment against Kavanaugh after

Blasey Ford came forward would be given even that small privilege of testifying. Most notable among them was the nominee's former Yale College classmate Deborah Ramirez, who claimed Kavanaugh had thrust his penis at her face at a party. Later, after a thorough investigation, reporters from the *New York Times* described both Blasey Ford's and Ramirez's stories as credible but said that Ramirez's "could be more fully corroborated" because it was "the talk of campus" at the time. The journalists identified at least seven people with knowledge of the event to whom the FBI or Judiciary Committee might have spoken, as well as a classmate who says he saw Kavanaugh similarly force his penis on another girl.

But Republicans weren't interested in investigating these allegations or allowing Ramirez to testify. They wouldn't even speak to her. Leaked staff emails revealed that while Republican senators publicly claimed to be seeking discussions with Ramirez's lawyers, their aides had actually shut down offers of phone calls with them. The *New Yorker* also reported that senior GOP staffers had learned of Ramirez the week before her story went public, and yet, during that gap, Senate Republicans had spoken out in favor of a rush to confirmation, rather than a pause to investigate the additional allegation.

A week and a half after Blasey Ford spoke publicly for the first time, she and Kavanaugh both testified before the Senate Judiciary Committee. No other witnesses or alleged victims spoke. Many readers, I am sure, remember the testimony vividly. Her assailants' laughter, Blasey Ford said, was "indelible in the hippocampus." Kavanaugh, red-faced with anger, insisted the allegation was "revenge on behalf of the Clintons."

The Senate Judiciary Committee voted on Kavanaugh's nomination the next day. After commotion and delay in the hearing room, Jeff Flake, a Republican senator from Arizona, forced a modest compromise: they would vote Kavanaugh out of committee for consideration by the full Senate, but only if the FBI would conduct an investigation. Later, Flake would attribute his decision, in part, to the many survivors he had heard from, including a group who confronted him in a Senate elevator. "I got calls and texts from women I never thought I'd hear from in that regard, saying, 'Here's what happened to me when I was young. Here's what happened to me 30 years ago,'" he explained.

Grassley agreed to the investigation, at least in theory. A final vote on Kavanaugh's confirmation would be delayed—briefly. But, in the end, the investigation was little more than political theater, a symbolic nod to the gravity of the allegations. The White House severely limited the scope of the FBI's inquiry, even as Trump falsely insisted on Twitter that he had not done so. FBI officers interviewed only ten people, despite the fact that a far longer list of witnesses had been established by Senate Democrats, Blasey Ford, and Ramirez. Absent from the roster of interviewees were many central figures, including Judge's ex-girlfriend, whom he had told about the possible gang rape, and most of the women who had accused Kavanaugh of assault. They didn't even interview the nominee himself. In the end, after less than a week of investigation, the FBI reported that it found "no corroboration" for the allegations. And for senators on the fence, inheritors of the centuries-old corroboration requirement now abandoned by the courts, that was enough. The Senate confirmed Kavanaugh by a vote of 50–48.

In a long speech in which she announced her critical vote, the supposedly moderate Susan Collins, Republican from Maine, explained one reason for her vote: due process. "The Senate confirmation process is not a trial, but certain legal principles—about due process, the presumption of innocence, and fairness—do bear on my thinking and I cannot abandon them," she said.

The senator did not explain how voting against Kavanaugh would have denied him due process.

LISTENING TO HIS conservative defenders, you would think a star chamber of Senate Democrats had interrogated Brett Kavanaugh on the rack. From the time Blasey Ford came forward, they bemoaned the Democrats' supposed disregard for due process—even though it was the Republicans who fought against process every step of the way. On *Fox News*, conservative author Victor Davis Hanson framed the issue as a Manichean choice between law and chaos. "Are you for due process or are you for revolutionary fervor?" he asked. "Are you for reason or are you for emotion? Are you for the street antics that Antifa brought into the Senate or are you for custom and practice of the U.S. Congress?" His invocation of "Antifa," as best I can tell, was meant to refer to feminist activists with no known connections to the radical anti-fascist group, the ones who confronted legislators aggressively but nonviolently in the Senate halls—as though that protest had somehow overwhelmed Senate deliberations.

Hanson's assignment of "emotion" to Democrats and "reason" to Republicans reeked of obvious sexism: the hysterical ladies are out of control, and the logical men must put them in their place. It was also backward. The Democrats had demanded the opportunity for experts to collect and review evidence to make a determination of fact. The Republicans had, from the start, rallied against inquiry and reason, refusing under the pretext of fairness to gather relevant information. Indeed, many observers believe that Kavanaugh was saved by Lindsey Graham's fiery speech during the hearing, a highly emotional appeal to his colleagues, and the American public, to protect our good men.

On a similar note, conservative columnist Rich Lowry opined in the *New York Post*, "When our system of justice is at its best, it judges each individual . . . on the basis of the evidence, and with an adversarial process." To Lowry's mind, the Senate Democrats' approach was instead akin to "the infamous kangaroo-court apparatus for adjudicating sexual-harassment and assault cases from college campuses—which often denies the accused basic protections of due process." Lowry took particular issue with a statement from Senator Kirsten Gillibrand of New York. She had decried that "by refusing to treat [Ford's] allegations properly," the Republicans were "telling women across the country that they're not to be believed." "No, that's not what they're telling women, or anyone else," wrote Lowry. "The message is that they'll try to find the truth before crediting an accusation."

But, of course, the Republicans *hadn't* tried to find the truth through evidence and process. They had hampered any meaningful attempt to do so. With his reference to campus discipline, Lowry seemed to bristle at the very idea that the truth of a sexual assault might be investigated outside the context of a trial. He insisted on two contrary positions at once. Anything less than a full adversarial process in the style of a trial, he suggested, is a kangaroo court. But at the same time, Gillibrand and those like her were unreasonable, even "otherworldly," to expect the Senate to undertake the truth-seeking steps requested by Blasey Ford, most importantly an opportunity to present witnesses. The implication, given these premises, is that the Senate should not bother looking into the harassment allegations at all.

Some had hoped that the Kavanaugh confirmation would allow the Senate, and the country, to show it had grown up since Clarence Thomas's parallel battle decades before. Instead, many of the same notes were repeated. On the Newsmax website, Clarence McKee compared Democratic opposition to Brett Kavanaugh, who is white, to the lynching of Emmett Till. "For Kavanaugh, just as was the case for black males in the old South, there is no presumption of innocence and no requirement of due process by his enemies," he wrote, pointing out that multiple Senate Democrats had said they believed Blasey Ford. "Under the Democrats' new no-due-process standard, any accusation of sexual assault by a woman will be an education and career death sentence for fathers, husbands, and sons throughout the nation in all professions." The presumption of innocence, in McKee's telling, meant that Kavanaugh's version of the story had to be taken at face value, and no opportunity should be afforded to prove otherwise.

In *City Journal*, published by the right-wing Manhattan Institute think tank, Adam Freedman wrote an article titled, simply enough,

"Due Process for Judge Kavanaugh." There, he bemoaned that Senator Gillibrand and Connecticut Democrat Richard Blumenthal had professed to believing Ford's story "though she has yet to testify." "This should set off alarms for anyone concerned about the old-fashioned notion of due process—that is, the procedural fairness that Anglo-American law guarantees to those accused of crimes," Freedman wrote, eliding the fact that Kavanaugh was not facing criminal charges and the senators were expressly political actors, not judges sworn to neutrality. Nowhere did Freedman and his fellow commenters note that prior to the hearing, plenty of Republicans had already decided that Blasey Ford was lying. Before she testified, Lindsey Graham declared on *Fox News* that nothing she said could change his plan to vote for Kavanaugh's confirmation. "What am I supposed to do? Go ahead and ruin this guy's life based on an accusation?" Graham said. "Unless there's something more, no, I'm not going to ruin Judge Kavanaugh's life over this." Apparently, a decision-maker was only required to be neutral and open-minded if it benefited the accused.

There's one procedural objection made by Republicans that I think does have a shred of validity as a matter of ethics, if not law: that Democrats withheld the information until the last minute. Perhaps Feinstein truly wanted to respect Blasey Ford's wishes, as reporting by *New York Times* journalists indicates. Or perhaps Democrats concealed the information until just before a vote to maximize the chances of scuttling Kavanaugh's nomination altogether. Either way, they foreclosed the opportunity of having the allegation investigated in the normal course of events, prior to the first hearing. In criminal proceedings, prosecutors are allowed to add on new charges late in the game, to bring multiple cases against a defendant over many years, or (as New York allowed until 2020) to surprise defendants with last-minute evidence. Kavanaugh had no inherent right to have his entire background check completed in one single take with no interruption in the middle. But the timing has the appearance, if nothing else, of poor political sportsmanship on the Democrats' part.

That will trouble some and seem to others simply a reflection of the nature of the Senate in 2018.

Regardless, it's difficult to credit the Republicans' calls for due process when they were the ones, at every turn, demanding *less* process. The Republican senators were the ones who rejected the Democrats and Blasey Ford's call for an investigation before the hearing. They were the ones who refused to allow an investigation of other alleged victims' claims, at the hearing or otherwise. Though we have Flake to thank for the post-hearing investigation, it was the Republican administration that placed such absurd limits on that inquiry as to render it nothing more than theater, a box to be checked so the Senate could move on to a vote. And the conservative commentators decrying Kavanaugh's treatment as an affront to due process simultaneously derided Democrats' reasonable calls for a competent inquiry.

An ordered truth-seeking inquiry is not what Blasey Ford's critics meant by due process. What they meant was that the professor had somehow violated Kavanaugh's rights just by accusing him. They meant that it is unfair for a man of his stature to face sexual assault allegations—regardless of whether they are true. As my husband remarked at the time, that is not due process. It's dude process.

KAVANAUGH'S CONFIRMATION IS an obvious example of defenders of accused men wielding due process arguments disingenuously. We could leave it there, perhaps. But it would be unsatisfying, and naïve, to end on a note of outrage that Kavanaugh's supporters were less than consistent and honorable in their campaign. Of course they were hypocritical—this is politics! Kavanaugh's nomination held partisan, ideological, world-altering stakes that thoroughly dwarfed the personal consequences. In fighting for Kavanaugh, the Republicans were not fighting for a man they felt was innocent. They were fighting to fulfill an electoral promise they had been running on for decades: a true conservative majority on the Supreme Court.

The party, conservative commentators, big donors, and many voters knew that replacing the more moderate Justice Anthony Kennedy with his former clerk Kavanaugh would likely usher in a new legal era. Fighting for Kavanaugh meant fighting for a Supreme Court ready to outlaw affirmative action, turn away immigrants, halt and perhaps reverse progress on LGBTQ rights, gut voter protections, undermine the rights of criminal defendants, and, most importantly to the conservative movement, overturn *Roe v. Wade*.

For the same reasons, Democrats and their allies fought against Kavanaugh's nomination well before Blasey Ford's allegation became public. Certainly, in the final weeks of the confirmation process, many, including many grassroots feminist activists, were motivated by the belief that her account was true. They believed that allegations of sexual harm perpetrated by powerful men must not be brushed aside, as they have for so long. But this does not mean that fierce opposition to Kavanaugh was apolitical, or that it wasn't deeply intertwined with progressives' serious concerns about the positions Kavanaugh would take as a justice. It's hardly controversial to acknowledge that Senator Gillibrand was never going to vote for Kavanaugh. Of course her call for Trump to withdraw Kavanaugh's nomination was political. In this polarized age, how could any moment of the whole confirmation process not be?

After so much ink spilled over Kavanaugh and due process, then, I don't think there's actually much to learn about the latter from the former. What useful lessons could we draw about how to conduct an investigation, or how to structure a hearing, from such an exceptional circumstance, in which the truth of the matter was—for everyone involved—only one of many priorities? I think analyzing the whole mess is most useful, instead, to understand what Kavanaugh means not for due process itself but for how we talk about due process.

On this score, the Kavanaugh hearings served to launder bad due process arguments that had been floating around the national dialogue. In went conservative instincts about white male vulnerability;

out they came on the other side of the confirmation, cleaner and more legitimate-looking. During the Senate hearing, Graham warned that "good people" would no longer be willing to put themselves forward for government nominations "because of this crap"—presumably a reference to the Democrats probing allegations of sexual assault. Kimberley Strassel of the *Wall Street Journal* described the stakes similarly: "If we are willing to overthrow all of due process in the country and just say, OK, that won't be the standard anymore, one accusation is enough to lose you your job, your life, your home, we've got some really big problems." Never mind that Kavanaugh was at no risk of losing his life, his home, or his existing job, none of which were at stake in the confirmation process. He was guaranteed lifetime tenure in his judgeship; the senators were only considering whether he deserved to be given a new position.

It was during the Kavanaugh confirmation process that Trump issued his MRA-like warning that "it's a very scary time for young men in America." Meanwhile, an ad by "Moms for Kavanaugh" started with heartwarming images of a multiracial group of babies growing into honorable young men—before jumping to Kavanaugh bemoaning, during the hearing, that he had been "destroyed" by the allegations. In bold text, the ad warned, "If it can happen to him . . . it can happen to our sons." "I've got boys and I've got girls," the president's son Donald Trump Jr. told a British tabloid in the midst of Kavanaugh's confirmation process. "When I see what's going on right now, it's scary." Asked whether he feared more for his sons or daughters—that is, whether he feared more that a son would be falsely accused of sexual assault, or that a daughter would be assaulted—he chose his boys.

That false accusations are more of a threat than rape itself is an instinct as old as Lord Hale, as old as the Bible, and demonstrably false. To rehearse the statistics again: a young man is more likely to be sexually assaulted than to be falsely accused of rape. Even if Don Jr. only cared about his sons, he should have been more worried about them being assaulted than accused. But the outsize fear of good men being destroyed by false allegations was never about facts. It is about a millennia-old male hysteria that absolute male authority might be threatened, heightened today as white men—despite their continued dominance—feel the threat that progress poses to their power.

And it is, perhaps, for that reason that Kavanaugh serves for many as the perfect example of the excesses of Me Too. His ordeal, in their eyes, confirms everything they already knew about the precariousness of men now that women can so easily come forward with allegations. "You have a lot of women that are extremely happy" about Kavanaugh's ascension to the highest court, Trump said after the confirmation. "A tremendous number of women. Because they're thinking of their sons, they're thinking of their husbands and their brothers, their uncles, and others." More recently, conservative authors Mollie Hemingway and Carrie Severino marketed their book on the Kavanaugh confirmation process, *Justice on Trial*, as a warning about the risks of false accusations: "A good person might [hold] the naive belief that what happened to Kavanaugh won't happen to him because he is a good person. But it can happen, it does happen, and it just happened. The question is whether America will let it happen again." In 2019, in the right-wing *Federalist* magazine, writer Daniel Buck held up Kavanaugh and Tom Robinson—the Black man wrongly accused of rape in *To Kill a Mockingbird*—as parallel victims of failed process for sexual accusations. Robinson was, of course, convicted contrary to overwhelming evidence and then killed by prison guards. Kavanaugh is a Supreme Court justice.

At the end of the day, Justice Kavanaugh is a particularly poor example of the supposed outsize power of lying women over innocent men. Most of the allegations against him were dismissed out of hand. He was provided a decent process, and he and his supporters rejected calls for a better one. He got to present his side of the story. And then he got the job. Far from a poster boy for male vulnerability to false accusations, Kavanaugh is a much better counterexample. His confirmation serves as terrible proof, for the generations of women who

watched the hearings and believed Blasey Ford, that, even now, powerful men will be shielded from the consequences of their violence—
that no matter how credible we are, our stories and all the proof we
can muster will be sidelined, ignored, trivialized. Blasey Ford was
right: we will suffer annihilation, and it will not matter. Indelible in
the hippocampus is his confirmation.

Yet in the process of confirming base fears, Kavanaugh legiti-
mized them, replacing the stink of men's rights activism with the
familiar air of mainstream politics. One research firm found that
the confirmation process "may have increased hostile sexism" among
Republican men. They are, post-hearing, "less likely to believe
women in cases of sexual harassment and assault."

The most important lesson from Kavanaugh's confirmation, as
I see it, is that he does not stand for the putative crisis many insist
he does. He doesn't teach us what process should look like, nor does
his confirmation stand as a verdict against Me Too. Kavanaugh, as
a major figure in the history of sexual abuse allegations, is no more
than a vessel for conservatives' worst fears about the twilight of white
male impunity. And from his seat on the Supreme Court, surveying
the crowd in his long black robe, he is proof the sun has not yet set.

Conclusion

I wrote earlier in this book that I wish I could offer a perfect blueprint for a perfectly fair set of procedures that could be used in every context—prefab due process, if you will. But I hope that by this point, a reader understands why there can be no single solution that fits all situations, either ethically or legally. That's frustrating, but it is also right.

So I offered, instead, some essential fundamentals of a fair process where serious sanctions are on the line, which each institution and community will need to build on according to its resources, capacities, and values. They are worth reiterating here: Rules governing members' conduct should be clear and understandable. A harmed person should have the opportunity to lodge a complaint, and the other person should be informed of the details of the allegation. Both people should be told how the process will work and, if possible, assigned someone to help them navigate it. Each should be given the opportunity, with sufficient time, to present their side of the story and any supporting evidence, including witnesses. Both sides should be able to review the other's relevant evidence and rebut the account the other side gave. As part of that, they should both have the opportunity to present questions to the other, to solicit answers that might undermine the other's story. The complainant, not the accused, should bear the burden of proving the allegation. A conclusion should be made by unbiased decision-makers, who should explain their decision to the parties. Whenever possible, a party unsatisfied with the result should be able to appeal a decision where a procedural flaw has occurred or the result is not supported by evidence.

There are also many pieces of the fairness puzzle that go beyond issues of process. Definitions of sexual harassment should be neither under- nor over-inclusive. Supportive services should be available for victims who do not want to pursue any sort of investigation and punishment against their assailant. And any sanction should be proportional to the harm. These are vital considerations, but they go beyond the scope of this book.

Institutions and communities will have to make many decisions about how to give shape to these basic commitments and rights. There are three overall principles that I think should guide these efforts: end exceptionalism, use the civil rights lens, and promote transparency. I also have two recommendations specific to advocates fighting against sexual harassment: be open-minded but careful, and expand the frame.

END AN EXCEPTIONAL APPROACH TO ALLEGATIONS OF SEXUAL HARM

Unsurprisingly, I think the most important lesson for sexual harassment policies is to de-exceptionalize. As I've already said countless times, the problem of adjudicating allegations of sex-based harm is much less daunting when we realize that we investigate wrongdoing outside courts *all the time*. And we already have models in place. The question we must constantly ask ourselves is: "How would I feel about this if we were not talking about sex?" Substitute in all the other ways workers, students, and friends hurt each other.

What if we were talking about a fistfight? What if we were talking about an ethnic slur? Would this particular process seem fair then?

For those with the power to draft procedures, from CEOs to my sci-fi-loving brother, my central recommendation is to address sexual harassment through the same disciplinary process as other forms of comparable misconduct. I like an approach similar to that adopted by some schools, which I mentioned earlier, in which there is one disciplinary system for all violations "against the school," and a second for all allegations that one student has hurt another. The first process applies to offenses like vandalism or plagiarism, where the "victim" is not another student but the school itself. In those cases, the school can afford to tilt the scales a bit to benefit the accused—for example, by requiring clear and convincing evidence of wrongdoing. After all, no one else's education is at stake. The second process, in contrast, would involve complaints where two students' abilities to learn and participate in campus life are threatened. That would encompass sexual harassment, yes, but also harassment on the basis of race, religion, or disability. It would include a student accused of bullying a classmate, hazing a freshman pledging a frat, or assaulting a teammate at soccer practice. Here, the school should give equal consideration to both students.

At the *very* least, I feel strongly that sexual harassment allegations should be handled by the same process as other civil rights issues, such as race- and disability-based discrimination. This first step might be more accessible to under-resourced institutions that feel they must prioritize where to devote limited resources. So, for example, they might decide to start by assigning support staff to both sides of all discrimination allegations. The goal would be to eventually provide that service to everyone involved in an interpersonal dispute, related to civil rights or not. Not my favorite option—there is still a whiff of exceptionalism—but a place to start.

It may sometimes be hard for anti-harassment advocates to avoid encouraging exceptionalism. If you push to reform a system that fails survivors, you might end up with a whole new, separate process just for sexual harms, which is bound to attract criticism. What is an activist to do, then? My best recommendation is that organizers should push institutions to improve how they handle *all* allegations, so that sexual harassment reports can be treated sensitively without any kind of separate, siloed process. That will, I am sure, be a complicated message for advocates to convey. But I suspect it will be worth it in the long haul.

The work of de-exceptionalizing will require feminists to be more thoughtful about how our own policy proposals have not only maintained but exacerbated the problem. A few years back, a group of advocates championed proposals to add a special notation to the transcripts of students found responsible for sexual assault. The basic idea was that someone deemed too dangerous to remain in his own community should not be allowed to transfer to another without any warning. Notations, the logic went, would allow the other school to decide whether or not to admit that student based on full information, and to put protections in place for others if they did.

That reasoning makes sense to me. So do countervailing arguments about allowing wrongdoers to improve themselves and make amends without being haunted by a record of their past mistakes, however severe. Personally, I think the latter outweighs the former. But regardless of how one ranks those two sets of concerns, the whole debate again raises the question: Are the benefits from singling out sexual assault for extra punishment worth the costs of exceptionalizing it? At least one court has concluded that schools must use a standard higher than the preponderance of the evidence if they will impose transcript notations, though it later backtracked and reversed its own holding. Whether that court was right the first time or second time, transcript notations invite exceptional procedures: add extra punishment, and you risk having to put in extra process. Transcript notation policies would then make it harder for a victim to prove her case—and, as a result, to secure the support and protections she needs. Students would receive the message that accusations of sexual assault demand extra care and extra suspicion. Is that worth whatever benefits a transcription notation might bring? I think not.

USE THE CIVIL RIGHTS LENS

A key to resisting exceptionalism is retaining a civil rights lens on sexual harassment. Some of that work will be done by sharing the long history of feminist resistance to sexual harassment as a form of discrimination, a threat to equality and freedom. Central to that must be highlighting the anti-rape work done by the mid-twentieth-century Black civil rights movement.

But there are also other ways to ensure that we maintain a civil rights perspective. One is to use accurate language to describe internal processes, rather than importing a criminal law vocabulary. In describing workplace or school discipline, we should talk about "disciplinary investigations" and "hearings," not "rape trials." In describing people accused of sexual harassment through these processes, we should talk about "respondents" or "the accused," not "defendants." If the claim is substantiated, the accused has been "found responsible," not "convicted." Using the right words helps us remember the institutional context, instead of slipping into associations with criminal law and the courtroom. With an ear out for those subtle differences, it becomes clear how often critics who demand exceptional procedures for sexual harassment use criminal terminology. Perhaps they don't know better. Perhaps they do, and use incorrect terms because that subtle appeal to criminal standards helps their demands go down easier. Either way, we should resist those mistakes and correct our own.

The civil rights lens also demands that we pay attention to where the burden of procedural reforms falls. Throughout this book, I've drawn a distinction between two types of procedural protections. One type helps both parties, and the cost of adding that particular feature is borne by the institution. Examples include providing free legal counseling, offering clear explanations of what rights each party has throughout the process, and giving everyone involved access to the evidence. The second type of protection helps just one party, and the cost is borne by the opposing side. The most obvious example is increasing the standard of evidence, which helps the accused but hurts the complainant.

Maintaining a civil rights lens means keeping the rights of both parties in mind and extending fairness to both. Following from that commitment, procedural reforms of the first kind are a better fit with the equality principles that should motivate institutional responses to sexual harassment. The second kind of reforms—those that tilt the scales against one side—fit instead with a criminal law approach, in which the complainant's needs and future are invisible. We can do better than that.

PROMOTE TRANSPARENCY

We have only just begun trying to address sexual harms in our institutions. News articles talk about Me Too as though workplaces only discovered in 2017 that sexual harassment might be a problem. And it's telling how often mainstream media declared that the 2011 Dear Colleague Letter was the first time federal law required schools to address sexual assault, even though that requirement was decades old. Before that point, few schools were even trying to fulfill their Title IX responsibilities—no wonder the public thought those responsibilities were new. As sexual abuses and the institutional failures that follow them fill the news, many institutions of all kinds are only now recognizing their legal and ethical duty to develop anti-harassment policies. For too many, the project is new. We will get things wrong. We have a responsibility to get them right.

One of the most powerful tools for crafting smarter policies and fixing their flaws will be transparency. Community members should have an opportunity to provide input for any new procedures. Doing so will allow drafters to solicit good ideas, identify pitfalls, and secure buy-in. In contrast, closed-door policy drafting loses out on helpful suggestions and sows mistrust. Part of what frustrated the Harvard Law professors who wrote to the *Boston Globe* is that they never had the chance to help shape the policy that would govern their school; instead, a new sexual harassment plan was imposed from on high. Given an opportunity to consult, they may have been able to shape the policy for the better, and they also might have felt more comfortable with the result.

Once a process is in place, the institution should share as much information as it safely can about how the process is working. What kind of reports are coming in? What kind of results are coming out? What seems to determine the severity of sanctions doled out—is it the severity of misconduct, or is it the race of the complainant or accused? To protect the privacy of individuals, groups can release anonymized data along with case studies stripped of identifying details. Such a report might provide a few examples that describe the complaint, its outcome, and any reasoning in broad strokes. For example: "A worker reported that his boss verbally harassed him over the course of many months. He did not want to pursue a formal complaint. HR transferred the worker to a different shift and explained to the boss why the alleged conduct, if true, was inappropriate." Or: "A congregant reported that another member sexually assaulted her. The committee investigated and determined the assault had occurred. Because of the gravity of the harm, the offender is no longer permitted to attend congregation events, though he may continue to seek spiritual guidance from the rabbi. If he successfully engages in our restorative justice process, his membership will be reassessed in two years." (If a group is so small that even anonymized case studies and statistics risk identifying individuals, they can be aggregated over a number of years.)

Part of why I like case studies is that they give community members insight into what happens within the black box. If they don't like what they see, they can advocate for change. And if it's good, the explanations can become a kind of precedent, guiding decision-makers in the future to ensure consistency. I've seen this work in practice. As a result of its settlement of our Title IX complaint with the Department of Education, my alma mater now releases regular reports summarizing the kinds of sexual harassment reports received and how they were resolved. That anonymized overview gives the community a sense for how the process is working—and the chance to protest if it's not. Of course, I would be happier if the reports summarized all student discipline, rather than separating out sexual harms. But it's a start.

Transparency is also crucial for rooting out discrimination against both complainants and respondents. One of the most powerful tools for advocates fighting discriminatory student discipline has been the federal government's regular collection of data from K-12 schools about the racial breakdown of suspensions and expulsions. Those schools are legally required to tally who is getting punished for what, and turn over that information so the government can calculate whether students of color are disproportionately punished. In my experience working on this issue, that data has been one of the best ways to convince legislators and school district policymakers that they have a problem they need to fix, and fast.

For the same reason, all organizations should collect and publish anonymized data about the outcomes of all disciplinary proceedings—including but not limited to those for sexual harassment. Those numbers should reflect key demographic trends in who is reporting misconduct, whose reports the organization decides are founded, and who is punished. Crucially, this data must be shared with the community. That way, workers may discover, for example, that their Black colleagues are more likely to be disciplined for harassment—and also that Black colleagues who report harassment are less likely to be believed. And they can use that information to push their employer to do better, through public exposure, protests, strikes, or other tactics.

BE OPEN-MINDED, BUT CAREFUL OF BAD-FAITH ACTORS

Some of the most important but uncomfortable work of building common ground is listening—including listening to those on the "other side." I do not mean that we have to read every speech by militant anti-feminists. I certainly do not believe that survivors must talk to accused rapists in order to be good advocates. But to the extent we are able to do so, a little listening can usefully inform our work. Something a man accused of sexual assault said has stuck with me. He supports Me Too, though with some caveats, and has no interest in the men's rights movement. But the men's rights activists, he told me, are the only ones who want to hear his story.

For my part, before I started writing this book, I had only once spoken with someone about their experience of being accused of sexual harassment. When I undertook interviews with the accused for this project, they were often difficult for me. I felt empathy, talking directly to people whose lives had been disrupted by what nearly all of them insisted were false allegations. I was also wary of "himpathy," and afraid of being manipulated by an abuser eager to style himself as a victim. On some occasions I learned through fact-checking that I had been lied to, and felt foolish. And yet, I still feel very grateful for what I learned from those conversations. I do not think I could have written this book without them. Through those stories, I gained a sense for the human experience on the other side of an allegation: how their lives had changed, how bad procedures made them feel powerless and small. And I learned, in some slight way, what it feels like to care about someone accused of sexual harassment. I feel moved that people with no real reason to trust me did so anyway.

I'm also very grateful for the lawyers and advocates for the accused who, over the years, have been willing to hash out hard questions, especially where we have created room to express uncertainty. Even if we approached the issues with different priorities and experiences, we could often agree on concrete policies.

This wasn't true all the time, though. Sometimes, trying to establish common ground only served to illuminate how little there was. Sometimes, it just showed an advocate for who he was: a misogynist deeply invested in men's impunity. I think of one man who, in a discussion about standards of evidence, put his cards on the table: he thought that in every single case it was best to avoid a finding of responsibility. Well then.

That some bad actors, like that guy or Earl Ehrhart, seek some of the same reforms we do doesn't mean that all our efforts are tainted by the transitive property of misogyny. But it should give us some pause when misogynists or racists or bigots of any kind think we're right. A former professor of mine once told me that having strange bedfellows sometimes means that we are discerning, unconventional thinkers—and sometimes it just means we are wrong. Finding ourselves on the same team as people with values not only different from but *diametrically opposed to* our own requires us to do a little soul-searching to make sure the position we're taking really is consistent with our commitments.

Caution is particularly important here because the approval of the bad boys is often so seductive. That may sound callous and flippant. But many women advocates I have met take a certain pride in the fact that anti-feminist men think they are onto something, as though that strange endorsement speaks to a certain heterodox intellect. In writing this book, I've had to resist that same siren call to be "one of the boys," the temptation to distort my own commitments to win over those critics whose approval I'm least likely to receive.

Even when we're confident we're in the right, we have to remain aware of all the ways that concern about treatment of the accused can be co-opted by men's rights activists and others whose main aim is to stop progress on sexual harassment. Agreeing with people who usually disagree with us might be an opportunity for a powerful alliance that can shift political winds. But it also might be an opportunity for fringe figures to leverage our relationship in a bid for legitimacy. Consider again how many times men's rights activists and Trump's Department of Education pointed to the Harvard Law professors as evidence that their own right-wing agendas were valid. That, in and of itself, is not the professors' fault. But if they had foreseen that dynamic, they could have taken efforts to highlight the important difference between their campaign and that of the MRAs: the professors took issue with specific parts of Harvard's new policy, but the men's rights activists thought the whole project of addressing sexual harms was rotten to the core. At the very least, we all have a responsibility, in undertaking this work, to defend against co-optation by bad actors.

EXPAND THE FRAME

I've tried to acknowledge, throughout this book, the number of people—both victims and accused—who are currently left out of these conversations. We have plenty of work to do to improve institutions' internal procedures for sexual harassment reports. But a great hope of mine is that conversations about fair process in the context of sexual harassment may lead to an expansion of fair process for other harms, too.

That is one of the benefits of de-exceptionalizing. If we are angry about the treatment of men accused of sexual assault, let's spread some of that concern around to people facing institutional sanctions for other kinds of misconduct. Students suspended for fighting and employees fired for stealing are just as worthy of our concern. Creating better disciplinary systems to handle a wide range of complaints should, ultimately, serve as a rising tide that lifts all boats. I have faith that we may well see these victories in schools, already a target for disciplinary reform, and in less formal communities.

The workplace, I expect, will be a harder fight, because most employees are utterly without legal protection. The default for workers is that they can be fired for almost any reason, at any time, with no process. Also, the typical American workplace is fundamentally undemocratic: employees rarely have any say in how their company runs. To win meaningful procedural rights for workers would require first convincing management or legislators that they deserve any rights at all. The good news is that there are proven models to change this dynamic. States can outlaw at-will employment, for instance, as Montana has done. And, of course, workers can—and should—unionize.

We also need to extend protection to more victims, which requires expanding the civil rights laws that are already on the books. Laws against sexual harassment in the workplace, like Title VII, leave out many workers. Employees of small businesses are excluded from Title VII, as are "independent contractors," workers without the stability and formal legal status of employees. In 2019, Democratic legislators introduced a federal bill, the BE HEARD Act, that would close these loopholes. On the state level, domestic worker groups have successfully pushed for greater labor protections, including provisions that would allow them to make complaints to a civil rights commission, not just the police, when they face abuses at work—work that generally occurs in their clients' homes, leaving them isolated and particularly vulnerable. Contract workers—traditionally excluded from laws that protect full employees—have similarly fought, and in some states won, inclusion in existing antidiscrimination protections.

Harder but just as crucial is figuring out how to create alternative remedies for those who live within systems like prisons, immigration detention, and the military, where the line between internal discipline and criminal law is hard to maintain, if it exists at all. That is a task beyond my expertise and the limits of my legal imagination. But I am eager to follow the lead of those with deeper knowledge on the subject.

Congress might also revisit the most ambitious civil rights response to sexual abuses it ever passed: the private right of action included in the Violence Against Women Act of 1994, which allowed survivors to directly sue their assailants in federal court without some of the usual obstacles of civil litigation—at least until 2000, when it was struck down. In addition to its practical benefits, the civil rights remedy also served as a powerful recognition of sexual harms as an issue of equality. As feminist lawyer and scholar Julie Goldscheid later noted, the provision "sought to transform the terms of debate in which violence against women was framed, to bring public attention to its severity and impact, and to counter the historic subordination violence against women both reflects and perpetuates."

As the law's drafters had anticipated, men who were sued under the civil rights remedy challenged its constitutionality, arguing that Congress lacked the authority to pass the law because the matter should have been handled by the individual states. Goldscheid worked as part of a team of lawyers who defended the provision from legal challenges, eventually arguing before the Supreme Court. They drew on congressional fact-finding to demonstrate the national impact of violence against women. But a majority was not convinced: five justices voted to strike down VAWA's private right of action. In an opinion written by Chief Justice Rehnquist, who had criticized VAWA before it was even passed, the court ruled that gender violence did not have a sufficient impact on the national economy to justify federal intervention.

Perhaps Congress is up for trying again. Me Too has provided a whole new perspective on the impact of sexual violence on survivors' economic opportunities—one that has shifted public opinion and could make for persuasive evidence before the Supreme Court. Perhaps Brett Kavanaugh would not want to solidify his reputation by casting a vote against a key provision of the Violence Against Women Act. Or perhaps that hope is terribly naïve.

I'M NOT USED to being the optimist in the room. My life as a lawyer and my previous work as an organizer revolve around the many ways schools fail students. Yet despite all that, and despite all the messy public debate about harassment and due process, I believe it is possible for institutions to do right by their people. Putting together this book was often depressing. There are so few success stories. But there are some—small proofs of possibility. And I believe that with many more years of hard work in good faith, we will resolve the easy questions and come closer to answering the hardest ones. That change will come in part from law, but mostly from protest and storytelling. We can do it. More importantly, we have no choice but to try.

My purpose in writing this book wasn't to provide a perfect road map toward fairness and justice, though of course I hope the principles I've laid out will be useful along the way. My goal, instead, was more modest: to open up the opportunity for more productive conversations about fairness and sexual harassment—in opinion pages, in classrooms and boardrooms and union halls, across dinner tables. If I've managed to convince a reader of anything, I hope I've demonstrated that commitment to justice and safety for victims of sexual harassment and commitment to the fair treatment of people accused of these same harms are not mutually exclusive. Rather, they're deeply interdependent. That's true as a practical matter: success on one axis will not be possible without the other. And, fundamentally, both sets of concerns are, at their best, motivated by shared values of equality, dignity, opportunity, and freedom. If we remain vigilant, if we continue to examine our own internal biases, if we resist co-optation by those hostile to our shared principles, we can get it right.

Now, let's get to work.

NOTES

INTRODUCTION

2   **"repeating 'due process, due process'"**: Amber Jamieson, "Harvey Weinstein Turned Up at an Event for Young Actors. A Woman Confronted Him and Was Thrown Out," *BuzzFeed News*, Oct. 24, 2019, https://www.buzzfeednews.com/article/amberjamieson/harvey-weinstein -heckled-comedian-event-women-actors; Maanvi Singh, "'Freddy Krueger in the Room': Women Confront Harvey Weinstein at New York Event," *Guardian*, Oct. 24, 2019, https://www.theguardian.com/film/2019/oct /25/harvey-weinstein-women-confront-producer-new-york-actors-hour.

3   **Department of Education investigated Yale:** See Letter to Dorothy K. Robinson, Vice President and General Counsel of Yale University, from Thomas J. Hibino, U.S. Department of Education, June 15, 2012, https://www.ed.gov/news/press-releases/us-department-education -announces-resolution-yale-university-civil-rights-invest.

5   **earned Wesley a public reprimand:** Letter to Robert E. Clark II, President of Wesley College, from Beth Gellman-Beer, U.S. Department of Education, Oct. 12, 2016, https://www2.ed.gov/about/offices/list/ocr/docs /investigations/more/03152329-a.pdf.

5   **denied a meaningful chance to defend himself:** Doe v. Univ. of S. California, 246 Cal. App. 4th 221, 225 (2016).

7   **Privately, he bullied schools:** Tyler Kingkade, "The Men's Man," *BuzzFeed News*, Dec. 21, 2017, https://www.buzzfeednews.com/article /tylerkingkade/meet-the-republican-lawmaker-whos-taken-up-the-cause -of; Kathryn Joyce, "The Takedown of Title IX," *New York Times*, Dec. 5,

2017, https://www.nytimes.com/2017/12/05/magazine/the-takedown -of-title-ix.html.

12   **help the wrongdoer understand:** sujatha baliga, "A Different Path for Confronting Sexual Assault," *Vox*, Oct. 10, 2018, https://www.vox .com/first-person/2018/10/10/17953016/what-is-restorative-justice -definition-questions-circle; Alexandra Brodsky, "Can Restorative Justice Change the Way Schools Handle Sexual Assault?," *Nation*, Apr. 14, 2016, https://www.thenation.com/article/archive/what-if-punishment -wasnt-the-only-way-to-handle-campus-sexual-assault/.

12   **restorative options for survivors dramatically expanded:** Few restorative options are currently available for victims. Tyler Kingkade, "Sexual Assault Survivors Who Want Restorative Justice Have Limited Options," *Appeal*, Dec. 10, 2019, https://theappeal.org/sexual-assault-survivors-who -want-restorative-justice-have-limited-options/.

14   **sometimes people reserve "harassment":** For those who work in the field, I mean this term to be synonymous with a capacious understanding of "gender violence" or "gender-based violence," which I considered using instead. I've chosen the term "sexual harassment" primarily because of its use in the legal cases I discuss in this book and my own background as a civil litigator, and worried switching between "sexual" and "gender-based" harms might be confusing. But I recognize my use of "sexual harassment" risks prioritizing only that abuse that is recognizably sexual, which I regret.

15   **then sometimes we get worse:** Dana Bolger, "Hurry Up and Heal: Pain, Productivity, and the Inadequacy of Victim vs. Survivor," Feministing, Apr. 10, 2014, http://feministing.com/2014/12/10/hurry-up-and -heal-pain-productivity-and-the-inadequacy-of-victim-vs-survivor.

15   **"men's first role in this movement":** Alanna Vagianos, "Tarana Burke: 'Me Too Is Not A Women's Movement,'" *Huffington Post*, Apr. 24, 2019, https://www.huffpost.com/entry/tarana-burke-me-too-not-womens -movement_n_5cc06af3e4b0764d31db5d88.

CHAPTER 1: THE STORY OF AFTER

19   **president of the student council:** Rebecca Grant, "After Reporting Her Rape, a Teen Girl Says She Was Pushed Out of High School," *Vice*, Nov. 22, 2017), https://broadly.vice.com/en_us/article/gyj7y7/after-reporting -her-rape-a-teen-girl-says-she-was-pushed-out-of-high-school; Complaint, Goodwin v. Pennridge School District, https://nwlc.org/wp-content /uploads/2017/05/Goodwin-v.-Pennridge-Complaint-Filed-5.30.17.pdf.

20   **later admitted to the basic facts:** "On April 6, 2015, H. spoke with police and gave his version of events, which largely comported with Goodwin's account. H. agreed that Goodwin repeatedly said no and tried to stop the sexual activity, and that he physically moved her head to resume the activities she had declined. Their stories diverged in that H.

said he observed no bleeding or bruising and insisted the sexual activity was consensual, despite Goodwin's attempt to stop it." Goodwin v. Pennridge Sch. Dist., 389 F. Supp. 3d 304, 310 (E.D. Pa. 2019) (internal citations omitted).

21 **less likely to participate in class discussion:** Cecilia Mengo and Beverly M. Black, "Violence Victimization on a College Campus: Impact on GPA and School Dropout," *Journal of College Student Retention: Research, Theory & Practice* 18 (2016): 234, 326–27.

22 **with a GPA under 2.5:** Carol E. Jordan et al., "An Exploration of Sexual Victimization and Academic Performance Among College Women," *Trauma, Violence, & Abuse* 15 (2014): 191.

22 **"lost opportunities are devastating":** Cari Simon, "On Top of Everything Else, Sexual Assault Hurts the Survivors' Grades," *Washington Post,* Aug. 6, 2014, https://www.washingtonpost.com/posteverything/wp/2014/08/06/after-a-sexual-assault-survivors-gpas-plummet-this-is-a-bigger-problem-than-you-think.

22 **saddled with student debt:** Dana Bolger, "Gender Violence Costs: Schools' Financial Obligations Under Title IX," *Yale Law Journal* 125 (2016): 2106, 2115–19.

22 **often leave for a worse job:** Heather McLaughlin et al., "The Economic and Career Effects of Sexual Harassment on Working Women," *Gender & Society* 31 (2017): 333.

22 **"feel less empowered to negotiate":** National Partnership for Women and Families, "Sexual Harassment and the Gender Wage Gap," Mar. 2020, https://www.nationalpartnership.org/our-work/resources/economic-justice/fair-pay/sexual-harassment-and-the-gender-wage-gap.pdf.

22 **"I was to be his lunch":** Alicia P. Q. Wittmeyer, "Eight Stories of Men's Regret," *New York Times,* Oct. 18, 2018, https://www.nytimes.com/interactive/2018/10/18/opinion/men-metoo-high-school.html.

23 **A startling number of women in prison:** Elizabeth Swavola, Kristine Riley, and Ram Subramanian, *Overlooked: Women and Jails in an Era of Reform,* Vera Institute of Justice (2016), https://storage.googleapis.com/vera-web-assets/downloads/Publications/overlooked-women-and-jails-report/legacy_downloads/overlooked-women-and-jails-report-updated.pdf.

23 **77 percent had been abused by a partner:** Shannon M. Lynch et al., *Women's Pathways to Jail: The Roles and Intersections of Serious Mental Illness and Trauma* 32 (2012), https://www.bja.gov/Publications/Women_Pathways_to_Jail.pdf.

23 **abused before they turned thirteen:** Dana K. Smith, Leslie D. Leve, and Patricia Chamberlain, "Adolescent Girls' Offending and Health Risking Sexual Behavior: The Predictive Role of Trauma," *Child Maltreatment* 11 (Nov. 2006): 346, 350.

23 **boys in the juvenile justice system:** Marianne Hennessey, Julian D. Ford, Karen Mahoney, Susan J. Ko, and Christine Siegfried, *Trauma*

Among Girls in the Juvenile Justice System, National Child Traumatic Stress Network 5 (2014), https://www.nctsn.org/sites/default/files/resources /trauma_among_girls_in_the_jj_system.pdf.

23 **"sexual abuse to prison pipeline"**: Malika Saada Saar, Rebecca Epstein, Lindsay Rosenthal, and Yasmin Vafa, *The Sexual Abuse to Prison Pipeline: The Girls' Story*, Center on Poverty and Inequality, Georgetown Law (July 2015), https://www.law.georgetown.edu/poverty-inequality-center /wp-content/uploads/sites/14/2019/02/The-Sexual-Abuse-To-Prison -Pipeline-The-Girls'-Story.pdf.

23 **may skip school to avoid their harassers**: Saar et al., *The Sexual Abuse to Prison Pipeline*.

23 **harrowing likelihood of further abuse**: Amnesty International, *Women in Custody*, https://www.amnestyusa.org/pdf/custodyissues.pdf.

23 **far more often than men are**: Matthew J. Breiding et al., *Prevalence and Characteristics of Sexual Violence, Stalking, and Intimate Partner Violence Victimization—National Intimate Partner and Sexual Violence Survey, United States, 2011* (Atlanta), https://www.cdc.gov/mmwr/pdf/ss/ss6308.pdf.

24 **Queer people and people who are transgender**: Callie Marie Rennison, "Rape and Sexual Assault: Reporting to Police and Medical Attention, 1992–2000," U.S. Department of Justice, Office of Justice Programs, Bureau of Justice Statistics (Aug. 2002), https://www.bjs.gov/content/pub /pdf/rsarp00.pdf; *NISVS: An Overview of 2010 Findings on Victimization by Sexual Orientation*, Centers for Disease Control and Prevention, https:// www.cdc.gov/violenceprevention/pdf/cdc_nisvs_victimization_final-a .pdf; *Sexual Assault and the LGBTQ Community*, Human Rights Campaign, https://www.hrc.org/resources/sexual-assault-and-the-lgbt-community.

24 **People with disabilities**: Joseph Shapiro, "The Sexual Assault Epidemic No One Talks About," *All Things Considered*, Jan. 8, 2018, https://www .npr.org/2018/01/08/570224090/the-sexual-assault-epidemic-no-one -talks-about.

24 **Native American women**: André B. Rosay, "Violence Against American Indian and Alaska Native Women and Men," *National Institute of Justice Journal* (June 1, 2016), https://nij.ojp.gov/topics/articles/violence -against-american-indian-and-alaska-native-women-and-men; Department of Justice, Office of Justice Programs, Bureau of Justice Statistics, *American Indians and Crime, 1992–2002* (2004), https://www.bjs.gov /content/pub/pdf/aic02.pdf.

24 **Black women filed harassment complaints**: Amanda Rossie, Jasmine Tucker, and Kayla Patrick, *Out of the Shadows: An Analysis of Sexual Harassment Charges Filed by Working Women*, National Women's Law Center, Aug. 2, 2018, https://nwlc-ciw49tixgw5lbab.stackpathdns.com/wp -content/uploads/2018/08/SexualHarassmentReport.pdf.

25 **"a boy's future and her feelings"**: Kay Lazar, "'Better Dead Than Coed': Deerfield Academy Confronts Its Male-Only Past," *Boston Globe*, Dec. 28, 2018, https://www.bostonglobe.com/metro/2018/12

/28/better-dead-than-coed-deerfield-academy-confronts-its-male-only
-past/63sZu3NRllpW2N9cu1fGkM/story.html.

26   **"pressure of the books that are not there"**: Reina A. E. Gattuso,
      "Gender Gap," *Harvard Crimson*, Apr. 9, 2015, https://www.thecrimson
      .com/article/2015/4/9/gender-gap/.

CHAPTER 2: A CIVIL RIGHT

28   **Mechelle Vinson started work as a teller:** Much of this history is
      drawn from two extraordinary books: Gillian Thomas, *Because of Sex: One
      Law, Ten Cases, and Fifty Years That Changed American Women's Lives at
      Work* (New York: St. Martin's Press, 2016); and Fred Strebeigh, *Equal:
      Women Reshape American Law* (New York: W. W. Norton, 2009).

29   **eventually became MacKinnon's first book:** Alexandra Brodsky and
      Elizabeth Deutsch, "The Promise of Title IX: Sexual Violence and the
      Law," *Dissent* (Fall 2015), https://www.dissentmagazine.org/article/title
      -ix-activism-sexual-violence-law.

29   **attitudes pervade the workplace:** Catharine A. MacKinnon, *Sexual
      Harassment of Working Women: A Case of Sex Discrimination* (New Haven,
      CT: Yale University Press, 1979).

31   **"a technology of sexism":** Katherine M. Franke, "What's Wrong with
      Sexual Harassment?," *Stanford Law Review* 49 (1997): 691.

31   **required to dress the part:** Ted Gregory, "Sexual Harassment Lawsuits
      Put Casinos Under Microscope," *Chicago Tribune*, Aug. 6, 1998.

31   **"harassment feminized Steiner":** Franke, "What's Wrong with Sexual
      Harassment?," 764.

32   **"they are women in a *man's world*":** Kate Manne, *Down Girl: The Logic
      of Misogyny* (New York: Oxford University Press, 2018), 64.

32   **lived at home with his mother:** Goluszek v. Smith, 697 F. Supp. 1452
      (N.D. Ill. 1988).

33   **part of their general legal responsibility:** Franklin v. Gwinnett Cty.
      Pub. Sch., 503 U.S. 60 (1992).

33   **on the better-established principle:** Pat K. Chew and Robert E. Kel-
      ley, "Unwrapping Racial Harassment Law," *Berkeley Journal of Employment
      and Labor Law* 27 (2006): 49; Walker v. Ford Motor Co., 684 F.2d 1355
      (11th Cir. 1982).

33   **feminist groups drew the same analogy:** MacKinnon, *Sexual Harass-
      ment of Working Women,* 210; Brief of Respondent, Meritor Savings Bank
      v. Vinson, 1986 WL 728302; Brief of the Women's Bar Association of
      the State of New York, Meritor Savings Bank v. Vinson, 1983 U.S. S. Ct.
      Briefs LEXIS 1130; Brief of the Working Women's Institute et al., Meritor
      Savings Bank v. Vinson, 1986 WL 728236 (U.S.).

33   **poor but not "clearly unreasonable":** E.g., Davis Next Friend
      LaShonda D. v. Monroe Cty. Bd. of Educ., 526 U.S. 629, 633, 648–49
      (1999).

34   **only so much that law can do:** Catharine A. MacKinnon, "Where
      #MeToo Came From, and Where It's Going," *Atlantic*, Mar. 24, 2019,
      https://www.theatlantic.com/ideas/archive/2019/03/catharine-mackinnon
      -what-metoo-has-changed/585313/.

34   **most violations never lead to prosecution:** RAINN, "The Criminal Jus-
      tice System: Statistics," https://www.rainn.org/statistics/criminal-justice
      -system (drawing data from Department of Justice, Office of Justice Pro-
      grams, Bureau of Justice Statistics, National Crime Victimization Survey,
      2010–2016 [2017]; Federal Bureau of Investigation, National Incident-
      Based Reporting System, 2012–2016 [2017]; Department of Justice,
      Office of Justice Programs, Bureau of Justice Statistics, Felony Defendants
      in Large Urban Counties, 2009 [2013]).

CHAPTER 3: WHAT INSTITUTIONS CAN DO

38   **text messages or medical records:** Susan Antilla, "When #MeToo
      Investigations Go Wrong," *New York Times*, Dec. 6, 2018, https://www
      .nytimes.com/2018/12/06/opinion/me-too-movement-investigations
      .html.

44   **"it got better every day":** Megan Dutta, *Me, Too*, Musings of Megan,
      Oct. 20, 2017, https://www.meganadutta.com/blog/me-too.

45   **"individual's capacity to organize with DSA":** Harassment Pol-
      icy (Resolution 33), Democratic Socialists of America, https://www
      .dsausa.org/about-us/harassment-policy-resolution-33/; Letter from the
      Harassment Working Group, Nov. 22, 2017, https://d3n8a8pro7vhmx
      .cloudfront.net/dsausa/mailings/1795/attachments/original/Dear
      _Comrade_Letter.pdf?1511384153.

47   **pioneered by radical grassroots groups:** The seminal anthology *The
      Revolution Starts at Home* tracks, in essays, poems, and case studies, how
      such grassroots groups have responded to sexual violence in their ranks.
      Ching-In Chen, Jai Dulani, and Leah Lakshmi Piepzna-Samarasinha,
      *The Revolution Starts at Home: Confronting Intimate Violence Within Activist
      Communities*, preface by Andrea Smith (Brooklyn, NY: South End Press,
      2011), https://thequeerproject.files.wordpress.com/2016/01/revolution
      -starts-at-home.pdf.

47   **Communities Against Rape and Abuse:** Alisa Bierria et al., "Taking
      Risks: Implementing Grassroots Community Accountability Strate-
      gies," in Chen et al., *The Revolution Starts at Home*.

CHAPTER 4: WHY NOT THE POLICE?

52   **over 60 percent of batteries and robberies:** RAINN, "The Criminal
      Justice System: Statistics." The number of sexual assaults reported to police
      is especially small among certain populations. For example, one National
      Institute of Justice study found that "[f]ewer than 5 percent of completed

and attempted rapes [of college women] were reported to law enforcement officials." Bonnie Fisher, Francis Cullen, and Michael Turner, *The Sexual Victimization of College Women*, National Institute of Justice (Washington, D.C.: U.S. Department of Justice, December 2000).

52   **a reasoned cost-benefit analysis:** See Nancy Chi Cantalupo, "For the Title IX Civil Rights Movement: Congratulations and Cautions," *Yale Law Journal Forum* 125 (2016): 281, http://www.yalelawjournal .org/forum/for-the-title-ix-civil-rights-movement-congratulations-and -cautions.

52   **all of the ways criminal law fails victims:** Some recent books on the issue include Michelle Bowdler, *Is Rape a Crime? A Memoir, An Investigation, and a Manifesto* (New York: Flatiron Books, 2020); Rachel Louise Snyder, *No Visible Bruises: What We Don't Know About Domestic Violence Can Kill Us* (New York: Bloomsbury, 2019); Leigh Goodmark, *Decriminalizing Domestic Violence: A Balanced Policy Approach to Intimate Partner Violence* (Oakland: University of California Press, 2018); Andrea J. Ritchie, *Invisible No More: Police Violence Against Black Women and Women of Color* (Boston: Beacon Press, 2017); Beth Richie, *Arrested Justice: Black Women, Violence, and America's Prison Nation* (New York: New York University Press, 2012).

Readers might note that, in this chapter, I discuss sexual assault and nonsexual intimate partner violence in the same breath, and perhaps unfairly conflate the two. There are, undoubtedly, differences in the ways that the criminal system responds to these distinct crimes, and I wish I had the space to parse those distinctions more deeply. This book is concerned with both kinds of harms, though, and there are certainly common patterns in the criminal system's mistreatment of victims of different sexual and gender-based crimes. See, e.g., Julie Goldscheid et al., *Responses from the Field: Sexual Assault, Domestic Violence, and Policing* (University of Miami Legal Research Studies Paper No. 16-2, October 2015), https://academicworks.cuny.edu/cgi/viewcontent.cgi ?article=1075&context=cl_pubs.

53   **three times less likely to result in convictions:** RAINN, "The Criminal Justice System: Statistics."

53   **hear those messages loud and clear:** Megan Greeson et al., "'Nobody Deserves This': Adolescent Sexual Assault Victims' Perceptions of Disbelief and Victim Blame from Police," *Journal of Community Psychology* 44 (2016): 90; Shana L. Maier, "'I Have Heard Horrible Stories . . .': Rape Victim Advocates' Perceptions of the Revictimization of Rape Victims by the Police and Medical System," *Violence Against Women* 14 (2008): 786.

53   **victim-blaming ideologies and obsolete legal definitions:** Rebecca Campbell and Camille R. Johnson, "Police Officers' Perceptions of Rape: Is There Consistency Between State Law and Individual Beliefs?," *Journal of Interpersonal Violence* 12 (1997): 255.

54   **a matter of both ethics and law:** A 1978 study—old, but recent

enough to still be shocking—found that police officers' views about rape were strikingly similar to those of convicted rapists, and, on a number of metrics, were more closely aligned with the rapists' attitudes than with the general population's. In fact, on half of the tests, researchers found no difference between police and rapists at all. Hubert S. Feild, "Attitudes Toward Rape: A Comparative Analysis of Police, Rapists, Crisis Counselors, and Citizens," *Journal of Personality and Social Psychology* 36 (1978): 156.

54 **marital rape is now illegal:** Amy Dellinger Page, "True Colors: Police Officers and Rape Myth Acceptance," *Feminist Criminology* 5 (2010): 315, 326. In my view, Dellinger Page's diagnosis of police officer attitudes is overly sunny because her definitions of sexist ideologies are quite narrow.

54 **police officers themselves commit sexual violence:** Leigh Goodmark, "Hands Up at Home: Militarized Masculinity and Police Officers Who Commit Intimate Partner Abuse," *Brigham Young University Law Review* 2015 (2015): 1183, 1189–96; Alex Roslin, *Police Wife: The Secret Epidemic of Police Domestic Violence* (2018).

More than a quarter of surveyed Alaskan sex workers report having been sexually assaulted by a police officer. One told a researcher that a friend had shown up to her house in handcuffs: "She got away from a policeman who . . . threatened to throw her in the [river] if she didn't perform oral sex on him." Alaska Criminal Justice Commission, Staff Summary of Plenary Meeting, Oct. 13, 2016, https://web.archive.org/web /20180330035504/http://www.ajc.state.ak.us/sites/default/files/meeting -summaries/commission-meeting-summary/acjcmeetingsummaryofocto ber132016.pdf.

Amnesty International published the account of a transgender woman who called the police after her abusive partner choked her and chased her around their apartment. Not only was she arrested rather than her partner, but the police insisted on calling her "mister" and using male pronouns after they saw her identification. A Latina trans woman was called a "faggot" and told to "shut up" by police when she reported that her boyfriend had assaulted her. Amnesty International, *Stonewalled: Police Abuse and Misconduct Against Lesbian, Gay, Bisexual and Transgender People in the U.S.*, Sept. 2005, https://www.amnesty.org/download/Documents /84000/amr511222005en.pdf.

54 **popular model of the "perfect victim":** E.g., Ericka A. Wentz, "Funneled Through or Filtered Out: An Examination of Police and Prosecutorial Decision-Making in Adult Sexual Assault Cases," *Violence Against Women* 26 (2020): 1919, 1921–22; Goldscheid, *Responses from the Field*, 17–24.

54 **vast majority know their abuser:** RAINN, "Perpetrators of Sexual Violence: Statistics," https://www.rainn.org/statistics/perpetrators -sexual-violence.

54 **44 percent of officers felt:** Amy Dellinger Page, "Behind the Blue

Line: Investigating Police Officers' Attitudes Toward Rape," *Journal of Police and Criminal Psychology* 22, no. 1 (June 2007): 22. A study of the Detroit Police Department found that officers often assumed survivors were sex workers based on their appearance or the location of the assault. In the officers' minds, whatever had happened was therefore the victims' own fault. Police reports often referred to sexual assaults of suspected sex workers as "a deal gone bad." Rebecca Campbell et al., *The Detroit Sexual Assault Kit (SAK) Action Research Project (ARP), Final Report*, Dec. 2015, https://www.ncjrs.gov/pdffiles1/nij/grants/248680.pdf. Officers often misclassified the rape of sex workers as an "economic crime." Martin Schwartz, *National Institute Justice Visiting Fellowship: Police Investigation of Rape—Roadblocks and Solutions*, Dec. 2010, www.ncjrs.gov/pdffiles1/nij /grants/232667.pdf. Some police will simply not accept reports of sexual assault from street-based sex workers. Goldscheid, *Responses from the Field*, 22. And sex workers know this. One explained to a researcher that she screens clients to "make sure that it's a safe environment, because I know that if it wasn't I couldn't just call the police and know that everything would be okay. I couldn't call the police and be treated like a typical public person." Alaska Criminal Justice Commission, Staff Summary of Plenary Meeting, Oct. 13, 2016.

54 **"income, reputation, disability, [or] sexual identity"**: TK Logan and Rob Valente, National Domestic Violence Hotline, "Who Will Help Me? Domestic Violence Survivors Speak Out About Law Enforcement Responses," 2015, https://www.thehotline.org/wp-content/uploads /media/2020/09/NDVH-2015-Law-Enforcement-Survey-Report -2.pdf; see also Emma Sleath and Ray Bull, "Comparing Rape Victim and Perpetrator Blaming in a Police Officer Sample: Differences Between Police Officers With and Without Special Training," *Criminal Justice and Behavior* 39 (2012): 646; Goldscheid, *Responses from the Field*, 17–24.

55 **none "had heard of female-on-male rape"**: Schwartz, *National Institute Justice Visiting Fellowship*; Lara Stemple and Ilan H. Meyer, "Sexual Victimization by Women Is More Common Than Previously Known," *Scientific America*, Oct. 10, 2017, https://www.scientificamerican.com/article /sexual-victimization-by-women-is-more-common-than-previously -known/.

55 **"any man can be raped"**: Dellinger Page, "True Colors," 326.

55 **male victims are less likely**: Goldscheid, *Responses from the Field*, 8.

55 **between 2 and 8 percent**: Kimberly A. Lonsway, Sgt. Joanne Archambault (Ret.), and David Lisak, *False Reports: Moving Beyond the Issue to Successfully Investigate and Prosecute Non-Stranger Sexual Assault*, https:// www.nsvrc.org/sites/default/files/publications/2018-10/Lisak-False -Reports-Moving-beyond.pdf; Emily Moon, "False Reports of Sexual Assault are Rare. But Why Is There So Little Reliable Data About Them?," *Pacific Standard*, Oct. 7, 2018, https://psmag.com/news/false

-reports-of-sexual-assault-are-rare-but-why-is-there-so-little-reliable
-data-about-them.

55 **believed** *most rape reports were false*: Annelise Mennicke et al., "Law Enforcement Officers' Perception of Rape and Rape Victims: A Multi-method Study," *Violence and Victims* 29 (2014): 814, 822.

55 **"victim's conduct, lifestyle, and personal history"**: Louis A. Trosch Jr., "State v. Strickland: Evening the Odds in Rape Trials—North Carolina Allows Expert Testimony on Post Traumatic Stress Disorder to Disprove Victim Consent," *North Carolina Law Review* 69 (1991): 1624.

56 **"wasn't the victim she claimed to be"**: Jennifer Emily, "Judge Says Sexually Assaulted 14-year-old 'Wasn't the Victim She Claimed to Be,'" *Dallas Morning News*, May 1, 2014, https://www.dallasnews.com/news/crime/2014/05/01/judge-says-sexually-assaulted-14-year-old-wasn-t-the-victim-she-claimed-to-be.

56 **"as much in control of the situation"**: Paul Vercammen and Kyung Lah, "Prosecutors Weigh Appeal of 30-day Rape Sentence in Montana," CNN, Aug. 30, 2013, https://www.cnn.com/2013/08/28/justice/montana-teacher-rape-sentence/.

56 **ethically obligated to use them**: Tyler Kingkade, "Here's the Awful Reality of Being a Rape Victim in Criminal Trials," *Huffington Post*, July 27, 2016; Sokratis Dinos et al., "A Systematic Review of Juries' Assessment of Rape Victims: Do Rape Myths Impact on Juror Decision-making?," *International Journal of Law, Crime and Justice* 43 (2015): 36.

56 **police rather than complainants**: Cantalupo, "For the Title IX Civil Rights Movement," 281.

56 **a grand jury indicted Anderson**: Kristin Hoppa, "Baylor Fraternity President Charged with Sexual Assault," *Waco Tribune-Herald*, March 3, 2016, https://wacotrib.com/news/higher_education/baylor-fraternity-president-charged-with-sexual-assault/article_65235ab8-a07e-5107-b8ea-7d1cde2fb988.html.

56 **prosecutor Hilary LaBorde later explained**: Holly Yan, "A Prosecutor Refused to Try an Ex-Frat Leader's Sex Assault Case. Here Are Her Eye-Opening Reasons Why," CNN, Dec. 13, 2018, https://www.cnn.com/2018/12/12/us/baylor-rape-allegation-letter-from-prosecutor/index.html.

57 **"'looked like a rapist'"**: LaBorde also explained that the injuries of Anderson's victim from the rape were not persuasive evidence because she had been a virgin at the time, meaning that consensual sex, too, might have caused vaginal tears. Contrast this to the young girl who was told she was to blame for her assault because she was *not* a virgin. No one can win.

57 **then district attorney Kamala Harris**: Peter Jamison, "A Lack of Conviction," *SF Weekly*, May 5, 2010, https://archives.sfweekly.com/sanfrancisco/a-lack-of-conviction/Content?oid=2177022.

58 **"the scratches on his neck"**: Meg Crager, Merril Cousin, and Tara Hard, *Victim-Defendants: An Emerging Challenge in Responding to Domestic Violence in Seattle and the King County Region*, King County Coalition

Against Domestic Violence, Apr. 2003, https://endgv.org/wp-content /uploads/2016/03/victimdefendantfinalreport111.pdf.

58   **arrested or threatened with arrest:** Logan and Valente, "Who Will Help Me?"

58   **"get to the phone first":** Susan L. Miller, "The Paradox of Women Arrested for Domestic Violence: Criminal Justice Professionals and Service Providers Respond," *Violence Against Women* 7 (2001): 1339.

58   **introduction of mandatory arrest laws:** Carol Bohmer et al., "Domestic Violence Law Reforms: Reactions from the Trenches," *Journal of Sociology & Social Welfare* 29, no. 3 (September 2002): 71, 78; David Hirschel et al., "Domestic Violence and Mandatory Arrest Laws: To What Extent Do They Influence Police Arrest Decisions?," *Journal of Criminal Law and Criminology* 98, no. 1 (2007): 255–56, 259–61.

58   **unintended consequences of these laws:** For an extended discussion of mandatory arrest laws, see Goodmark, *Decriminalizing Domestic Violence.*

59   **exacerbated two dangerous patterns:** David Hirschel et al., *Explaining the Prevalence, Context, and Consequences of Dual Arrest in Intimate Partner Cases* (Washington, D.C.: U.S. Department of Justice, 2007), https://www .ncjrs.gov/pdffiles1/nij/grants/218355.pdf; Mary Haviland et al., *The Family Protection and Domestic Violence Intervention Act of 1995: Examining the Effects of Mandatory Arrest in New York City: A Report by the Family Violence Project of the Urban Justice Center* (New York: Urban Justice Center, 2001).

59   **they often arrest both parties:** Amy M. Zelcer, "Battling Domestic Violence: Replacing Mandatory Arrest Laws with a Trifecta of Preferential Arrest, Officer Education, and Batterer Treatment Programs," *American Criminal Law Review* 51, no. 2 (Spring 2014): 541, 550.

59   **ten times more likely to arrest both partners:** David Hirschel, *Domestic Violence Cases: What Research Shows About Arrest and Dual Arrest Rates* (Washington, D.C.: U.S. Department of Justice, July 25, 2008), https:// www.ncjrs.gov/pdffiles1/nij/222679.pdf.

59   **"mutual abuse":** National Center for Victims of Crime and the National Coalition of Anti-Violence Programs, *Why It Matters: Rethinking Victim Assistance for Lesbian, Gay, Bisexual, Transgender, and Queer Victims of Hate Violence & Intimate Partner Violence,* Mar. 2010, http://avp.org/wp-content /uploads/2019/02/WhyItMatters.pdf.

59   **scratched up from the victim's self-defense:** Hillary Potter, *Battle Cries: Black Women and Intimate Partner Abuse* (New York: New York University Press, 2008), 178–79.

59   **In Harris County, Texas:** Leon Neyfakh, "A Texas Prosecutor Jailed a Rape Victim," *Slate,* July 22, 2016, https://slate.com/news-and-politics/2016/07/a -texas-prosecutor-jailed-a-rape-victim-to-ensure-her-testimony-against-her -attacker.html.

59   **she was imprisoned for a month:** While incarcerated, this woman later alleged in a lawsuit, she was assaulted by both another inmate and a guard. In another case, a Sacramento judge ordered that a seventeen-year-old be

detained in a juvenile detention facility for refusing to testify against the man who raped her; after three weeks, she was released wearing a GPS ankle monitor. Anginas Becker Stevens, "17-Year-Old Imprisoned for Failing to Testify Against Her Alleged Rapist," *Ms.*, Apr. 16, 2012, http://msmagazine.com/blog/2012/04/16/17-year-old-imprisoned-for -failing-to-testify-against-her-alleged-rapist/.

60   **Houston, Los Angeles, San Diego:** Cora Engelbrecht, "Fewer Immigrants Are Reporting Domestic Abuse. Police Blame Fear of Deportation," *New York Times*, June 3, 2018, https://www.nytimes.com/2018/06/03/us /immigrants-houston-domestic-violence.html.

60   **"increase in fear of immigration consequences":** ACLU, *Freezing Out Justice: How Immigration Arrests at Courthouses Are Undermining the Justice System* (2018), https://www.aclu.org/report/freezing-out-justice; see also Tahirih Justice Center, *May 2019 Advocate Survey: Immigrant Survivors Fear Reporting Violence*, May 2019.

60   **before she could exit the courthouse:** Aaron Martinez, "Transgender Woman Gets Time Served, Stays Jailed," *El Paso Times*, Apr. 13, 2017, https://www.elpasotimes.com/story/news/crime/2017/04/13/transgender -woman-gets-time-served-stays-jailed/100430560/.

60   **"no ability to apply for a U visa":** Human Rights Watch, *Cultivating Fear: The Vulnerability of Immigrant Farmworkers in the US to Sexual Violence and Sexual Harassment* 56 (2012), https://www.hrw.org/sites/default/files /reports/us0512ForUpload_1.pdf.

61   **the Colemans' home burning down:** Laura Collins, "With Frostbite on Her Hands and Hair Frozen to the Ground, 14-year-old Daisy Coleman Was Raped and Dumped by High School Footballers. Now She Speaks Out About Her Ordeal," *Daily Mail*, Feb. 2, 2017, https:// www.dailymail.co.uk/news/article-4176786/Teen-rape-victim-Daily -Coleman-speaks-out.html.

61   **Daisy Coleman died by suicide:** Eric Levenson and Kay Jones, "Daisy Coleman, Student Featured in Netflix Documentary on Sexual Assault, Dies by Suicide," CNN, Aug. 7, 2020, https://www.cnn.com/2020/08 /06/us/daisy-coleman-suicide-trnd/index.html.

61   **Melinda followed her four months after:** EJ Dickson, "The Mother of Daisy Coleman from 'Audrie & Daisy' Has Died by Suicide," *Rolling Stone*, Dec. 7, 2020, https://www.rollingstone.com/culture/culture-news/audrie -daisy-doc-daisy-coleman-mother-melinda-coleman-suicide-1099884/.

61   **Audrie Pott, a fifteen-year-old:** Nina Burleigh, "Sexting, Shame and Suicide," *Rolling Stone*, Sept. 17, 2013, https://www.rollingstone.com /culture/culture-news/sexting-shame-and-suicide-72148/.

61   **"Messing with Notre Dame football":** Melinda Henneberger, "Reported Sexual Assault at Notre Dame Campus Leaves More Questions Than Answers," *National Catholic Reporter*, Mar. 26, 2012, https://www.ncronline .org/news/accountability/reported-sexual-assault-notre-dame-campus -leaves-more-questions-answers.

61   **DOJ's National Crime Victimization Survey:** Michael Planty et al.,

Female Victims of Sexual Violence, 1994–2010 (Washington, D.C.: U.S. Department of Justice, Office of Justice Programs, Bureau of Justice Statistics, May 31, 2016), https://www.bjs.gov/content/pub/pdf/fvsv9410 .pdf; Lynn Langton et al., *Victimizations Not Reported to the Police, 2006– 2010* (Washington, D.C.: U.S. Department of Justice, Office of Justice Programs, Bureau of Justice Statistics, Aug. 2012), https://www.bjs.gov /content/pub/pdf/vnrp0610.pdf.

61   **"making the situation worse"**: Logan and Valente, "Who Will Help Me?," 3.

61   **#WhyIDidntReport**: Christine Marley-Frederick (@drcmarley), Twitter, Sept. 20, 2018, 8:12 p.m., https://twitter.com/drcmarley/status /1042929468761927681.

62   **under the guise of "protection"**: Dorothy Thomas et al., *All Too Familiar: Sexual Abuse of Women in U.S. State Prisons*, Human Rights Watch, Dec. 1996, https://www.hrw.org/legacy/reports/1996/Us1.htm.

62   **"negative consequences for the offender's life"**: Logan and Valente, "Who Will Help Me?," 4.

62   **ranked concern for their assailant**: Marjorie R. Sable et al., "Barriers to Reporting Sexual Assault for Women and Men: Perspectives of College Students," *Journal of American College Health* 55 (2006): 157.

63   **Ray Rice's abuse of his then fiancée**: Feminista Jones, "Why Black Women Struggle More with Domestic Violence," *Time*, Sept. 10, 2014, http://time.com/3313343/ray-rice-black-women-domestic-violence/.

CHAPTER 5: WHEN INSTITUTIONS FAIL

65   **"how many penises she could take"**: Kelly Weill, "McDonald's Workers in 10 Cities Strike over Sexual Harassment by Bosses," *Daily Beast*, Sept. 18, 2018, https://www.thedailybeast.com/mcdonalds-workers-in -10-cities-strike-over-sexual-harassment-by-bosses.

65   **"it's 'America's best first job'"**: Daniella Silva, "McDonald's Workers Go on Strike over Sexual Harassment," NBC News, Sept. 18, 2018, https://www.nbcnews.com/news/us-news/mcdonald-s-workers-go-strike -over-sexual-harassment-n910656.

65   **rampant in the fast-food industry**: Hart Research Associates, *Key Findings from a Survey of Women Fast Food Workers*, Oct. 5, 2016, https:// hartresearch.com/wp-content/uploads/2016/10/Fast-Food-Worker-Survey -Memo-10-5-16.pdf.

65   **cheese it must put on a Big Mac**: David Yaffe-Bellany, "McDonald's Lawsuit Targets 'Pervasive' Culture of Sexual Harassment," *New York Times*, Nov. 12, 2019. One appeals court has already ruled for McDonald's on this issue.

65   **rely significantly on undocumented laborers**: Ariel Ramchandani, "There's a Sexual-Harassment Epidemic on America's Farms," *Atlantic*, Jan. 29, 2018, https://www.theatlantic.com/business/archive/2018/01 /agriculture-sexual-harassment/550109/.

66   Brigham Young University came under fire: Christina Cauterucci, "BYU's
      Honor Code Sometimes Punishes Survivors Who Report Their Rapes,"
      Slate, Apr. 15, 2016, https://slate.com/human-interest/2016/04/byu-s-honor
      -code-sometimes-punishes-survivors-who-report-their-rapes.html.

66   instituted an amnesty clause: Associated Press, "BYU Amends Honor
      Code That Shamed Students Who Reported Sexual Assault," *Guardian*,
      Oct. 26, 2016, https://www.theguardian.com/us-news/2016/oct/26
      /brigham-young-university-sexual-assault-policy-changes.

66   the girl had broken its rules: Eric Stirgus, "Gwinnett School Bun-
      gled Sex Assault Claim, Alleged Victim Says," *Atlanta Journal-
      Constitution*, Sept. 20, 2016, https://www.ajc.com/news/local-education
      /gwinnett-school-bungled-sex-assault-claim-alleged-victim-says
      /c7aXDNpFa2dY4SQVS3UhwL/.

66   "internal" allegations to law enforcement: E.g., PREA § 115.271.
      Even when no criminal prosecution results, the outcomes of internal
      complaints against other detained people are often inherently criminal,
      like extended incarceration and solitary confinement. The military suf-
      fers from a similar problem: its internal governance structure includes
      internal criminal law enforcement.

68   "played out quite a bit differently": Susan Fowler, "Reflecting on
      One Very, Very Strange Year at Uber," Feb. 19, 2017, https://www
      .susanjfowler.com/blog/2017/2/19/reflecting-on-one-very-strange-year
      -at-uber; Mike Isaac, "Uber Investigating Sexual Harassment Claims
      by Ex-Employee," *New York Times*, Feb. 19, 2017, https://www.nytimes
      .com/2017/02/19/business/uber-sexual-harassment-investigation.html.

69   Avendaño left the company: Daisuke Wakabayashi, "Former Uber
      Engineer's Lawsuit Claims Sexual Harassment," *New York Times*, May
      21, 2018, https://www.nytimes.com/2018/05/21/technology/uber-sexual
      -harassment-lawsuit.html.

69   termination of at least twenty: Olivia Solon, "Uber Fires More Than
      20 Employees After Sexual Harassment Investigation," *Guardian*, June
      6, 2017, https://www.theguardian.com/technology/2017/jun/06/uber
      -fires-employees-sexual-harassment-investigation.

69   released a set of public recommendations: Meghann Farnsworth,
      "Read the Full Investigation into Uber's Troubled Culture and Manage-
      ment," *Vox*, June 13, 2017, https://www.vox.com/2017/6/13/15794412
      /read-entire-investigation-uber-culture-management-ethics-eric-holder.

69   Uber's founder, Travis Kalanick, resigned: Julia Carrie Wong, "Uber
      CEO Travis Kalanick Resigns Following Months of Chaos," *Guardian*,
      June 21, 2017, https://www.theguardian.com/technology/2017/jun/20
      /uber-ceo-travis-kalanick-resigns.

69    $4.4 million to settle charges: Andrew J. Hawkins, "Uber Will Pay
      $4.4 Million to Settle a Federal Probe into Sexual Harassment and Retal-
      iation," *Verge*, Dec. 19, 2019, https://www.theverge.com/2019/12/19
      /21029831/uber-settles-federal-probe-sexual-harassment-retaliation.

70   forced arbitration agreements: Daisuke Wakabayashi, "Uber

Eliminates Forced Arbitration for Sexual Misconduct Claims," *New York Times*, May 15, 2018, https://www.nytimes.com/2018/05/15/technology /uber-sex-misconduct.html.

70 **38 percent as often as their counterparts:** Katherine V. W. Stone and Alexander J. S. Colvin, *The Arbitration Epidemic: Mandatory Arbitration Deprives Workers and Consumers of Their Rights* (Washington, D.C.: Economic Policy Institute, Dec. 7, 2015), https://www.epi.org/publication /the-arbitration-epidemic/#epi-toc-20.

71 **outcry against Google's reliance on them:** Daisuke Wakabayashi, "Google Ends Forced Arbitration for All Employee Disputes," *New York Times*, Feb. 21, 2019, https://www.nytimes.com/2019/02/21/technology /google-forced-arbitration.html.

71 **domestic violence calls about fellow cops:** Conor Friedersdorf, "Police Have a Much Bigger Domestic-Abuse Problem Than the NFL Does," *Atlantic*, Sept. 19, 2014, https://www.theatlantic.com/national /archive/2014/09/police-officers-who-hit-their-wives-or-girlfriends /380329/.

71 **"The abuser is still in DSA":** Allison Geroi [Hrabar], "The Chips Are Down," Medium, Apr. 3, 2019, https://medium.com/@allisongeroi/the -chips-are-down-8ab1777f3865.

72 **"leadership that is, at best, apathetic":** The most obvious and historically significant example of an institution using the opacity of its own internal systems to protect sexual abusers is, of course, the Catholic Church. Shielded from public scrutiny by its own internal governance, as well as a leadership that shamed and manipulated victims into silence, the Church long faced no repercussions when it ignored victims' stories about abuse at the hands of priests. I don't think it is a particularly useful example to understand what drives institutional failures and how advocates can fix them, though, because the Church is truly sui generis. What other institution is so immune from public pressure?

72 **a sea change in schools' responses:** The story at McDonald's is still incomplete. McDonald's has now begun to implement some reforms, like anti-harassment trainings. But organizers feel these are baby steps at best. Future legal victories will hopefully spur further meaningful change. Bryce Covert, "McDonald's Has a Real Sexual Harassment Problem," *Nation*, July 28, 2020, https://www.thenation.com/article/society /mcdonalds-sexual-harassment-feature/.

72 **Coalition of Immokalee Workers (CIW):** "Fair Food Code of Conduct," Fair Food Standards Council, http://www.fairfoodstandards.org /resources/.fair-food-code-of-conduct/.

73 **"eliminate horrendous human rights abuses":** Kerstin Lindgren, *Justice in the Fields: A Report on the Role of Farmworker Justice Certification and an Evaluation of the Effectiveness of Seven Labels* 17, Fair World Project (2016), https://fairworldproject.org/wp-content/uploads/2016 /10/Justice-In-The-Fields-Report.pdf.

75 **"first thing you need to give up":** Sara Ahmed (@SaraNAhmed), Twitter,

May 14, 2019, 1:55 a.m., https://web.archive.org/web/20190515124925
/https://twitter.com/SaraNAhmed/status/1128222193735950337.

76   **the Ya Basta! coalition:** Bernice Yeung, "A Group of Janitors Started
a Movement to Stop Sexual Abuse," *Reveal*, Jan. 16, 2018, https://www
.revealnews.org/article/a-group-of-janitors-started-a-movement-to-stop
-sexual-abuse/.

76   **not simple outsourcing to cops:** "Fair Food Code of Conduct," Fair
Food Standards Council, http://www.fairfoodstandards.org/resources/.fair
-food-code-of-conduct/.

CHAPTER 6: "THE OTHER SIDE"

80   **wasn't a onetime mistake:** Letter to Robert E. Clark II, President of
Wesley College, from Beth Gellman-Beer, U.S. Department of Education,
Oct. 12, 2016, https://www2.ed.gov/about/offices/list/ocr/docs/investigations
/more/03152329-a.pdf.

80   **"conduct inconsistent with our values":** Richard Johnson, "Ex-
Congressman Axed by Morgan Stanley Prepping for a Comeback," *Page
Six*, Jan. 10, 2018, https://pagesix.com/2018/01/10/ex-congressman-axed
-by-morgan-stanley-prepping-for-a-comeback.

80   **did not identify the actual reason:** Ford was, however, reportedly
"accused at Morgan Stanley of padding his expense account and mistreating his assistants," so alternative explanations exist. Kate Kelly, "Morgan Stanley Says Harold Ford Jr. Wasn't Fired for Sexual Misconduct,"
New York Times, Jan. 22, 2018, https://www.nytimes.com/2018/01/22
/business/morgan-stanley-harold-ford-sexual-misconduct.html.

81   **cast a shadow over Tecedor's efforts:** Sarah Viren, "The Accusations Were
Lies. But Could We Prove It?," *New York Times*, Mar. 18, 2020, https://
www.nytimes.com/2020/03/18/magazine/title-ix-sexual-harassment
-accusations.html.

82   **now required under California law:** California's intermediate appeals
courts currently require schools to provide live hearings with some form
of indirect cross-examination. Doe v. Westmont Coll., 34 Cal. App. 5th
622 (Cal. Ct. App. 2019). At the time of this writing, the California
Supreme Court has agreed to review the question, and may either limit
or expand the rule.

83   **In a series of focus groups:** National Center for Victims of Crime,
unpublished data.

CHAPTER 7: WHAT IS DUE

88   **$33.5 million to the families:** B. Drummond Ayres Jr., "Jury Decides
Simpson Must Pay $25 Million in Punitive Award," *New York Times*,
Feb. 11, 1997, https://www.nytimes.com/1997/02/11/us/jury-decides
-simpson-must-pay-25-million-in-punitive-award.html.

88   **convinced *beyond a reasonable doubt*:** Cal. Pen. Code § 1096.

88   the "preponderance of the evidence": Cal. Evid. Code. § 115.

90   **Kelly sued the responsible public officials:** Goldberg v. Kelly, 397 U.S. 254, 255–57 (1970); Deborah J. Cantrell, "A Short History of Poverty Lawyers in the United States," *Loyola Journal of Public Interest Law* 5 (2003): 11.

90   **can be relatively simple and informal:** The balancing test reinforces the first principle of due process: fairness comes in many forms. Courts recognize that a lot of government decision-making happens outside of lawsuits. Such decision-making must still be consistent with due process, but that does not require a courtroom. A welfare hearing does not violate due process simply because it does not look much like a trial. The interests are different in the two contexts; so are the resources available.

90   **The court ruled in Kelly's favor:** *Goldberg*, 397 U.S. at 261–69. The same kind of balancing test is used to assess disciplinary systems in publicly run workplaces and schools, where employees and students have due process rights when they face removal. See Cleveland Bd. of Ed. v. Loudermill, 470 U.S. 532, 546 (1985); Goss v. Lopez, 419 U.S. 565, 583 (1975). I'll discuss school rules further shortly.

91   **an "asymmetry of representation":** Turner v. Rogers, 564 U.S. 431, 447 (2011). I should say that I don't know enough about child support proceedings to know if the Supreme Court was right in this particular instance—that is, whether, as it claimed, other procedural protections for the noncustodial parent were sufficient without a guarantee of free legal services. But the case illustrates the principle that due process inquiries should account for the interests of third parties with direct stakes in the outcome.

91   **need to be part of the equation:** Sage Carson and Sarah Nesbitt, "Balancing the Scales: Student Survivors' Interests and the Mathews Analysis," *Harvard Journal of Law & Gender* 43 (2020): 319, 343.

93   **termination, or demotion, or suspension:** See, e.g., Fed. R. Civ. Pro. 2 ("There is one form of action—the civil action."); Paul D. Carrington, "Making Rules to Dispose of Manifestly Unfounded Assertions: An Exorcism of the Bogy of Non-Trans-Substantive Rules of Civil Procedure," *University of Pennsylvania Law Review* 137 (1989): 2067, 2069–81 (explaining history and purpose of trans-substantive procedural rules).

There is one narrow exception to the general rule that we do not scale process to the specific offense, but it does not undermine the overarching principle. Some courts require a higher "clear and convincing" standard of evidence, rather than the usual "preponderance of the evidence," for civil fraud lawsuits. Courts sometimes suggest that this is because fraud reflects poorly on the defendant, but the scholarly consensus is that it is a historical accident, perhaps due to unusual overlaps between contract and tort law. John Terrence A. Rosenthal and Robert T. Alter, "Clear and Convincing to Whom? The False Claims Act and Its Burden of Proof Standard: Why the Government Needs a Big Stick," *Notre Dame Law Review* 75 (2000): 1409, 1432–45; Restatement (Third) of Torts: Liab. for Econ. Harm § 9 TD No. 2 (2014). The rule is truly anomalous: However painful it might be to lose a fraud suit, it is certainly a harder reputational hit to lose a civil suit for killing someone, which uses the preponderance of the evidence.

Some might also note that there are special rules of evidence, known as "rape shield laws," that exclude evidence about parties' and victims' sexual history and preferences. Personally, I am ambivalent about these rules. I don't love singling out sexual evidence, but I also recognize that these rules were created to address jurors' deep-seated biases that derailed meritorious cases. Regardless, those aren't really procedural rules. And there are other rules that single out certain kinds of evidence that are too likely to prejudice the proceedings. For example, evidence of some kinds of prior bad acts, but not others, are not admissible to impeach a witness.

94   **from an entirely separate prosecution:** Parties to civil suits who may risk criminal prosecution by testifying are allowed to refuse to testify without it reflecting poorly on their case, as part of their right to avoid self-incrimination. That is an accommodation to deliver defendants from a double bind with high stakes, not an allegation-specific procedural requirement.

94   **it had "nearly ruined" his life:** Patrick Witt, "A Sexual Harassment Policy That Nearly Ruined My Life," *Boston Globe*, Nov. 3, 2014, https://www.bostonglobe.com/opinion/2014/11/03/sexual-harassment-policy -that-nearly-ruined-life/hY3XrZrOdXjvX2SSvuciPN/story.html.

95   **stigma attached to the specific offense:** For some lawyers, the discussion of stigma might call to mind the still-developing doctrine known as "stigma-plus." See generally Linnet Davis-Stermitz, "Stigma Plus Whom? Evaluating Causation in Multiple-Actor Stigma-Plus Claims," *University of Chicago Law Review* 84 (2017): 1883.

The basic idea of stigma-plus is this: to have due process rights, you need to have a "liberty or property interest" in whatever the government is trying to take away from you. Some examples are your interest in your tenured public job, or your interest in freedom from incarceration. Generally, if you don't have that kind of interest, you don't get due process protections. An injury to your reputation—for example, the government saying something negative about you publicly—won't trigger those protections on its own. But, courts say, you might be owed due process if the government embarrassed you publicly in the process of taking something concrete away from you—even if that thing alone wasn't a sufficient "interest." For example, you might not have a recognizable interest in your untenured seat on the local parks committee, so if your fellow members want to remove you from the committee, they won't need to provide you a hearing or anything like that. But let's say that when the committee kicks you off, they put out a press release explaining that you have been dismissed for some embarrassing reason, like theft. Now you have a hit to your reputation "plus" the deprivation itself, so might be owed a hearing to clear your name.

"Stigma-plus" means that yes, sometimes the law cares about the government hurting your reputation. But this isn't inconsistent with our rule. Even here, once your right to due process has been triggered, you don't get extra process based on how shameful the allegation is.

CHAPTER 8: AN INCOMPLETE BLUEPRINT

97 **The complainant, not the accused:** As a technical matter, the institution might place the burden on its own investigators to prove an allegation. (This is the uncharacteristically reasonable approach taken by Betsy DeVos's Title IX regulations, the topic of much discussion in this book.) In doing so, the institution recognizes that it must take an active role in figuring out what happened, rather than merely waiting on the two sides to provide evidence. Either way, the key point is that the respondent does not have the burden of disproving the allegation.

98 **"truncated trial-type procedures":** Goss v. Lopez, 419 U.S. 565, 584 (1975).

99 **American Bar Association's Commission on Domestic & Sexual Violence:** See generally ABA Commission on Domestic & Sexual Violence, *Recommendations for Improving Campus Student Conduct Processes for Gender-Based Violence*, 2019, https://www.americanbar.org/content/dam/aba/publications/domestic-violence/campus.pdf.

99 **evidence that she is nervous:** Suzanne B. Goldberg, "Keep Cross-Examination Out of College Sexual-Assault Cases," *Chronicle of Higher Education*, Jan. 10, 2019, https://www.chronicle.com/article/Keep-Cross-Examination-Out-of/245448.

100 **more room for a single person's biases:** It's not inevitable that an interview will be conducted by fewer people than would sit on a hearing board. But the general trend makes sense: an interview by three people won't look too different from a hearing, and lacks the intimacy that may make an interview model more comfortable for a victim.

100 **at a large and unfair advantage:** This is a view shared by some who represent accused students. See, e.g., Max Larkin, "New Federal Guidance Will Remake System for Handling Sexual Assault, Harassment on Campus," WBUR, May 6, 2020.

101 **when in untrained hands:** Haidak v. Univ. of Massachusetts-Amherst, 933 F.3d 56, 68–69 (1st Cir. 2019); see also Doe v. Univ. of Arkansas-Fayetteville, 974 F.3d 858, 868 (2020).

101 **almost all federal appellate courts:** E.g., Walsh v. Hodge, 975 F.3d 475, 485 (5th Cir. 2020); *Univ. of Arkansas-Fayetteville*, 974 F.3d at 867–78; Doe v. Colgate Univ., 760 F. App'x 22, 33 (2nd Cir. 2019); *Haidak*, 933 F.3d at 68–70; Nash v. Auburn Univ., 812 F.2d 655, 664 (11th Cir. 1987); Doe v. Westmont Coll., 34 Cal. App. 5th 622, 635 (Cal. Ct. App. 2019).

One court, the U.S. Court of Appeals for the Sixth Circuit, has held that, where "credibility is in dispute and material to the outcome," a public university must allow an accused student to cross-examine witnesses either directly or through a representative. In doing so, it did not explain its departure from past precedent allowing "indirect" cross-examination. Doe v. Baum, 903 F.3d 575, 584 (6th Cir. 2018).

101 **administrators can pose each side's questions:** Those skeptical that institutions like schools and employers have the capacity to handle

complex disciplinary cases may find some solace in these debates. Even the courts that demand the most trial-like processes still tailor these rules to fit within the institutions' capacity. Whether, for example, one federal appeals court is right to require live, direct cross-examination for student discipline is an open question (which I'll discuss shortly). But there is little doubt that schools are *able* to provide exactly what it requires.

101   **universities should provide some kind of hearing:** As courts have noted, this hearing is more likely to be helpful where the school's determination turns on questions of credibility than where, for example, everyone agrees as to what occurred and the question is simply whether those facts constitute sexual harassment. In the latter case, the decision-makers do not need to hear from the parties to make a determination.

102   **the best parts of each approach:** The ABA's Commission on Domestic & Sexual Violence has identified two possible "hybrid" models, and endorsed one. ABA Commission on Domestic & Sexual Violence, *Recommendations for Improving Campus Student Conduct Processes for Gender-Based Violence*, 62.

102   **into a witch-hunting ground:** For example, Daphne Merkin, "Publicly, We Say #MeToo. Privately We Have Misgivings," *New York Times*, Jan. 5, 2018, https://www.nytimes.com/2018/01/05/opinion/golden -globes-metoo.html?smid=tw-nytimes&smtyp=cur&_r=1.

103   **set of rules applies to all students:** Of course, wealthy students can hire lawyers to advise them, prepare them for interviews, write their statements, and sometimes participate in the hearings. I would guess they are, statistically, more likely to get away with these behaviors because of their access to lawyers, or the school's hope that Mom and Dad will finance new tennis courts. But there is no equivalent to the CEO contract for rich college students; they cannot negotiate for permission to sexually harass their peers just a little, or demand specific procedural protections unavailable to their classmates.

104   **extremely carefully in disciplining top executives:** Rachel Arnow-Richman, "Of Power and Process: Handling Harassers in an At-Will World," *Yale Law Journal Forum*, June 18, 2018, https://www .yalelawjournal.org/forum/of-power-and-process.

CHAPTER 9: WHY PROCESS MATTERS FOR ALL

106   **despite everything, a good guy at heart:** Sam Levin, "Stanford Sexual Assault: Read the Full Text of the Judge's Controversial Decision," *Guardian*, June 14, 2016, https://www.theguardian.com/us-news/2016 /jun/14/stanford-sexual-assault-read-sentence-judge-aaron-persky.

106   **"into the victim of his own crimes":** Manne, *Down Girl*, 197–98.

107   **After all, what Manne criticizes:** Here is what Manne said in an interview with the *New Yorker*'s Isaac Chotiner: "I think we can be sympathetic toward someone within the criminal-justice system, to the extent

that that's appropriate, when we're not thinking about victim vs. perpetrator, but when we are thinking that the state is trying to make a case that the accused committed the crime beyond a reasonable doubt.

"And that's a very different set of propositions and provides a very different, potentially sympathetic lens for thinking about crime or a criminal act, as opposed to a public reaction to a rape case, where there is a more straightforward question of who you sympathize with primarily, the victim or the perpetrator. So I am saying that criminal law is a pretty different context than media discussions or initial reactions to someone telling you a crime was committed against them. There are interesting cases where, within a friend group, a man is accused of raping a woman in the friend group, and it is a common experience that people are disbelieving or more sympathetic toward him. And in that kind of context, I think it is pretty clear you should sympathize with the victim first and foremost."

Isaac Chotiner, "Kate Manne on the Costs of Male Entitlement," *New Yorker*, Sept. 4, 2020, https://www.newyorker.com/news/q-and-a/kate-manne-on-the-costs-of-male-entitlement.

109　**"as objects, subject to infinite manipulation"**: Jerry L. Mashaw, "Administrative Due Process: The Quest for a Dignitary Theory," *Boston University Law Review* 61 (1981): 885, 901.

109　**more likely to buy into the result**: Tom R. Tyler, "Procedural Justice, Legitimacy, and the Effective Rule of Law," *Crime and Justice* 30 (2003): 283, 286.

110　**contributed to greater pay satisfaction**: Robert Folger and Mary A. Konovsky, "Effects of Procedural and Distributive Justice on Reactions to Pay Raise," *Academy of Management Journal* 32 (Mar. 1989): 115.

110　**respond less negatively to the outcome**: Joel Brockner et al., "Interactive Effects of Procedural Justice and Outcome Negativity on Victims and Survivors of Job Loss," *Academy of Management Journal* 37 (1994): 397.

111　**"will fall to vigilantes like Tehlirian"**: David Luban, "Folktales of International Justice," *Proceedings of the Annual Meeting of the American Society of International Law* 98 (2004): 182.

111　**"citizens are left with little option"**: Paul H. Robinson and Sarah M. Robinson, *Shadow Vigilantes: How Distrust in the Justice System Breeds a New Kind of Lawlessness* (Amherst, NY: Prometheus Books, 2018), 43.

113　**provost refused to remove**: Tamar Lewin, "Handling of Sexual Harassment Case Poses Larger Questions at Yale," *New York Times*, Nov. 1, 2014, https://www.nytimes.com/2014/11/02/us/handling-of-sexual-harassment-case-poses-larger-questions-at-yale.html.

113　**could not share such warnings except anonymously**: George Joseph and Jon Swaine, "Behind Columbia's 'Rape Lists': 'When Existing Systems Fail, What Then?,'" *Guardian*, June 26, 2014, https://www.theguardian.com/education/2014/jun/26/columbia-university-students-rape-list-mishandle-sexual-assault.

114 **That woman, Moira Donegan, identified herself:** Moira Donegan, "I Started the Media Men List," *The Cut*, Jan. 10, 2018, https://www.thecut .com/2018/01/moira-donegan-i-started-the-media-men-list.html.

114 **famed rape apologist Katie Roiphe:** For a background on Roiphe's rape politics, see Jennifer Gonnerman, "The Selling of Katie Roiphe," *Baffler*, Dec. 1994, https://thebaffler.com/salvos/the-selling-of-katie-roiphe.

116 **who would be on the disciplinary panel:** The accused student victim was also allowed to decide whether the victim could bring her adviser to the hearing. Anne McClintock, "Who's Afraid of Title IX?," *Jacobin*, Oct. 2017, https://www.jacobinmag.com/2017/10/title-ix-betsy-devos -doe-colleges-assault-dear-colleague.

116 **a swinging "pendulum" or "overcorrection":** Alexandra Brodsky, "A Rising Tide: Learning About Fair Disciplinary Process from Title IX," *Journal of Legal Education* 66 (2017): 822; David G. Savage and Timothy M. Phelps, "How a Little-Known Education Office Has Forced Far-Reaching Changes to Campus Sex Assault Investigations," *Los Angeles Times*, Aug. 17, 2015, https://www.latimes.com/nation/la-na-campus-sexual-assault-20150817-story.html; Emily Yoffe, "The College Rape Overcorrection," *Slate*, Dec. 8, 2014, http://www.slate.com/articles /double_x/doublex/2014/12/college_rape_campus_sexual_assault_is_a _serious_problem_but_the_efforts.html; Robby Soave, "As the Campus Rape Narrative Unravels, Will Due Process Strike Back in 2015?," *Reason*, Dec. 30, 2014.

117 **2020 survey by Know Your IX:** Know Your IX, *The Cost of Reporting: Perpetrator Retaliation, Institutional Betrayal, and Student Survivor Pushout*, 2021.

CHAPTER 10: THE LIMITS OF PROCESS

118 **allow attorneys to remove potentially biased jurors:** See, e.g., Vivien Toomey Montz and Craig Lee Montz, "The Peremptory Challenge: Should It Still Exist? An Examination of Federal and Florida Law," *University of Miami Law Review* 54 (2000): 451, 455–56.

118 **seminal 1986 opinion *Batson v. Kentucky*:** Batson v. Kentucky, 476 U.S. 79, 96–97 (1986).

118 **Justice Thurgood Marshall, while concurring:** *Batson*, 476 U.S. at 102–8 (Marshall, J., concurring).

118 **too eager to accept ridiculous explanations:** Shari Seidman Diamond et al., "Realistic Responses to the Limitations of Batson v. Kentucky," *Cornell Journal of Law and Public Policy* 7 (1997): 77.

119 **found this post hoc justification reasonable:** United States v. Romero-Reyna, 889 F.2d 559, 561–62 (5th Cir. 1989).

119 **"the greatest legal engine ever invented":** 5 Wigmore on Evidence § 1367; Stuart v. Alabama, 139 S. Ct. 36 (2018).

119 **"a witness's nervous or stumbling response":** Goldberg, "Keep Cross-Examination Out of College Sexual-Assault Cases."

119 **what is called an inquisitorial model:** For an explanation of inquisitorial models, see David Alan Sklansky, "Anti-Inquisitorialism," *Harvard Law Review* 122 (2009): 1634, 1688.

120 **"let them eat due process":** Craig Haney, "The Fourteenth Amendment and Symbolic Legality: Let Them Eat Due Process," *Law and Human Behavior* 15 (1991): 183.

120 **violent and corrupt Chicago Police Department:** Debbie Southorn and Sarah Lazare, "Officers Accused of Abuses Are Leading Chicago Police's 'Implicit Bias' Training Program," *Intercept*, Feb. 3, 2019, https://theintercept.com/2019/02/03/chicago-police-procedural-justice-training-complaints-lawsuits-racism/; Maudlyne Ihejirika, "'Procedural Justice': A Day at CPD's Sensitivity-Training Course," *Chicago Sun-Times*, Jan. 20, 2017, https://chicago.suntimes.com/news/procedural-justice-a-day-at-cpds-sensitivity-training-course/; Simone Weichselbaum, "The 'Chicago Model' of Policing Hasn't Saved Chicago," Marshall Project, Apr. 19, 2016, https://www.themarshallproject.org/2016/04/19/the-chicago-model-of-policing-hasn-t-saved-chicago.

120 **as the theorist Dennis Fox puts it:** Dennis R. Fox, "Psychological Jurisprudence and Radical Social Change," *American Psychologist* 48 (1993).

120 **people's investment in the end result:** The fact that outcome matters to people is not only common sense, but also supported by research. See, for example, Sveinung Arnesen, "Legitimacy from Decision-Making Influence and Outcome Favourability: Results from General Population Survey Experiments," *Political Studies* 65 (2017); Honorata Mazepus, "What Makes Political Authorities Legitimate? Students' Ideas About Legitimacy in Five European Democracies and Hybrid Regimes," *Contemporary Politics* 23 (2017).

121 **Franken called for an investigation:** Jane Mayer, "The Case of Al Franken," *New Yorker*, July 22, 2019, https://www.newyorker.com/magazine/2019/07/29/the-case-of-al-franken.

124 **"odious," a "smear":** Bret Stephens, "This I Believe About Blasey v. Kavanaugh," *New York Times*, Sept. 21, 2018, https://www.nytimes.com/2018/09/21/opinion/blasey-kavanaugh-assault-allegations-truth.html; Bret Stephens, "The Smearing of Woody Allen," *New York Times*, Feb. 9, 2018, https://www.nytimes.com/2018/02/09/opinion/smearing-of-woody-allen.html.

CHAPTER 11: STRAW FEMINISTS

127 **"I told them all men were rapists":** Kate Beaton, "Straw Feminists in the Closet," *Hark! A Vagrant*, http://www.harkavagrant.com/?id=341. In a later comic on the same theme, straw feminists explain to a girl at the mall to buy her first bra, "You don't want a training bra little girl. You want all the men in the world to be *dead*." Kate Beaton, "Straw Feminists

in 'Feminist Fun!,'" *Hark! A Vagrant*, http://www.harkavagrant.com /index.php?id=382.

128 "smug pundits / naive critics": Sam Huber (@hubersamj), Twitter, July 9, 2019, 9:08 p.m., https://twitter.com/hubersamj/status /1148760983126650883.

128 Death Star to his Luke Skywalker: KC Johnson and Stuart Taylor Jr., "The ACLU's 'Death Star' Client in Its Title IX Lawsuit," *RealClearPolitics*, June 21, 2020, https://www.realclearpolitics.com/articles/2020/06 /21/the_aclus_death_star_client_in_its_title_ix_lawsuit_143490.html; "Title IX Changes Are Coming. Can the Warring Sides Find Common Ground?," *BuzzFeed News*, Sept. 22, 2017, https://www.buzzfeednews .com/article/tylerkingkade/title-ix-changes-are-coming-can-the-sides -find-common-ground.

128 Emily Yoffe posed a question: Emily Yoffe, "Does Anyone Still Take Both Sexual Assault and Due Process Seriously?," *Atlantic*, Oct. 13, 2018, https://www.theatlantic.com/ideas/archive/2018/10/sexual -assault-has-become-partisan-issue/572893/.

129 "seek truth without bias": Hanna Stotland, "I Advise Students Accused of Sexual Assault. Expelling Them Isn't the Answer," *New York Times*, July 9, 2019, https://www.nytimes.com/2019/07/09/opinion/sexual -assault-students-campus.html.

129 self-proclaimed feminist comedian Aziz Ansari: Katie Way, "I Went on a Date with Aziz Ansari. It Turned into the Worst Night of My Life," Babe, Jan. 13, 2018, https://babe.net/2018/01/13/aziz-ansari -28355.

130 critics like Bari Weiss and Caitlin Flanagan: Bari Weiss, "Aziz Ansari Is Guilty. Of Not Being a Mind Reader," *New York Times*, Jan. 15, 2018, https://www.nytimes.com/2018/01/15/opinion/aziz-ansari-babe-sexual -harassment.html; Caitlin Flanagan, "The Humiliation of Aziz Ansari," *Atlantic*, Jan. 14, 2018, https://www.theatlantic.com/entertainment/archive /2018/01/the-humiliation-of-aziz-ansari/550541/.

130 guidance documents that detailed schools' obligations: See, e.g., Russlynn Ali, Assistant Secretary for Civil Rights, Dear Colleague Letter on Bullying, U.S. Department of Education, Oct. 26, 2010, https://tinyurl.com/y7d8ubgb; *Revised Sexual Harassment Guidance: Harassment of Students by School Employees, Other Students, or Third Parties*, U.S. Department of Education, Office for Civil Rights, Jan. 2001, https://tinyurl.com/yaeajxkz; Norma V. Cantu, Assistant Secretary for Civil Rights, Dear Colleague Letter on Prohibited Disability Harassment, U.S. Department of Education, July 25, 2000, https://tinyurl .com/yb5jobbn; *Racial Incidents and Harassment Against Students at Educational Institutions, Investigative Guidance*, 59 Fed. Reg. 11448 (Mar. 10, 1994), https://tinyurl.com/y86mu9tw.

130 known as the "Dear Colleague Letter": Russlynn Ali, Assistant Secretary for Civil Rights, Office for Civil Rights, U.S. Department of

Education, Dear Colleague Letter: Sexual Violence, Apr. 4, 2011, http://www2.ed.gov/about/offices/list/ocr/letters/colleague-201104.pdf.

131 **historically given educators considerable discretion:** See, e.g., Goss v. Lopez, 419 U.S. 565, 577–84 (1975); U.S. Department of Education, Office for Civil Rights, *Questions and Answers on Title IX and Sexual Violence*, Apr. 29, 2014, 13–14, https://www2.ed.gov/about/offices/list/ocr/docs/qa-201404-title-ix.pdf; U.S. Department of Education, *Revised Sexual Harassment Guidance*, 19–22.

131 **must offer each side of an accusation the same rights:** In doing so, I think the Dear Colleague Letter created what was then the most robust statement of accused students' rights in federal law, an irony given the deluge of criticism. Alexandra Brodsky, "A Rising Tide: Learning About Fair Disciplinary Process from Title IX," *Journal of Legal Education* 66 (2017): 822.

131 **if the school allowed one side to appeal:** Some critics have taken issue with the Department of Education permitting alleged victims to appeal. They analogize to criminal law, where prosecutors are not permitted to appeal a "not guilty" verdict. But in civil trials, plaintiffs do have the right to appeal. The Trump administration initially provided greater appellate rights to respondents than complainants, but, after criticism, decided to grant both sides an equal opportunity. See 34 C.F.R. § 106.45(b)(8).

131 **might implement sloppy, unfair policies:** Samuel R. Bagenstos, "What Went Wrong with Title IX?," *Washington Monthly*, Sept./Oct. 2015, https://washingtonmonthly.com/magazine/septoct-2015/what-went-wrong-with-title-ix/.

132 **a few different models for disciplinary procedures:** In 2014, a White House task force announced the Department of Justice would research an array of models to identify best practices. Unfortunately, one model identified in that announcement as a promising possibility was a "single-investigator" process that many advocates on all sides have since criticized. The task force's follow-up report in the last month of the Obama administration included general guidelines for fair discipline but no recommended models. *The Second Report of the White House Task Force to Protect Students from Sexual Assault*, Jan. 5, 2017, https://www.whitehouse.gov/sites/whitehouse.gov/files/images/Documents/1.4.17.VAW%20Event.TF%20Report.PDF; *Not Alone: The First Report of the White House Task Force to Protect Students from Sexual Assault*, Apr. 2014, 14, https://www.justice.gov/archives/ovw/page/file/905942/download.

132 **procedural errors were absolutely not required:** Erin E. Buzuvis, "Title IX and Procedural Fairness: Why Disciplined-Student Litigation Does Not Undermine the Role of Title IX in Campus Sexual Assault," *Montana Law Review* 78 (2017): 71; Brodsky, "A Rising Tide"; Bagenstos, "What Went Wrong with Title IX?" As I will discuss in more detail, some critics were displeased that the department required schools to use the preponderance of the evidence in disciplining students for sexual harassment. But courts are clear that standard is consistent with due

process. See, e.g., Doe v. Univ. of Arkansas-Fayetteville, 974 F.3d 858, 869 (8th Cir. Sept. 4, 2020).

132 **forbidden schools from providing hearings:** E.g., Shikha Dalmia, "In Defense of Betsy DeVos' Title IX Plan," *The Week*, Nov. 29, 2018, https://theweek.com/articles/808638/defense-betsy-devos-title-ix-plan. The closest the Dear Colleague Letter got to this was discouraging schools from allowing students to question each other *directly*, which it noted could be traumatizing. Even the Trump administration agreed, requiring schools to instead require students to question each other through representatives. See Alexandra Brodsky, "Repealing Title IX Guidelines on Sexual Assault: A Dialogue," *American Prospect*, Oct. 27, 2017, https://prospect.org/education/repealing-title-ix-guidelines-sexual-assault-dialogue; 34 C.F.R. §106.45(b)(6).

132 **groundbreaking work *promoting* fair discipline:** U.S. Department of Education, "U.S. Departments of Education and Justice Release School Discipline Guidance Package to Enhance School Climate and Improve School Discipline Policies/Practices," Jan. 8, 2014, https://www.ed.gov/news/press-releases/us-departments-education-and-justice-release-school-discipline-guidance-package-.

132 **approached the writer Ijeoma Oluo:** Ijeoma Oluo, "Due Process Is Needed for Sexual Harassment Accusations—but for Whom?," *Establishment*, Nov. 30, 2017, https://theestablishment.co/due-process-is-needed-for-sexual-harassment-accusations-but-for-whom-968e7c81e6d6/index.html.

134 **"remain largely divided along party lines":** Caroline Kitchener, "How Campus Sexual Assault Became So Politicized," *Atlantic*, September 22, 2017, https://www.theatlantic.com/education/archive/2017/09/how-campus-sexual-assault-became-so-politicized/540846/.

134 **"don't assume women as a gender are especially deceptive":** Jude Ellison S. Doyle, "Despite What You May Have Heard, 'Believe Women' Has Never Meant 'Ignore Facts,'" *Elle*, Nov. 29, 2017, https://www.elle.com/culture/career-politics/a13977980/me-too-movement-false-accusations-believe-women/.

134 **"Treat women seriously":** Monica Hesse, "'Believe Women' Was a Slogan. 'Believe All Women' Is a Straw Man," *Washington Post*, May 12, 2020, https://www.washingtonpost.com/lifestyle/style/believe-women-was-a-slogan-believe-all-women-is-a-strawman/2020/05/11/6a3ff590-9314-11ea-9f5e-56d8239bf9ad_story.html.

135 **#BelieveWomen and #BelieveAllWomen:** Susan Faludi, "'Believe All Women' Is a Right-Wing Trap," *New York Times*, May 18, 2020, https://www.nytimes.com/2020/05/18/opinion/tara-reade-believe-all-women.html.

136 **"If you're explaining, you're losing":** Hesse, "'Believe Women' Was a Slogan. 'Believe All Women' Is a Straw Man."

137 **vote of two-thirds of their chamber:** U.S. Const. art. I, § 5.

138 **"outweigh the loss of any one man's reputation":** Emily Lindin (@

EmilyLindin), Twitter, Nov. 21, 2017, 3:45 p.m., https://twitter.com
/emilylindin/status/933073784822579200?lang=en.

CHAPTER 12: AN "EXCEPTIONAL" HARM

141   the "Pence Rule": Aaron Blake, "Mike Pence Doesn't Dine Alone with
Other Women. And We're All Shocked," *Washington Post*, Mar. 30, 2017,
https://www.washingtonpost.com/news/the-fix/wp/2017/03/30/mike
-pence-doesnt-dine-alone-with-other-women-and-were-all-shocked/.

141   "new terrain for us societally": Kathleen Parker, "The Inevitable
Unintended Consequences of #MeToo," *Washington Post*, Dec. 4, 2018,
https://www.washingtonpost.com/opinions/the-inevitable-unintended
-consequences-of-metoo/2018/12/04/9c7e0418-f80e-11e8-8d64
-4e79db33382f_story.html.

142   leaving messages in fake blood: See Isaac Arnsdorf, "Branford '11
Aims to Move Beyond Rocky Start to Year," *Yale Daily News*, Nov. 7,
2007, https://yaledailynews.com/blog/2007/11/07/branford-11-aims-to
-move-beyond-rocky-start-to-year/.

143   they had *more* legal rights: The Campus SaVE Act requires schools to
provide certain procedural protections in student discipline for sexual
harassment. 20 U.S.C.A. § 1092.

145   not formally reported to the correct official: Under employment law,
by contrast, an institution is responsible for responding to harassment
that it either knew or should have known about. That was also the standard used by the Department of Education until the new rules promul-
gated under Trump in 2020.

145   unable to answer basic questions: Katie Reilley, "Here's a Look at the
Education Questions Betsy DeVos Struggled to Answer," *Time*, Jan. 18,
2017, https://time.com/4637642/betsy-devos-confirmation-education
-policy/.

145   closest she had to qualifications: See, e.g., Kristina Rizga, "Betsy DeVos
Wants to Use America's Schools to Build 'God's Kingdom,'" *Mother Jones*,
Mar./Apr. 2017, https://www.motherjones.com/politics/2017/01/betsy
-devos-christian-schools-vouchers-charter-education-secretary/; Paul Fain
and Rick Seltzer, "Family Ties," *Inside Higher Ed*, Feb. 7, 2017, https://
www.insidehighered.com/news/2017/02/07/betsy-devoss-connection
-college-fix-conservative-higher-education-news-site; Annie Waldman,
"DeVos' Code Words for Creationism Offshoot Raise Concerns About
'Junk Science,'" *ProPublica*, Jan. 29, 2017, https://www.propublica.org
/article/devos-education-nominees-code-words-for-creationism-offshoot
-raise-concerns.

145   vice president's tie-breaking vote: U.S. Senate Historical Office,
"Occasions When Vice Presidents Have Voted to Break Tie Votes in
the Senate," Nov. 9, 2018, 9 n.3, https://www.senate.gov/artandhistory
/history/resources/pdf/VPTies.pdf; Emmarie Huetteman and Yamiche

Alcindor, "Betsy DeVos Confirmed as Education Secretary; Pence Breaks Tie," *New York Times*, Feb. 7, 2017, https://www.nytimes.com/2017/02 /07/us/politics/betsy-devos-education-secretary-confirmed.html. Some have suggested that, because she was not confirmed by a majority of the Senate, DeVos never actually became the secretary of education as a matter of constitutional law. National Center for Youth Law, Comment on Proposed Title IX Regulations 1–3, Jan. 30, 2019, https://youthlaw .org/wp-content/uploads/2018/01/NCYL-Comment-on-Title-IX-regs -1.pdf.

146   **"90 percent" of campus rape allegations were illegitimate:** Sarah Brown, "Ed. Dept. Official Apologizes for '90%' Remark on Campus Rape. What's the Research?," *Chronicle of Higher Education*, July 12, 2017, https://www.chronicle.com/article/ed-dept-official-apologizes-for -90-remark-on-campus-rape-whats-the-research/.

146   **past statements are admissible:** Fed. R. Evid. 801(d)(2)(A).

146   **much harder time proving her claim:** Nicole Bedera, Seth Galanter, and Sage Carson, "A New Title IX Rule Essentially Allows Accused Sexual Assailants to Hide Evidence Against Them," *Time*, August 14, 2020, https://time.com/5879262/devos-title-ix-rule. I found it telling that DeVos's supporters' reaction to this article was that the provision it criticized was so ridiculous it couldn't possibly be real. Even they thought it was absurd.

147   **victim can be cross-examined directly:** 34 C.F.R. § 106.45.

147   **School professionals prefer this preponderance standard:** "[The Association for Student Conduct Administration] recommends [the preponderance of the evidence] because it is the only standard that reflects the integrity of equitable student conduct processes which treat all students with respect and fundamental fairness." Chris Loschiavo and Jennifer Waller, *The Preponderance of Evidence Standard: Use In Higher Education Campus Conduct Processes*, Association for Student Conduct Administration, https://www.theasca.org/files/The%20Preponderance%20of%20 Evidence%20Standard.pdf.

148   **reserve it for harms like cheating and vandalism:** The University of Maryland is one such school. It requires clear and convincing evidence of academic dishonesty, but uses the preponderance standard for all other student conduct matters. University of Maryland Code of Student Conduct, Aug. 24, 2020, 2; University of Maryland Code of Academic Integrity, Apr. 1, 2020, 3.

148   **under DeVos's proposed rule:** Ultimately, after advocates objected, DeVos achieved the same end through different means. She dropped the requirement that schools must use clear and convincing evidence for sexual harassment if they did the same for any other student discipline. But she required that schools use the same standard for sexual harassment complaints against students and faculty. Some schools use the preponderance of the evidence for all student discipline, but, due to

long-negotiated contracts, can only fire staff using a higher standard. As a result, the final rule required many schools to use a higher standard for sexual harassment than all other student discipline, without actually having to say so—a wiser legal strategy for the Department of Education.

148　**The supposed "heightened stigma":** Nondiscrimination on the Basis of Sex in Education Programs or Activities Receiving Federal Financial Assistance, 83 *Fed. Reg.* 61,462, 61,477 (Proposed Nov. 29, 2018), https://www.govinfo.gov/content/pkg/FR-2018-11-29/pdf/2018-25314 .pdf.

149　**Missouri Republicans pushed legislation:** Edward McKinley, "Proposed Missouri Title IX Changes Would Give Accused More Power Than Any Other State," *Kansas City Star*, Jan. 30, 2019, https://www .kansascity.com/news/politics-government/article225240190.html.

149　**As originally drafted, the bill:** For drafts and legislative histories of the House and Senate versions of the bill, see "MO SB259 | 2019 | Regular Session," May 17, 2019 *LegiScan*, https://legiscan.com/MO/bill/SB259 /2019, and "MO HB573 | 2019 | Regular Session," March 14, 2019 *LegiScan*, https://legiscan.com/MO/bill/HB573/2019. On some provisions, the House and Senate versions of the bills differed slightly, and some parts of the bills were amended in committee.

150　**his mother was a presiding judge:** Elena Quinones, "Changing the Rules: Lobbyist Pressing Title IX Changes Motivated by Son's Expulsion from WU," *Student Life*, Apr. 25, 2019, https://www.studlife.com/news /2019/04/25/changing-the-rules-lobbyist-pressing-title-ix-changes -motivated-by-sons-expulsion-from-wu/; Edward McKinley, "Lobbyist's Crusade to Change Title IX in Missouri Stems from His Son's Expulsion," *Kansas City Star*, Apr. 23, 2019, https://www.kansascity.com/news /politics-government/article228733614.html.

152　**law or regulation that guaranteed the same:** Under the Spending Clause, Congress could pass a law requiring certain disciplinary procedures at all schools that receive federal funds. To the extent the Department of Education has authority to promulgate regulations for the procedures schools use to investigate sexual harassment, it could do the same for all misconduct that schools are required by department-enforced law to investigate, including all sex-, race-, and disability-based discrimination. More broadly, though, I believe the department has authority to require certain basic procedural protections in *all* school discipline—not just those that so directly implicate civil rights laws—as a prophylactic against discriminatory discipline.

152　**known as the "Discipline Guidance":** Andrew Ujifusa, "Betsy DeVos Revokes Obama Discipline Guidance Designed to Protect Students of Color," *Education Week*, Dec. 21, 2018, https://blogs.edweek.org/edweek /campaign-k-12/2018/12/betsy_devos_revokes_obama_discipline _guidance_students_of_color_protect.html.

152　**identify any troubling patterns:** Catherine E. Lhamon, Assistant

Secretary for Civil Rights, Office for Civil Rights, U.S. Department of Education, and Jocelyn Samuels, Acting Assistant Attorney General, Civil Rights Division, U.S. Department of Justice, Dear Colleague Letter on the Nondiscriminatory Administration of Student Discipline, Jan. 8, 2014, https://www2.ed.gov/about/offices/list/ocr/letters/colleague -201401-title-vi.html. The guidance document also included interpretations of Title IV, another race discrimination statute, though the letter is best known for its discussion of Title VI.

152   **more than** *five times as likely*: District of Columbia Office of the State Superintendent of Education, *State of Discipline: 2017–2018 School Year*, https://osse.dc.gov/sites/default/files/dc/sites/osse/page_content /attachments/2017-18%20School%20Year%20Discipline%20Report.pdf.

152   **rates had been even worse:** District of Columbia Office of the State Superintendent of Education, *Reducing Out-of-School Suspensions and Expulsions in District of Columbia Public and Public Charter Schools*, https:// osse.dc.gov/sites/default/files/dc/sites/osse/page_content/attachments /2013-14%20School%20Year%20OSSE%20Discipline%20Report .pdf.

153   **published a letter in the** *New York Times*: Hans Bader, Letter to the Editor, *New York Times*, Dec. 11, 2018, https://www.nytimes.com/2018 /12/11/opinion/letters/colleges-sexual-assault.html.

153   **Yet he had long waged war:** Hans Bader, "The Trump Administration Got It Right on School-Discipline Policy," *Washington Post*, Dec. 26, 2018, https://www.washingtonpost.com/opinions/the-trump-administration -got-it-right-on-school-discipline-policy/2018/12/26/0e4ed27e-07ba -11e9-8942-0ef442e59094_story.html; Hans Bader et al., "A Review of Department of Education Programs: Transgender Issues, Racial Quotas in School Discipline, and Campus Sexual Assault Mandates," Regulatory Transparency Project of the Federalist Society, Sept. 12, 2017, https:// regproject.org/wp-content/uploads/RTP-Race-Sex-Working-Group-Paper .pdf; Russell Skiba et al., "Race Is Not Neutral: A National Investigation of African American and Latino Disproportionality in School Discipline," *School Psychology Review* 40 (2011).

153   **if it benefited white people:** Professor Nancy Chi Cantalupo argues that the new Title IX regulations' focus on protecting accused students' rights served as an anti–civil rights "beachhead," "a foothold, one that can be used to launch an effort to expand" the Trump and DeVos administration's assault on student civil rights. Nancy Chi Cantalupo, "Dog Whistles and Beachheads: The Trump Administration, Sexual Violence & Student Discipline in Education," *Wake Forest Law Review* 54 (2019): 303, 306–7.

154   **According to the Department of Education's data:** In that year, 0.1 percent of Asian boys and 0.2 percent of white boys in K-12 schools were "disciplined for engaging in harassment or bullying" based on sex, compared to 0.3 percent of Black and Hispanic boys and 0.4 percent

of American Indian/Alaska Native boys. United States Government Accountability Office, *Report to Congressional Requesters, K-12 Education: Discipline Disparities for Black Students, Boys, and Students with Disabilities* 89 (Mar. 2018), https://www.gao.gov/assets/700/690828.pdf.

My friend Kayla Patrick, an education policy expert and statistics whiz, crunched some numbers for me and concluded that, nationally, 35 percent of Black boys were disciplined by their schools, which was three times the rate at which white boys were disciplined. That is twice the disparity related to sex-based misconduct.

None of this is to say we shouldn't be worried about race-based disparities for sexual harassment, even if they are worse for other misconduct. And I could believe that ameliorating discriminatory patterns may be particularly difficult for student discipline that depends on another student's allegation, since race will affect not only how a school responds to a report but also which reports classmates lodge in the first place—an issue process cannot cure.

Take Colgate University. The school was the subject of an antidiscrimination complaint with the Department of Education for mistreatment of students of color accused of sexual assault. Black and Asian students made up a disproportionate number of the forty-four students reported to Colgate for sexual assault over the three academic years between 2012 and 2015, fourteen of whom were referred to formal disciplinary hearings. Yet the department found no legal violation because it concluded Black and Asian students who were accused of sexual assault were not more likely than white students reported for the same offenses to be referred to a formal hearing or, if found responsible, expelled. See Closure Letter to Melissa Kagle from Anna Moretto Cramer, Department of Education, Apr. 19, 2017.

It's hard to draw any definite lessons from such a small number of cases. But the complaint against Colgate points to the issue of racially disparate *inputs* to a disciplinary system, which are harder to solve precisely because they can't be directly attributed to the school's policies or procedures. Racially disparate reporting patterns may result both from over-reporting of students of color due to racism in the student body and the under-reporting of white students due to their social dominance. Both are urgent issues, and neither is susceptible to an obvious legal intervention or solved by new procedures.

CHAPTER 13: THE ROOTS OF EXCEPTIONALISM

155   "inconsistent with due process for accused sex criminals": Graeme Wood, "Harvard's Feast of Grievance," *Atlantic*, May 15, 2019, https://www.theatlantic.com/ideas/archive/2019/05/ronald-sullivan-was-fired-harvard-does-it-matter/589471.

155   "sexual conduct and quasi-judicial tribunals": Judith Levine, "Is

Stealthing a Sex Crime?," *Boston Review*, June 21, 2017, http://bostonreview
.net/gender-sexuality/judith-levine-stealthing-sex-crime/.

156   **"turning {Keillor} into a criminal"**: Abby Ohlheiser, "Here's Why the
Garrison Keillor Allegations Stand Out," *Washington Post*, Dec. 1, 2017,
https://www.washingtonpost.com/news/arts-and-entertainment/wp
/2017/12/01/heres-why-the-garrison-keillor-allegations-stand-out/.

156   **Even before the 2011 letter, most schools:** Jake New, "Burden
of Proof in the Balance," *Inside Higher Ed*, Dec. 26, 2016, https://
www.insidehighered.com/news/2016/12/16/will-colleges-still-use
-preponderance-evidence-standard-if-2011-guidance-reversed.

156   **best balances the interests of both people:** William Kidder, "(En)forcing
a Foolish Consistency? A Critique and Comparative Analysis of the Trump
Administration's Proposed Standard of Evidence Regulation for Campus
Title IX Proceedings," *Journal of College and University Law* 45 (2020): 1.

156   **discipline can come with serious stakes:** I think this is particularly
true for students. My unscientific assumption is that expulsion is more
likely to have a profound effect on a person than termination is, especially since employers are, for legal reasons, often unable to disclose
the reasons a worker was fired. One possible compromise would be to
use the preponderance standard to come to any finding that bears on
the complainant's rights (for example, requiring the harasser to move
out of the victim's dorm, or suspending him until she graduates), but
to require clear and convincing evidence for punishment that does not
serve to protect the complainant's education, such as permanently expelling the harasser. That calculus, of course, ignores the threat the accused
might pose to other students upon his return, even if the victim has
since graduated.

156   **its use in student discipline is constitutional:** See, e.g., Doe v. Univ. of
Arkansas-Fayetteville, 974 F.3d 858, 868 (8th Cir. 2020) ("While there
is a substantial legal and policy debate about whether a more demanding
standard is appropriate . . . we do not think a higher standard of proof is
compelled by the Constitution. The preponderance standard 'is commonly
used in civil proceedings, even to decide matters of great importance.' . . .
As the district court observed, a civil action for sexual battery is governed
by a preponderance standard, despite the potential for damages and similar consequences for an accused's reputation. . . . Doe cites no authority
holding that due process requires a higher standard of proof in university
disciplinary proceedings or comparable civil actions. A heightened burden of proof may lessen the risk of erroneous deprivations for an accused,
but it also could frustrate legitimate governmental interests by increasing
the chance that a true victim of sexual assault is unable to secure redress
and a sexual predator is permitted to remain on campus. We conclude that
the choice between the competing standards of proof is within the range
of options available to a public university under the Constitution.").

156   **Even the Trump administration required schools:** See, e.g., Resolution

Agreement, Indep. Sch. Dist. No. 1 of Woods City, Oklahoma , OCR Case No. 07–15–1154, 9 (Sept. 28, 2017) (requiring school use preponderance standard for disability-based harassment), https://tinyurl.com/yak27ens; Resolution Agreement, BASIS Scottsdale, OCR Case No. 08–16–1676, 2 (Mar. 20, 2017) (requiring school use preponderance standard for racial harassment), https://tinyurl.com/y7kkzr66.

157   **"When Does a Watershed Become a Sex Panic?"**: Masha Gessen, "When Does a Watershed Become a Sex Panic?," *New Yorker*, Nov. 14, 2017, https://www.newyorker.com/news/our-columnists/when-does-a -watershed-become-a-sex-panic. Gessen's article is full of significant errors. For one, it inaccurately describes the preponderance standard as a mechanism to "shift the burden of proof from the accuser to the accused." That would, indeed, be an affront to fairness. But it is simply not true. Whether the standard is "preponderance" or "clear and convincing," it is the injured party who must provide evidence to meet that line. Gessen also wrongly identified the source of the policy as the Justice Department, rather than the Department of Education. That might seem like a petty quibble, but it speaks to how frequently high-profile writers opine on this subject without, it seems, doing basic research.

157   **"conflicts with due-process protections"**: American Association of University Professors, *The History, Uses, and Abuses of Title IX*, 2016, https://www.aaup.org/report/history-uses-and-abuses-title-ix.

157   **"a presumption of male guilt"**: Peter Berkowitz, "College Rape Accusations and the Presumption of Male Guilt," *Wall Street Journal*, Aug. 20, 2011, https://www.wsj.com/articles/SB10001424053111903596904576 516232905230642.

157   **sued Harvard for denying him tenure:** "Case Dismissed," *Harvard Magazine*, Sept.–Oct. 2003, https://web.archive.org/web/20071005205654 /http://www.harvardmagazine.com/on-line/090364.html; Mark Brodin and Michael Avery, *Handbook of Massachusetts Evidence* § 3.3.2 (8th ed. 2020).

157   **closer to that used in criminal trials:** Foundation for Individual Rights in Education, *Standard of Evidence Survey*, Oct. 28, 2011, https:// www.thefire.org/standard-of-evidence-survey-colleges-and-universities -respond-to-ocrs-new-mandate/.

157   **not only used for suits for money damages:** The preponderance standard is also used in civil lawsuits where the plaintiff seeks other outcomes, including what are known as "injunctions"—basically, a court order for the other side to do or not do something. The consequences of that injunction can be sweeping: a state might be required to reduce its prison population dramatically, or a business might be ordered to stop selling its product. The preponderance standard is also used for serious disciplinary matters like the revocation of professional licenses due to misconduct. See Kidder, "(En)forcing a Foolish Consistency?"

159   **"imposed upon without great care and vigilance"**: Matthew Hale,

The History of the Pleas of the Crown, vol. 1 (London: Professional Books, 1972 [1678]), 635.

159   **Hale's views were animated:** Peggy Reeves Sanday, *A Woman Scorned: Acquaintance Rape on Trial* (Berkeley: University of California Press, 1997), 58.

159   **"out to blackmail the man who seduced her":** Sanday, *A Woman Scorned*, 59.

159   **"giving defendants in witchcraft trials the same benefit":** Sanday, *A Woman Scorned*, 61–63.

159   **"entertained friends with jokes about it":** G. Geis, *Lord Hale, Witches, and Rape*, British Journal of Law and Society 5 (1978): 26–27, www.jstor .org/stable/1409846.

159   **more women were executed for witchcraft:** Sanday, *A Woman Scorned*, 63.

160   **the lowest of any capital crime:** Sanday, *A Woman Scorned*, 58.

160   **unusually suspicious of the charges before them:** People v. Rincon–Pineda, 538 P.2d 247, 254–55 (1975); A. Thomas Morris, "The Empirical, Historical and Legal Case Against the Cautionary Instruction: A Call for Legislative Reform," *Duke Law Journal* 1988 (1988): 154.

160   **"difficulty of determining the truth":** Model Penal Code § 213.6(4).

160   **amendments to the Model Penal Code's treatment:** American Law Institute, "Model Penal Code: Sexual Assault and Related Offenses," https://www.ali.org/projects/show/sexual-assault-and-related-offenses/ (as of December 8, 2020).

160   **stop requiring judges to echo Lord Hale's words:** See, e.g., Michelle J. Anderson, "The Legacy of the Prompt Complaint Requirement, Corroboration Requirement, and Cautionary Instructions on Campus Sexual Assault," *Boston University Law Review* 84 (2004): 945, 973–77.

161   **"fraud and narcotics transactions":** Rincon-Pineda, 538 P.2d at 254.

161   **effectively "he said, she said" situations:** Michelle Sharpe, "The Justice System Runs on Testimonial, 'He-Said She-Said' Evidence," Establishment, Jan. 8, 2019, https://theestablishment.co/the-justice-system -runs-on-testimonial-he-said-she-said-evidence/.

163   **converge on rates between 2 and 8 percent:** Lonsway et al., *False Reports*. The upper end of the range is slightly higher than the corresponding rate for some (though not all) other crimes, but derives from studies that applied less scrutiny to police classifications of reports. David Lisak et al., "False Allegations of Sexual Assault: An Analysis of Ten Years of Reported Cases," *Violence Against Women* 16 (2010): 1318, https://journals.sagepub.com/doi/10.1177/1077801210387747; Emily Moon, "False Reports of Sexual Assault are Rare. But Why Is There So Little Reliable Data About Them?," *Pacific Standard*, Oct. 7, 2018, https://psmag.com/news/false-reports-of-sexual-assault-are-rare-but -why-is-there-so-little-reliable-data-about-them.

One study came to a 10 percent rate by including reports filed by the alleged victims' relatives or boyfriends. If the study was limited to reports only from the putative victims themselves, the number drops to 6 percent. Lisak et al., "False Allegations of Sexual Assault: An Analysis of Ten Years of Reported Cases," 1324.

163   **significantly more likely to be sexually assaulted:** Cindy Dampier, "Your Son Is More Likely to Be Sexually Assaulted Than to Face False Allegations. Explaining the Fear of #HimToo," *Chicago Tribune*, Oct. 12, 2018, https://www.chicagotribune.com/lifestyles/ct-life-false-rape -allegations-20181011-story.html; Tyler Kingkade, "Males Are More Likely to Suffer Sexual Assault Than to Be Falsely Accused of It," *Huffington Post*, Dec. 8, 2014.

163   **1994 study by Eugene Kanin:** Eugene J. Kanin, "False Rape Allegations," *Archives of Sexual Behavior* 23 (1994): 81.

163   **"violates a cardinal rule of science":** David Lisak, "False Allegations of Rape: A Critique of Kanin," *Sexual Assault Report* 11 (2007): 1, quoted by Lonsway et al., *False Reports*.

163   **"the greater the scrutiny applied":** Lisak et al., "False Allegations of Sexual Assault," 1331.

164   **a then recent Pentagon study:** Rowan Scarborough, "False Sex Assault Reports Not as Rare as Reported, Studies Say," *Washington Times*, Oct. 7, 2018, https://apnews.com/b5c40b513448cfc1269d51d 923bb76f7.

164   **retained it, though, for sexual violence:** State v. Hill, 578 A.2d 370, 374–75 (N.J. Sup. Ct. 1990).

164   **all-male Utah Supreme Court postulated:** State v. Neel, 60 P. 510, 511 (Utah 1900).

164   **Supreme Court of Illinois reinforced:** People v. Lawler, 568 N.E.2d 895, 901 (Ill. 1991).

165   *three months* **for sexual offenses:** Model Penal Code § 213.6(4); Susan Estrich, "Rape," *Yale Law Journal* 95 (1986): 1087, 1139.

165   **except for murder, which has none:** Model Penal Code § 1.06.

165   **"The requirement of prompt complaint springs":** Model Penal Code § 213.6 comment at 421.

165   **"attentive to the problem of the vindictive, spurned woman":** Estrich, "Rape," 1150.

165   **Luckily, the states have outpaced the Model Penal Code:** Anderson, "The Legacy of the Prompt Complaint Requirement," 964–68.

165   **New York legislature in 1886:** Anderson, "The Legacy of the Prompt Complaint Requirement," at 956–57.

165   **corroboration was required only for the rape:** People v. Moore, 245 N.E.2d 710 (N.Y. 1969).

166   **"most women" have rape fantasies:** Note, "The Corroboration Rule and Crimes Accompanying a Rape," *University of Pennsylvania Law Review* 118 (1970): 458. In 1967, the *Columbia Law Review* published another article about the corroboration requirement, which opined on "the inordinate danger that innocent men will be convicted of rape."

Note, "Corroborating Charges of Rape," *Columbia Law Review* 67 (1967): 1137–38. "Surely the simplest, and perhaps the most important reason not to permit conviction for rape on the uncorroborated word of the prosecutrix is that that word is very often false," the author wrote without any citation to supporting evidence.

166   **"the man is powerless":** Davis v. State, 48 S.E. 180, 181–82 (Ga. 1904).

166   **in a rare moment of insight:** Hale, *The History of the Pleas of the Crown*, 633. The dissent to the same Georgia case points this out, citing William Blackstone, whose *Commentaries on the Laws of England* devoted significant space to Hale's views.

166   **"The unchaste (let us call it) mentality":** State v. Anderson, 137 N.W.2d 781 (1965).

167   **"all too frequently have an urge to fantasize":** United States v. Wiley, 492 F.2d 547, 550 (D.C. Cir. 1973) (internal quotation marks omitted). I find the concurrence to this opinion very interesting. There, progressive Chief Judge David L. Bazelon acknowledged feminist critiques of the corroboration rule. He also acknowledged that the usual justifications for the rule were unsupported by evidence, and seemed aware that this rule would be looked upon unfavorably by future generations of lawyers. And yet he nonetheless joined the majority opinion requiring corroboration.

167   **though only a handful of states today:** Benjamin Rachlin, "Who to Believe," *New Republic*, Dec. 3, 2018, https://newrepublic.com/article /152305/who-to-believe-sexual-assault; Kathleen Ronayne, "State Considers Requiring Corroboration in Sex Assault Cases," Associated Press, Jan. 17, 2017, https://apnews.com/94305d0b97a34eedbd77cd0332904 890; Anderson, "The Legacy of the Prompt Complaint Requirement," 968–73.

167   **"cultural dirt from the criminal law":** Anderson, "The Legacy of the Prompt Complaint Requirement," 950.

167   **That adjacent room includes institutional responses:** Anderson, "The Legacy of the Prompt Complaint Requirement," 950; Michelle J. Anderson, "Campus Sexual Assault Adjudication and Resistance to Reform," *Yale Law Journal* 125 (2016): 1940, 2000.

167   **We see it, unsubtly, in the "justifications":** See, e.g., Barclay Sutton Hendrix, "A Feather on One Side, A Brick on the Other: Tilting the Scale Against Males Accused of Sexual Assault in Campus Disciplinary Proceedings," *Georgia Law Review* 47 (2013): 591, 615–16 (claiming rape accusations "nearly always involve a 'he said, she said' dispute"); Stephen Henrick, "A Hostile Environment for Student Defendants: Title IX and Sexual Assault on College Campuses," *Northern Kentucky Law Review* 40 (2013): 49, 66 ("The evidence of what happened in a typical sexual assault case is usually murky and prone to an increased risk of erroneous conviction."); Berkowitz, "College Rape Accusations and the Presumption of Male Guilt."

168   "where erotic desire is involved": Berkowitz, "College Rape Accusa-
       tions and the Presumption of Male Guilt."

CHAPTER 14: EXCEPTIONS TO EXCEPTIONALISM

170   As Michelle Anderson has extensively documented: Anderson, "The
       Legacy of the Prompt Complaint Requirement," 950, 990–95.
171   submitted a list of fifteen witnesses: Anderson, "The Legacy of the
       Prompt Complaint Requirement," 991.
171   weren't allowed to tell their side of the story: Letter of Findings
       to Martha Minow from Joel J. Berner, Department of Education, Dec.
       30, 2014, https://www.clearinghouse.net/chDocs/public/ED-MA-0005
       -0001.pdf.
171   a new university-wide disciplinary system for sexual harassment:
       Resolution Agreement, Harvard Law School, Dec. 2014, https://www.
       clearinghouse.net/chDocs/public/ED-MA-0005-0002.pdf.; Harvard
       University, Procedures for Handling Complaints Involving Students
       Pursuant to the Sexual and Gender-Based Harassment Policy, 2014,
       https://hls.harvard.edu/content/uploads/2014/09/harvard_sexual_
       harassment_procedures_student1.pdf.
171   no live, adversarial hearing with cross-examination: Peer Dispute,
       Student Conduct Process, Harvard College Administrative Board, https://
       adboard.fas.harvard.edu/peer-dispute-0 (as of June 2020); Governance,
       Harvard University Graduate School of Arts and Sciences, https://gsas
       .harvard.edu/codes-conduct/governance (as of June 2020). Older copies
       on file with the author.
       One difference was that, for nonsexual grievances handled by the col-
       lege and Faculty of Arts and Sciences graduate schools, generally a group
       of people make a decision about whether the conduct occurred, while
       the default was for a single person to make the decision when it came to
       sexual harassment. Some believe that the latter alternative is better for
       victims, because it allows them to recount their experiences privately. I
       am not convinced. Plenty of victim-advocates think this model is faulty,
       too, because they are just as likely to be hurt by a bad investigator. I'd
       prefer a multi-person decision. That said, there is nothing inherently
       unfair about one person, rather than a group, making a factual decision.
       Trial-level judges do it all the time.
171   be "sufficiently persuaded": Brief in Support of Defendants' Memo-
       randum in Support of Their Motion to Dismiss the Complaint, Sonoiki
       v. Harvard University et al., ECF No. 24 at 13.
171   used live hearings with cross-examination: Harvard Law School Hand-
       book of Academic Policies 2020–2021, Procedures for Disciplinary Cases,
       https://hls.harvard.edu/dept/academics/handbook/rules-relating-to-law
       -school-studies/xii-administrative-board/b-procedures-for-disciplinary
       -cases-except-for-cases-covered-under-the-law-schools-interim-sexual

-harassment-policies-and-procedures-see-appendix-viii/. Older policies on file with the author.

172   **public letter in the *Boston Globe*:** These criticisms were: "[1] The absence of any adequate opportunity to discover the facts charged and to confront witnesses and present a defense at an adversary hearing; [2] The lodging of the functions of investigation, prosecution, fact-finding, and appellate review in one office, and the fact that that office is itself a Title IX compliance office rather than an entity that could be considered structurally impartial; [3] The failure to ensure adequate [legal] representation for the accused, particularly for students unable to afford representation." Elizabeth Bartholet et al., "Rethink Harvard's Sexual Harassment Policy," *Boston Globe*, Oct. 14, 2014, https://www.bostonglobe.com/opinion/2014/10/14/rethink-harvard-sexual-harassment-policy/HFDDiZN7nU2UwuUuWMnqbM/story.html. Despite public commentary to the contrary, none of the specific procedures the professors were concerned about had been required by the Department of Education.

172   **Anderson, the rape law scholar, notes:** Anderson, "Campus Sexual Assault Adjudication," 1985.

172   **legal theorist Katharine Baker points out:** Katharine A. Baker, "Campus Misconduct, Sexual Harm and Appropriate Process: The Essential Sexuality of It All," *Journal of Legal Education* 66 (2017): 4.

173   **One signatory, Jeannie Suk Gersen:** There was no legal impediment to Harvard Law correcting this asymmetry by using the same procedures and standards for racial harassment that it was, by university policy, required to use for sexual harassment.

173   **in that way, anti-exceptional:** One demand was exceptional even in the context of the law school. The professors demanded that law students facing discipline for sexual allegations be provided free counsel; this was not guaranteed for students facing discipline for nonsexual harms, though the law school says it will "attempt to assist a student who needs and desires but cannot afford counsel." See Harvard Law School Handbook of Academic Policies, 90; Anderson, "Campus Sexual Assault Adjudication," 1985.

173   **much more like its usual discipline process:** HLS Sexual Harassment Resources and Procedures for Students, Dec. 18, 2014, https://hls.harvard.edu/content/uploads/2019/08/HLS-Student-Procedure-Re-Posted-8-15-19-accessible.pdf.

173   **allies cited the Harvard Law episode:** E.g., Nondiscrimination on the Basis of Sex in Education Programs or Activities Receiving Federal Financial Assistance, 83 *Fed. Reg.* 61,462, 61,464 at nn.2 & 3 (Proposed Nov. 29, 2018), https://www.govinfo.gov/content/pkg/FR-2018-11-29/pdf/2018-25314.pdf; George Leef, "New Title IX Regulations Restore Due Process—But There's a Battle Ahead," James G. Martin Center, May 15, 2020, https://www.jamesgmartin.

center/2020/05/new-title-ix-regulations-restore-due-process-but-theres-a-battle-ahead/; KC Johnson, "Four Reasons to Support the DeVos Title IX Rewrite," *Minding the Campus*, Feb. 6, 2019, https://www.mindingthecampus.org/2019/02/06/four-reasons-to-support-the-devos-title-ix-rewrite; Betsy Devos, "Secretary DeVos Prepared Remarks on Title IX Enforcement," U.S. Department of Education, Sept. 7, 2017, https://www.ed.gov/news/speeches/secretary-devos-prepared-remarks-title-ix-enforcement.

173 **so it seemed at first glance:** The letter writers did not, in fact, support the full DeVos regulations, which prohibited some parts of the new process they designed after their successful protest. Three of the signatories to the *Boston Globe* letter submitted a comment to the Education Department explaining that while they agreed with parts of the new regulations, they disagreed with others, including the direct cross-examination requirement and the narrow definition of sexual harassment. Simon C. Chu and Iris M. Lewis, "Harvard Law School Professors Issue Comment on Title IX Changes," *Harvard Crimson*, Jan. 31, 2019, https://www.thecrimson.com/article/2019/1/31/devos-faculty-members-respond/.

175 **Not all sexual harassment victims find it life-changing:** For feminist criticisms of exceptionalizing rape as a uniquely devastating harm, see, e.g., Charlotte Shane, "Live Through This," *New Inquiry*, July 26, 2012, http://thenewinquiry.com/essays/live-through-this/ ("It is unforgivable to publicly question the mythologizing of rape's status as the ruination of all women who go through it."); Jenny Diski, "Diary: Rape-Rape," *London Review of Books* 31 (Nov. 5, 2009): 52, http://www.lrb.co.uk/v31/n21/jenny-diski/diary ("I didn't think that it was the most terrible thing that had ever happened to me. It was a very unpleasant experience, it hurt and I was trapped. But I had no sense that I was especially violated by the rape itself, not more than I would have been by any attack on my person and freedom. In 1961 it didn't go without saying that to be penetrated against one's will was a kind of spiritual murder.").

CHAPTER 15: UGLY HISTORIES

177 **Chief Judge David L. Bazelon:** United States v. Wiley, 492 F.2d 547, 555–56 (D.C. Cir. 1973) (Bazelon, C.J., concurring).

178 **influential defenders of DeVos's rules:** See, e.g., Bader, Letter to the Editor; Dalmia, "In Defense of Betsy DeVos' Title IX Plan"; Lara Bazelon, "I'm a Democrat and a Feminist. And I Support Betsy DeVos's Title IX Reforms," *New York Times*, December 4, 2018, https://www.nytimes.com/2018/12/04/opinion/-title-ix-devos-democrat-feminist.html. See also Madison Pauly, "It's Hard Enough for Student Sexual Assault Survivors. Missouri Lawmakers Are Trying to Make It Even Worse," *Mother Jones*, April 1, 2019, https://www.motherjones.com/politics/2019/04/missouri-student-sexual-assault-title-ix-mcintosh-steward/, noting

defense of exceptionalist Missouri bill on the basis of a unique threat to Black men. Notably, none of these defenses suggest expanding proposed rights for accused harassers to students accused of other misconduct. Relatedly, critiques that post–Dear Colleague Letter, pre-DeVos disciplinary procedures for sexual harassment disproportionately affected men of color were nearly always divorced from any concern about, or even acknowledgment of, race discrimination in student discipline writ large. See, e.g., Emily Yoffe, "The Question of Race in Campus Sexual-Assault Cases," *Atlantic*, Sept. 11, 2017.

178 **that research is limited:** Student discipline rates were discussed in chapter 12. That data is self-reported by K-12 schools, and we lack analogous national data for higher education or employment. For discussion of racial disparities in convictions of sex offenses, see Judith Levine and Erica Meiners, "Are Sex Offenders White?," *Counterpunch*, Apr. 11, 2016, https://www.counterpunch.org/2016/04/11/are-sex -offenders-white.

179 **"Lynching was merely an excuse":** Chris Linder, "Reexamining Our Roots: A History of Racism and Antirape Activism" in *Intersections of Identity and Sexual Violence on Campus: Centering Minoritized Students' Experience,* eds. Jessica C. Harris and Chris Linder (Sterling, VA: Stylus Publishing, 2017), chapter 3; see also Crystal Nicole Feimster, *Southern Horrors: Women and the Politics of Rape and Lynching* (Cambridge, MA: Harvard University Press, 2009).

179 **"The closer a Negro got to the ballot box":** E. C. L. Adams and R. G. O'Meally, *Tales of the Congaree* (Chapel Hill: University of North Carolina Press, 2014), lxi.

179 **sex between Black men and white women was presumptively criminal:** Dorsey v. State, 34 S.E. 135, 136–37 (Ga. 1899); see also Estelle B. Freedman, *Redefining Rape: Sexual Violence in the Era of Suffrage and Segregation* (Cambridge, MA: Harvard University Press, 2013), 94.

180 **fifteen-year-old Willie James Howard:** Gilbert King, *Devil in the Grove: Thurgood Marshall, the Groveland Boys, and the Dawn of a New America* (New York: Harper, 2012).

180 **her claim was "not true":** Richard Pérez-Peña, "Woman Linked to 1955 Emmett Till Murder Tells Historian Her Claims Were False," *New York Times*, Jan. 27, 2017, https://www.nytimes.com/2017/01/27/us /emmett-till-lynching-carolyn-bryant-donham.html.

180 **still overrepresented on sex offender registries:** Levine and Meiners, "Are Sex Offenders White?"

180 **Black defendants are wrongfully convicted of rape:** Samuel R. Gross, Maurice Possley, and Klara Stephens, "Race and Wrongful Convictions in the United States," National Registry of Exonerations, Newkirk Center for Science and Society 2017, 11–15, https://repository.law .umich.edu/other/122/. Surprisingly, there is some data that Black people arrested for sexual assault are less likely to be convicted and receive

shorter sentences than their white counterparts (though that isn't true for other violent crimes). One explanation might be that police arrest Black people for sexual assault on thinner evidence than they arrest white people. Another is that because rape is overwhelmingly intra-racial, these discrepancies may reflect disparate concern for Black and white victims. Christopher D. Maxwell, Amanda L. Robinson, and Lori A. Post, "The Impact of Race on the Adjudication of Sexual Assault and Other Violent Crimes," *Journal of Criminal Justice* 31 (2003): 523, 533–34, https://doi .org/10.1016/j.jcrimjus.2003.08.005.

181   **as of 2019, Trump remained unshaken:** Jan Ransom, "Trump Will Not Apologize for Calling for Death Penalty over Central Park Five," *New York Times*, June 18, 2019, https://www.nytimes.com/2019/06/18 /nyregion/central-park-five-trump.html.

181   **very same white men who lynched Black men:** Feimster, *Southern Horrors*, 37 (citing Wells's memoir *Crusade for Justice*).

181   **KKK used the gang rape of Black women:** Carolyn M. West and Kalimah Johnson, "Sexual Violence in the Lives of African American Women," VAWnet.org, Mar. 2013, https://vawnet.org/sites/default /files/materials/files/2016-09/AR_SVAAWomenRevised.pdf.

181   **"practically unheard of":** Sharon Block, *Rape and Sexual Power in Early America* (Chapel Hill: University of North Carolina Press, 2006), 65.

181   **not legally permitted to even file a rape charge:** Crystal N. Feimster, "When Black Women Reclaimed Their Bodies," *Slate*, Feb. 2, 2018, https://slate.com/human-interest/2018/02/how-formerly-enslaved-black -women-fought-for-human-dignity-and-sexual-justice.html.

182   **"a trespass against the slave woman's master":** Peter W. Bardaglio, "Rape and the Law in the Old South: 'Calculated to Excite Indignation in Every Heart,'" *Journal of Southern History* 60 (1994): 749, 756.

182   **"The crime of rape does not exist":** Bardaglio, "Rape and the Law in the Old South," 758–59 (quoting George [a Slave] v. the State, 37 Miss., 316 [1859]).

182   **declined to place any restrictions on white men's legal right:** Jennifer Wriggins, "Rape, Racism, and the Law," *Harvard Women's Law Journal* 6 (1983): 103, 118 n.93.

182   **judge held that a "master":** "Sexual Exploitation of Black Women," Equal Justice Initiative, Aug. 8, 2016, https://eji.org/news/history-racial -injustice-sexual-exploitation-black-women/.

182   **were lynched by mobs:** Freedman, *Redefining Rape*, 98.

182   **"traded sex for candy":** Brittany Slatton and April Richard, "Black Women's Experiences of Sexual Assault and Disclosure: Insights from the Margins," *Sociology Compass* 14 (2020); Freedman, *Redefining Rape*, 87.

183   **"from 25 cents to $1":** L. F. Litwack, *Trouble in Mind: Black Southerners in the Age of Jim Crow* (New York: Knopf, 1998), 269.

183   **less likely to be chaste than white women:** Darci E. Burrell, "Myth,

Stereotype, and the Rape of Black Women," *UCLA Women's Law Journal* 4 (1993): 87, 93, and n.31.

183 **unusually untrustworthy and unusually promiscuous:** Comment, "Police Discretion and the Judgment That a Crime Has Been Committed: Rape in Philadelphia," *University of Pennsylvania Law Review* 117 (1968): 277, 304; see also Wiggins, *Rape, Racism, and the Law*, 122.

183 **groundwork for what became the civil rights movement:** Danielle L. McGuire, *At the Dark End of the Street: Black Women, Rape, and Resistance—A New History of the Civil Rights Movement from Rosa Parks to the Rise of Black Power* (New York: Vintage Books, 2011); Feimster, *Southern Horrors*.

183 **In 1944, Recy Taylor:** Allyson Hobbs, "One Year of #MeToo: The Legacy of Black Women's Testimonies," *New Yorker*, Oct. 10, 2018, https:// www.newyorker.com/culture/personal-history/one-year-of-metoo-the -legacy-of-black-womens-testimonies.

183 **case never went to trial:** Sewell Chan, "Recy Taylor, Who Fought for Justice After a 1944 Rape, Dies at 97," *New York Times*, Dec. 29, 2017, https://www.nytimes.com/2017/12/29/obituaries/recy-taylor-alabama -rape-victim-dead.html.

183 **direct predecessors of the Montgomery bus boycotts:** McGuire, *At the Dark End of the Street*.

183 *The Rape of Recy Taylor*: Hobbs, "One Year of #MeToo."

184 **stereotypes that persist today:** See, e.g., Burrell, "Myth, Stereotype, and the Rape of Black Women," 92–93; Wiggins, *Rape, Racism, and the Law*, 122.

184 **refused to cooperate with prosecutors:** Elizabeth A. Harris and Robert Chiarito, "In Turnabout, a Key Witness Is Cooperating in R. Kelly Case," *New York Times*, July 16, 2019, https://www.nytimes.com/2019 /07/16/arts/music/r-kelly-sexual-assault-tape.html.

185 **Audience dollars and tax dollars:** Motolani Alake, "Meet Oronike Odeleye, the Co-founder of the #MuteRKelly Campaign," *Pulse*, Aug. 16, 2018, https://www.pulse.ng/gist/profile-meet-oronike-odeleye-the -co-founder-of-the-muterkelly-campaign/pj2shcj.

185 **an ill-advised interview with Gayle King:** Elizabeth A. Harris, "How Gayle King Kept Her Cool in the R. Kelly Interview," *New York Times*, Mar. 8, 2019, https://www.nytimes.com/2019/03/08/arts/gayle-king-r -kelly-interview.html.

185 **idea that Black girls are "fast":** Saida Grundy, "The Flawed Logic of R. Kelly's Most Unlikely Supporters," *Atlantic*, Jan. 10, 2019, https://www .theatlantic.com/entertainment/archive/2019/01/why-some-women-still -support-r-kelly/579985/.

186 **"a knee-jerk reaction to protect Black men":** Terry Gross, "'Surviving R. Kelly' Producer Dream Hampton Takes On Ecosystem That Supported the Star," NPR, Feb. 20, 2019, https://www.npr.org/2019/02 /20/695083431/surviving-r-kelly-producer-dream-hampton-takes-on -ecosystem-that-s-supported-him/.

186   "'Save Our Brotha' ('SOB') playbook": Kimberlé Williams Crenshaw, "I Believe I Can Lie," *Baffler*, Jan. 17, 2019, https://thebaffler.com/latest /i-believe-i-can-lie-crenshaw.

187   "a white preoccupation incompatible with antiracism": Kimberlé Crenshaw, "We Still Haven't Learned from Anita Hill's Testimony," *New York Times*, September 27, 2018, https://www.nytimes.com/2018/09 /27/opinion/anita-hill-clarence-thomas-brett-kavanaugh-christine-ford .html.

187   "they're slipping through the cracks": Nia Evans, "Dear Betsy DeVos: Fighting for Survivors of Sexual Violence Is a Racial Justice Fight," Feministing, Dec. 15, 2017, http://feministing.com/2017/12/15/dear -betsy-devos-fighting-for-survivors-of-sexual-violence-is-a-racial-justice -fight/.

187   "rendering Black sexual assault survivors invisible": Wagatwe Wanjuki, "How Betsy DeVos' Proposed Title IX Changes Would Hurt Black Campus Rape Survivors," Medium, Jan. 30, 2019, https://medium.com /@wagatwe/how-betsy-devos-proposed-title-ix-changes-would-hurt -black-campus-rape-survivors-46652869b06f.

187   Lara Bazelon, a lawyer and professor: Bazelon, "I'm a Democrat and a Feminist. And I Support Betsy DeVos's Title IX Reforms."

188   letter to the editor revealed: Amelia W., Letter to the Editor, *New York Times*, December 11, 2018, https://www.nytimes.com/2018/12/11/ opinion/letters/colleges-sexual-assault.html.

188   "tend to omit race in the discussions of accusers": Nancy Chi Cantalupo, "And Even More of Us Are Brave: Intersectionality & Sexual Harassment of Women Students of Color," *Harvard Journal of Law & Gender* 42, no. 1 (2019): 18.

188   "race-less (and implicitly white) group of accusers": Deborah L. Brake, "Fighting the Rape Culture Wars Through the Preponderance of the Evidence Standard," *Montana Law Review* 78 (2017): 109, https:// scholarship.law.umt.edu/mlr/vol78/iss1/6/.

188   erasure of survivors of color: Wagatwe Wanjuki (@wagatwe), Twitter, Dec. 5, 2018, 10:24 a.m., https://twitter.com/wagatwe/status /1070338207923884032. She points out, too, that the most prominent voices criticizing Title IX protections as bad for Black men are white women, like Bazelon and the writer Emily Yoffe. Wagatwe Wanjuki (@wagatwe), Twitter, Dec. 5, 2018, 10:19 a.m., https://twitter .com/wagatwe/status/1070336980603424773.

188   knew about the predation: Grace Elletson, "Morehouse Is Criticized— Again—for Its Handling of Sexual Misconduct," *Chronicle of Higher Education*, July 22, 2019, https://www.chronicle.com/article/Morehouse-Is -Criticized-/246749.

189   "Black men are insatiable": Tommy J. Curry, "Expendables for Whom: Terry Crews and the Erasure of Black Male Victims of Sexual Assault and Rape," *Women's Studies in Communication* 42 (2019): 287.

189   "'240 lbs. Black Man stomps out Hollywood Honcho'": Gwilym
       Mumford, "Actor Terry Crews: I Was Sexually Assaulted by Hollywood
       Executive," *Guardian*, Oct. 11, 2017, https://www.theguardian.com
       /film/2017/oct/11/actor-terry-crews-sexually-assaulted-by-hollywood
       -executive.

189   **queer people are also at tremendous risk:** American law and ethics
       have historically failed to distinguish between sexually harmful behav-
       ior, like rape, and consensual sex that deviates from mainstream, vanilla
       expectations, like gay sex or kink. This toxic conflation of "deviant" sex
       with violent sex contributed to sexually oppressive legal regimes, often
       motivated—at least ostensibly—by fears about sexual violence. Gayle
       Rubin, "Thinking Sex: Notes for a Radical Theory of the Politics of Sex-
       uality" in *Culture, Society and Sexuality: A Reader*, eds. Richard Parker and
       Peter Aggleton (New York: Routledge, 2007), 144. See also Scott De
       Orio, "Punishing Queer Sexuality in the Age of LGBT Rights" (PhD
       diss., University of Michigan, 2017), 25, https://deepblue.lib.umich.edu
       /bitstream/handle/2027.42/138757/sadeorio_1.pdf; Tamara Rice Lave,
       "Only Yesterday: The Rise and Fall of Twentieth Century Sexual Psycho-
       path Laws," *Louisiana Law Review* 69 (2009): 549; Edwin H. Sutherland,
       "The Sexual Psychopath Laws," *Journal of Criminal Law and Criminology*
       40 (1949–50): 543; Group for the Advancement of Psychiatry, Commit-
       tee on Psychiatry and Law, *Psychiatry and Sex Psychopath Legislation: The
       30s to the 80s* (1977).
           In light of this history, some now worry that institutional efforts to
       address sexual harassment may end up targeting queer people dispropor-
       tionately. See, e.g., Lisa Duggan, "Bad Girls: On Being the Accused,"
       Bully Bloggers, Dec. 21, 2017, https://bullybloggers.wordpress.com
       /2017/12/21/bad-girls-on-being-the-accused/. Yet queer people are also
       at tremendous risk for sexual victimization from which they will need
       protection from institutions. Nearly half of bisexual women have been
       raped, according to the Centers for Disease Control and Prevention's
       findings, compared to 17 percent of straight women. *NISVS: An Overview
       of 2010 Findings on Victimization by Sexual Orientation*, CDC, https://www
       .cdc.gov/violenceprevention/pdf/cdc_nisvs_victimization_final-a.pdf.
       Gay and bisexual men are more than five times as likely to be raped in
       adulthood as heterosexual men. Kimberly F. Balsam et al., "Victimiza-
       tion over the Life Span: A Comparison of Lesbian, Gay, Bisexual, and
       Heterosexual Siblings," *Journal of Consulting and Clinical Psychology*
       73 (2005): 477. This violence is often used as a homophobic tool. That
       is perhaps clearest from the long history of so-called corrective rape, sexual
       assaults meant to "turn" the victim straight. One scholar writes, "The
       rapist believes that his act of corrective rape is not only the victim's fault
       because if she chose to behave differently, she would not have to suf-
       fer, but also that the act is in the victim's interest." Sarah Doan-Minh,
       "Corrective Rape: An Extreme Manifestation of Discrimination and the

State's Complicity in Sexual Violence," *Hastings Women's Law Journal* 30 (2019): 167. She gets, as one survivor of corrective rape recounted, "a real fuck from real men." Consuelo Rivera-Fuentes and Linda Birke, "Talking with/in Pain: Reflections on Bodies Under Torture," *Women's Studies International Forum* 24 (2001): 653, 663.

190   **"more believable but also more tragic and compelling"**: Jessica C. Harris, "Center Women of Color in the Discourse on Sexual Violence on College Campuses" in *Intersections of Identity and Sexual Violence on Campus*.

190   **"clear and convincing"** victims: Wanjuki, "How Betsy DeVos' Proposed Title IX Changes Would Hurt Black Campus Rape Survivors"; Brake, "Fighting the Rape Culture Wars Through the Preponderance of the Evidence Standard," 137; see also Ruth Lawlor, "How the Trump Administration's Title IX Proposals Threaten to Undo #MeToo," *Washington Post*, Feb. 4, 2019, https://www.washingtonpost.com/outlook/2019/02/04/how-trump-administrations-title-ix-proposals-threaten-undo-metoo/.

CHAPTER 16: OF MEN'S RIGHTS AND FAMOUS MEN

196   **"indentured servants to a malicious matriarchy"**: Michael S. Kimmel, *Angry White Men: American Masculinity at the End of an Era* (New York: Nation Books, 2017).

196   **gender pay gap is nonexistent**: This is untrue, according to economists. Niamh McIntyre, "Gender Pay Gap Figures: Debunking the Myths," *Guardian*, Apr. 5, 2019, https://www.theguardian.com/world/2019/apr/05/gender-pay-gap-figures-debunking-the-myths.

196   **as much domestic labor as their wives**: Untrue, sociologists show. Pew Research Center, "Americans' Time at Paid Work, Housework, Child Care, 1965 to 2011," https://www.pewsocialtrends.org/2013/03/14/chapter-5-americans-time-at-paid-work-housework-child-care-1965-to-2011/; Claire Cain Miller, "Young Men Embrace Gender Equality, but They Still Don't Vacuum," *New York Times*, February 11, 2020, https://www.nytimes.com/2020/02/11/upshot/gender-roles-housework.html.

196   **women are equal perpetrators**: Also untrue. Michael S. Kimmel, "'Gender Symmetry' in Domestic Violence: A Substantive and Methodological Research Review," *Violence Against Women* 8 (2002): 1332.

196   **Post-*Roe*, women gained control**: "Male supremacy," Southern Policy Law Center, https://www.splcenter.org/fighting-hate/extremist-files/ideology/male-supremacy, as of June 11, 2020.

197   **"Two firefighters died"**: Warren Farrell, *The Myth of Male Power: Why Men Are the Disposable Sex* (New York: Berkley Books, 2001).

197   **"There is now a second sexism"**: Arthur Goldwag, "Men's Rights Activists Battle 'Misandry' on College Campuses," Hatewatch, Southern Poverty Law Center, Dec. 18, 2013, https://www.splcenter.org/hatewatch/2013/12/18/men%E2%80%99s-rights-activists-battle-%E2%80%98misandry%E2%80%99-college-campuses.

197   "male studies," a right-wing discipline: Charles McGrath, "The Study
       of Man (or Males)," *New York Times*, Jan. 7, 2011, https://www.nytimes
       .com/2011/01/09/education/09men-t.html; Miles Groth, "Prof. Miles
       Groth Explains Need for Men's Studies," Wagner College Newsroom,
       Feb. 28, 2010, https://wagner.edu/newsroom/node-510.

197   "history of human beings who are male": Groth, "Prof. Miles Groth
       Explains Need for Men's Studies." But see Edward Gibbon, *The History
       of the Decline and Fall of the Roman Empire* (1776–1789).

197   "a lazy and incompetent Latina": Nicole Hong, Mihir Zaveri, and
       William K. Rashbaum, "Inside the Violent and Misogynistic World
       of Roy Den Hollander," *New York Times*, July 26, 2020, https://www
       .nytimes.com/2020/07/26/nyregion/roy-den-hollander-judge.html.

197   "a male-only chastity belt": Pamela Warrick, "A New Role for Men:
       Victim: Former Feminist Warren Farrell Says He's Sick and Tired of
       Guys Getting Bashed. 'Male Power,' He Proclaims, Is Just a Myth," *Los
       Angeles Times*, Aug. 9, 1993, https://www.latimes.com/archives/la-xpm
       -1993-08-09-vw-22148-story.html.

197   thousands of innocent men to prison: "False Accusations of Rape,"
       National Coalition For Men, Jan. 11, 2009, https://ncfm.org/2009/01
       /news/issues/false-accusations/.

198   "brainwashed public cheers it all on": Paul Elam, "Jury Duty at a
       Rape Trial? Acquit!," *A Voice for Men*, July 20, 2010, https://archive.is
       /TGaGX#selection-483.37–483.52.

198   only a third were expelled: Tyler Kingkade, "Fewer Than One-Third
       of Campus Sexual Assault Cases Result in Expulsion," *Huffington Post*,
       Dec. 6, 2017, https://www.huffpost.com/entry/campus-sexual-assault_n
       _5888742.

198   "hypocrisy [that] borders on treason": Paul Elam, "The Death of
       Due Process for Males in Higher Education," *A Voice for Men*, Aug. 26,
       2011, https://avoiceformen.com/government-tyranny/the-death-of-due
       -process-for-males-in-higher-education/.

198   Farrell later concurred, citing the preponderance standard: Warren
       Farrell, "Why This Is a Very Scary Time for Young Men," *Minding the
       Campus*, Nov. 6, 2018, https://www.mindingthecampus.org/2018/11/06
       /why-this-is-a-very-scary-time-for-young-men/.

198   "the system is rigged" against men: Elam, "Jury Duty at a Rape Trial?
       Acquit!"

198   "Voting not guilty on any charge": Elam, "Jury Duty at a Rape Trial?
       Acquit!"

199   who are "false accusers": Ted Scheinbar, "Silencing Women: Inside the
       National Coalition for Men," *Pacific Standard*, Nov. 12, 2014, https://
       psmag.com/news/silencing-women-inside-national-coalition-men-rape
       -sexual-assault-harry-crouch-94284.

199   shorter identifier "this cunt": The Beat Man, "Suspected False Rape
       Accuser Alexandra Brodsky: 'Campus Sexual Assault Cases Should Not

Be Turned Over to the Police,'" Living in Anglo-America, Mar. 15, 2015, https://angloamerica101.wordpress.com/2015/03/15/suspected-false -rape-accuser-alexandra-brodsky-campus-sexual-assault-cases-should -not-be-turned-over-to-the-police/.

199 **first and foremost a dog whistle:** Cantalupo, "Dog Whistles and Beach-heads," 303.

199 **"if she hadn't aggravated him":** Scheinbar, "Silencing Women: Inside the National Coalition For Men."

199 **decriminalizing rape on private property:** Roosh V, "How to Stop Rape," Feb. 16, 2015, https://www.rooshv.com/how-to-stop-rape.

199 **"Bash a Violent Bitch Month":** Paul Elam, "October Is the Fifth Annual Bash a Violent Bitch Month," *A Voice for Men*, Sept. 30, 2015, https://avoiceformen.com/featured/october-is-the-fifth-annual-bash-a -violent-bitch-month/.

200 **"loses a wallet full of cash":** Paul Elam, "Challenging the Etiology of Rape," *A Voice For Men*, Nov. 14, 2020, https://archive.fo/eIlgf#selection -623.8–631.178.

200 **a *Nation* exposé uncovered:** Hélène Barthélemy, "How Men's Rights Groups Helped Rewrite Regulations on Campus Rape," *Nation*, Aug. 14, 2020, https://www.thenation.com/article/politics/betsy-devos-title -ix-mens-rights/.

200 **Bill Barr, blurbed a book:** Heidi Przybyla, "Barr Praised 2017 Book That Claims Colleges Unfairly Went After Male Students Accused of Sexual Assault," NBC News, Sept. 19, 2019, https://www.nbcnews.com /politics/justice-department/barr-praised-2017-book-claims-colleges -unfairly-went-after-male-n1056141.

201 **"you're automatically guilty":** Tovia Smith, "On #MeToo, Americans More Divided by Party Than Gender," NPR, Oct. 31, 2018, https://www .npr.org/2018/10/31/662178315/on-metoo-americans-more-divided-by -party-than-gender.

201 **women "are doing great":** Philip Bump, "Trump Says It's 'a Very Scary Time' for Young Men—but That Women Are 'Doing Great,'" *Washington Post*, Oct. 2, 2018, https://www.washingtonpost.com/politics/2018 /10/02/trump-says-its-very-scary-time-young-men-that-women-are -doing-great/.

201 **ran through standard MRA talking points:** Farrell, "Why This Is a Very Scary Time for Young Men."

202 **"No one's perfect," he explained:** Smith, "On #MeToo, Americans More Divided by Party Than Gender."

202 **long history of left-wing apologists and enablers:** Linda Hirshman, *Reckoning: The Epic Battle Against Sexual Abuse and Harassment* (Boston: Houghton Mifflin Harcourt, 2019).

202 **sanitizing language of due process:** These actors' invention of a new, less obviously objectionable rationale for their long-standing position—that men should be allowed to hurt women without consequence—is

reminiscent of a dynamic Reva Siegel has diagnosed and dubbed "preservation through transformation." See Reva B. Siegel, "'The Rule of Love': Wife Beating as Prerogative and Privacy," *Yale Law Journal* 105 (1996): 2117.

202 **"I can't and won't point fingers"**: Brady MacDonald, "So Who Has Dared to Defend Harvey Weinstein?," *Los Angeles Times*, Oct. 16, 2017, https://www.latimes.com/entertainment/movies/la-et-mn-harvey-weinstein-defenders-20171013-story.html.

203 **compared him to Freddy Krueger**: Singh, "'Freddy Krueger in the Room.'"

203 **they had feared reprisal**: Melena Ryzik, Cara Buckley, and Jodi Kantor, "Louis C.K. Is Accused by 5 Women of Sexual Misconduct," *New York Times*, Nov. 9, 2017, https://www.nytimes.com/2017/11/09/arts/television/louis-ck-sexual-misconduct.html.

203 **"I will now step back"**: Louis C.K., "Louis C.K. Responds to Accusations: 'These Stories Are True,'" *New York Times*, Nov. 10, 2017, https://www.nytimes.com/2017/11/10/arts/television/louis-ck-statement.html.

204 **did not address the reason for his absence**: Interrobang Staff, "Louis C.K.'s Return to the Cellar Makes Headlines Everywhere and None of Them Are Happy He's Back," Interrobang, Aug. 28, 2018, https://theinterrobang.com/louis-c-k-s-return-cellar-makes-headlines-everywhere/.

204 **"one biased inconsistent mess"**: Interrobang Staff, "Louis C.K.'s Return to the Cellar Makes Headlines Everywhere and None of Them Are Happy He's Back."

CHAPTER 17: THE PEOPLE WHO WANT TO BRING YOU MANDATORY REFERRAL

206 **"a lightning rod around social issues"**: Kingkade, "The Men's Man."

207 **"My advice is to shut down this office"**: Kingkade, "The Men's Man."

208 **recognized as a sexual assault**: Kathryn Joyce, "The Takedown of Title IX," *New York Times*, Dec. 5, 2017, https://www.nytimes.com/2017/12/05/magazine/the-takedown-of-title-ix.html.

209 **The language is worth noting**: Melissa Block, "The Racially Charged Meaning Behind the Word 'Thug,'" *All Things Considered*, April 30, 2015, https://www.npr.org/2015/04/30/403362626/the-racially-charged-meaning-behind-the-word-thug.

210 **"That's where we are at Tech"**: Jim Galloway, "A Georgia Tech Fraternity Fight Spills into the State Capitol," *Atlanta Journal-Constitution*, Jan. 23, 2016, https://www.ajc.com/blog/politics/georgia-tech-fraternity-fight-spills-into-the-state-capitol/Y86xl0zdsnHaJsrjHocU3L/.

210 **more than two-thirds male**: Georgia Institute of Technology, *Complete College Georgia 2016 Status Report*, Oct. 28, 2016, https://oue

.gatech.edu/sites/default/files/CCG%20Status%20Report%202016%20 FINAL%20Georgia%20Tech.pdf.

210 **"don't come looking to us for money":** Kingkade, "The Men's Man."

211 **until there is a conviction or guilty plea:** Alexandra Brodsky, "Against Taking Rape 'Seriously': The Case Against Mandatory Referral Laws for Campus Gender Violence," *Harvard Civil Rights-Civil Liberties Law Review* 53 (2018): 131.

211 **seem to place them in a *worse* position:** A high priority for students facing both school and criminal proceedings at once is avoiding incriminating themselves for purposes of one in an attempt to defend against charges in the other. There are ways to ameliorate those concerns. Plenty of schools have instituted rules whereby disciplinarians will not hold an accused student's silence against him if he also faces criminal charges, for example. That's an idea borrowed from civil trials. Usually juries can make what is called an "adverse inference" from a civil defendant's silence, meaning that his refusal to speak reflects poorly on his case. But the jury is forbidden to do so when the civil defendant is also at risk of criminal consequences for the same conduct.

212 **survivors would be less likely to report:** Know Your IX, "Resisting Mandatory Police Referral Efforts," http://knowyourix.org/mandatory-referral.

213 **"Any policy that takes away choice":** Jill Filipovic, "Making It Harder to Punish Campus Rapists Won't Help Stop Campus Rape," *Washington Post*, Aug. 10, 2015, https://www.washingtonpost.com/posteverything /wp/2015/08/10/making-it-harder-to-punish-campus-rapists-wont-help -stop-campus-rape/.

213 **"Survivors need to feel like they have choices":** Tyler Kingkade, "28 Groups That Work with Rape Victims Think the Safe Campus Act Is Terrible," *Huffington Post*, Sept. 13, 2015, http://www.huffingtonpost.com /entry/rape-victims-safe-campus-act_us_55f300cce4b063ecbfa4150b.

214 **"trigger somewhere else":** "Rep. Ehrhart to Rape Survivors: 'Trigger Somewhere Else,'" *Better Georgia*, March 18, 2017, https://www .bettergeorgia.org/2017/03/18/rep-ehrhart-to-rape-survivors-trigger -somewhere-else/ (video embedded).

214 **"hoot and holler and act ridiculous":** Tyler Kingkade, "Georgia Bill Designed to Limit College Rape Investigations Advances," *BuzzFeed News*, Mar. 1, 2017, https://www.buzzfeednews.com/article/tylerkingkade/ georgia-bill-campus-rape.

214 **"Could you grow up?":** Grace Starling, "Opinion: Senate Listens to Student Survivors of Sexual Assault; House Mocked Them," *Atlanta Journal-Constitution*, Mar. 26, 2017, https://www.ajc.com/blog/get-schooled /opinion-senate-listened-student-survivors-sexual-assault-house-mocked -them/A0ePD0oJvTBNEyPcS2KNGL/.

214 **"pretty little liar":** Starling, "Opinion: Senate Listens to Student Survivors of Sexual Assault."

214 **"untrained college bureaucrats":** Jeremy Bauer-Wolf, "Who Should

Investigate Sexual Assaults?," *Inside Higher Ed*, April 11, 2017, https://
www.insidehighered.com/news/2017/04/11/controversial-georgia
-sexual-assault-bill-prompts-debate-reporting/.

215 **pressuring KSU to punish cheerleaders:** Lindsay Gibbs, "University
Officials Tried to Stop This Cheerleader from Taking a Knee. Now She's
Suing Them," *ThinkProgress*, Sept. 8, 2018, https://thinkprogress.org/ex
-cheerleader-sues-university-for-conspiring-to-prevent-her-from-taking
-a-knee-during-anthem-83f4cc900196/.

215 **From the start, FIRE had led:** Ari Cohn, "Did the Office for Civil
Rights' April 4 'Dear Colleague' Letter Violate the Law?," FIRE, Sept.
12, 2011, https://www.thefire.org/did-the-office-for-civil-rights-april-4
-dear-colleague-letter-violate-the-law/.

216 **"courts of law—not campus administrators":** Alex Morey, "Baylor
Rape Controversy More Evidence College Unequipped to Decide Sexual Assault Cases," FIRE, Sept. 14, 2015, https://www.thefire.org/baylor
-rape-controversy-more-evidence-colleges-unequipped-to-decide-sexual
-assault-cases/.

216 **"highly inflated notion of an 'epidemic'":** Will Creeley, "Cathy
Young Highlights New Threats to Due Process on Campus," FIRE,
Nov. 7, 2011, https://www.thefire.org/cathy-young-highlights-new
-threats-to-due-process-on-campus/.

216 **rampant just like COVID-19:** Samantha Harris and Michael Thad
Allen, "Epidemics on Campus, Real and Imagined," *Reason*, May 20,
2020, https://reason.com/2020/05/20/epidemics-on-campus-real-and
-imagined/.

216 **spread of an airborne communicable disease:** "Is It Safe to Go to
College? Health Experts Weigh In," CNN, 2020, https://www.cnn
.com/interactive/2020/health/reopening-coronavirus/college.html; Sofi
Sinozich and Lynn Langston, *Rape and Sexual Assault Victimization Among
College-Aged Females, 1995–2013*, https://www.bjs.gov/content/pub/pdf
/rsavcaf9513.pdf.

216 **schools would sex-segregate their dorms:** Emily Yoffe, "The Problem
with Campus Sexual Assault Surveys," *Slate*, Sept. 24, 2015, https://slate
.com/human-interest/2015/09/aau-campus-sexual-assault-survey-why
-such-surveys-dont-paint-an-accurate-portrait-of-life-on-campus.html.

216 **Laura Kipnis's book on campus "sexual paranoia":** Peter Bonilla,
"'Unwanted Advances' Shows Laura Kipnis' Critiques of Academic
Culture More Relevant Than Ever," FIRE, Apr. 11, 2017, https://
www.thefire.org/unwanted-advances-shows-laura-kipnis-critiques-of
-academic-culture-more-relevant-than-ever/; see also McClintock, "Who
Is Afraid of Title IX?" (describing FIRE's affection for Kipnis).

216 **has aged poorly:** Kipnis has since settled a lawsuit brought by one of
her colleague's alleged victims. Brian Leiter, "Doe v. Kipnis, Harper-
Collins Has Settled," *Leiter Reports*, Nov. 10, 2018, https://leiterreports
.typepad.com/blog/2018/11/doe-v-kipnis-harpercollins-has-settled
.html; Maddie Burakoff, "Kipnis Lawsuit Moves Forward as Judge

Declines Motion to Dismiss the Case," *Daily Northwestern*, Mar. 9, 2018, https://dailynorthwestern.com/2018/03/09/campus/kipnis-lawsuit -moves-forward-as-judge-declines-motion-to-dismiss-the-case; Stassa Edwards, "Laura Kipnis Sued for Defamation over Book That Characterized Campus Sexual Assault as 'Romance,'" *Jezebel*, May 17, 2017, https://jezebel.com/laura-kipnis-sued-for-defamation-over-book-that -charact-1795303051.

217   **than their non-Greek peers:** John Foubert, "'Rapebait' E-Mail Reveals Dark Side of Frat Culture," CNN, October 9, 2013, https://edition.cnn .com/2013/10/09/opinion/foubert-fraternities-rape/.

217   **essentially House Bill 51:** Tyler Kingkade, "How Rolling Stone's UVA Story Sparked a Controversial Frat Lobbying Effort," *Huffington Post*, Dec. 11, 2015, https://www.huffpost.com/entry/fraternity-lobbying-campus -rape_n_566062bae4b08e945fee3f79.

217   **At Thurmond's party, Lott declared:** Thomas B. Edsall and Brian Falser, "Lott Remarks on Thurmond Echoed 1980 Words," *Washington Post*, Dec. 11, 2002, https://www.washingtonpost.com/archive/politics /2002/12/11/lott-remarks-on-thurmond-echoed-1980-words/c613ae1c -e17d-41c1-836a-4dd0741ec7c8/.

218   **"should be prosecuted to the fullest extent":** Cleta Mitchell and Trent Lott, "Safe Campus Act Sends Campus Sex Assaults to Police," *Columbia Daily Tribune*, last updated Oct. 6, 2015, 1:00 p.m., https:// www.columbiatribune.com/article/20151006/Opinion/310069968 ?template=ampart. In 2021, Mitchell made headlines by reportedly helping Trump pressure elections officials to "find" votes for him in Georgia. Michael S. Schmidt and Maggie Haberman, "Lawyer on Trump Election Call Quits Firm After Uproar," *New York Times*, Jan. 5, 2021, https://www.nytimes.com/2021/01/05/us/politics/cleta-mitchell-foley -lardner-trump.html.

218   **"police involvement sends a strong message":** Filipovic, "Making It Harder to Punish Campus Rapists."

218   **to advocate only for the latter:** See, e.g., Motion to Intervene, Pennsylvania v. DeVos, No. 1:20-cv-01468, ECF 27 at 12 (D.D.C. June 25, 2020); Motion to Intervene, Know Your IX v. Devos, No. 1:20-cv-01224, ECF 20–1 at 12 (D.Md. June 24, 2020).

219   **least popular member of Trump's cabinet:** For a summary of polling on Trump's cabinet members' popularity, see Amy Sherman, "How Unpopular Is Betsy DeVos?," PolitiFact, Jan. 6, 2020, https://www.politifact.com /factchecks/2020/jan/06/frederica-wilson/how-unpopular-betsy-devos/.

219   **"Secretary DeVos is a breath of fresh air":** Mary Kate McGowan, "Ehrhart Discusses Campus Rape Bill During Meeting with DeVos," *Marietta Daily Journal*, Apr. 24, 2017, https://www.mdjonline.com /news/ehrhart-discusses-campus-rape-bill-during-meeting-with-devos /article_4ce4bace-2956-11e7-975f-57efc5c7d6a7.html.

220   **"shielding institutions from liability":** Dana Bolger, "Betsy DeVos's New Harassment Rules Protect Schools, Not Students," *New York Times*,

Nov. 27, 2018, https://www.nytimes.com/2018/11/27/opinion/betsy-devos-title-ix-schools-students.html.

220   *"weakening* its due-process standards": Editors, "The ACLU's Absurd Title IX Lawsuit," *National Review*, May 19, 2020, https://www.nationalreview.com/2020/05/the-aclus-absurd-title-ix-lawsuit/.

220   focused on DeVos's substantive redefinition: David Cole, "The Absurd Attacks on the ACLU," ACLU, May 21, 2020, https://www.aclu.org/news/womens-rights/the-absurd-attacks-on-the-aclu/.

221   "the ACLU vs. due process": KC Johnson and Justin Dillon, "The ACLU vs. Due Process: The Nonprofit Takes a Surprising Stand Against More Rights for Those Accused on Campus," *New York Daily News*, May 21, 2020, https://www.nydailynews.com/opinion/ny-oped-the-aclu-vs-due-process-20200521-jtqqglschfdgxmmpwduipmvhku-story.html.

CHAPTER 18: INDELIBLE IN THE HIPPOCAMPUS

222   "Why suffer through the annihilation": Emma Brown, "California Professor, Writer of Confidential Brett Kavanaugh Letter, Speaks Out About Her Allegation of Sexual Assault," *Washington Post*, Sept. 16, 2018, https://www.washingtonpost.com/investigations/california-professor-writer-of-confidential-brett-kavanaugh-letter-speaks-out-about-her-allegation-of-sexual-assault/2018/09/16/46982194-b846-11e8-94eb-3bd52dfe917b_story.html.

224   it was the Senate's job to make a decision: Li Zhou and Tara Goldshan, "The Fight over Reopening the FBI Investigation into Brett Kavanaugh, Explained," *Vox*, Sept. 30, 2018, https://www.vox.com/policy-and-politics/2018/9/20/17879284/democrats-fbi-investigation-kavanaugh.

225   Judge's college girlfriend would say: Ronan Farrow and Jane Mayer, "Senate Democrats Investigate a New Allegation of Sexual Misconduct, from Brett Kavanaugh's College Years," *New Yorker*, Sept. 23, 2018, https://www.newyorker.com/news/news-desk/senate-democrats-investigate-a-new-allegation-of-sexual-misconduct-from-the-supreme-court-nominee-brett-kavanaughs-college-years-deborah-ramirez.

226   force his penis on another girl: Robin Pogrebin and Kate Kelly, "Brett Kavanaugh Fit In with the Privileged Kids. She Did Not," *New York Times*, Sept. 14, 2019, https://www.nytimes.com/2019/09/14/sunday-review/brett-kavanaugh-deborah-ramirez-yale.html/.

226   shut down offers of phone calls: Ronan Farrow and Jane Mayer, "E-mails Show That Republican Senate Staff Stymied a Kavanaugh Accuser's Effort to Give Testimony," *New Yorker*, Sept. 18, 2018, https://www.newyorker.com/news/news-desk/e-mails-show-republican-senate-staff-stymied-a-kavanaugh-accusers-effort-to-give-testimony.

226   rather than a pause to investigate: Farrow and Mayer, "Senate

Democrats Investigate a New Allegation of Sexual Misconduct, from Brett Kavanaugh's College Years."

227 "'Here's what happened to me 30 years ago'": Farah Stockman, "Jeff Flake Says Brett Kavanaugh Inquiry Should Look at Any 'Credible Allegation,'" *New York Times*, Oct. 1, 2018, https://www.nytimes.com/2018/10/01/us/senator-jeff-flake-kavanaugh-boston.html.

227 **White House severely limited the scope**: Ken Dilanian, Geoff Bennett, and Kristen Welker, "Limits to FBI's Kavanaugh Investigation Have Not Changed, Despite Trump's Comments," NBC News, Sept. 30, 2018, https://www.nbcnews.com/politics/politics-news/white-house-limits-scope-fbi-s-investigation-allegations-against-brett-n915061.

227 **a far longer list of witnesses had been established**: Senate Judiciary Committee, "Supplemental FBI Investigation Executive Summary," Oct. 4, 2018, https://www.judiciary.senate.gov/press/rep/releases/supplemental-fbi-investigation-executive-summary; Karen Yourish and Troy Griggs, "The F.B.I. Investigation into Kavanaugh Has Ended. Here's Who Was Questioned, and Who Was Not," *New York Times*, Oct. 4, 2018, https://www.nytimes.com/interactive/2018/10/01/us/politics/kavanaugh-fbi-investigation-witnesses.html.

227 **"the presumption of innocence, and fairness"**: "Senator Collins announces she will vote to confirm Judge Kavanaugh," Oct. 5, 2018, https://www.collins.senate.gov/newsroom/senator-collins-announces-she-will-vote-confirm-judge-kavanaugh.

228 **"the street antics that Antifa brought"**: Ian Schwartz, "Victor Davis Hanson: Dr. Blasey Ford's Story Has 'Collapsed'; She Gave 'One Too Many Narratives,'" *RealClearPolitics*, Oct. 4 2018, https://www.realclearpolitics.com/video/2018/10/04/victor_davis_hanson_dr_christine_blasey_fords_story_has_collapsed_she_gave_one_too_many_narratives.html.

228 **Lindsey Graham's fiery speech**: Transcript of Graham's Remarks on Kavanaugh Nomination, https://www.lgraham.senate.gov/public/index.cfm/2018/9/transcript-of-graham-s-remarks-on-kavanaugh-nomination.

229 **"try to find the truth"**: Rich Lowry, "Democrats Have Abandoned the Presumption of Innocence," *New York Post*, Sept. 20, 2018, https://nypost.com/2018/09/20/democrats-have-abandoned-the-presumption-of-innocence/.

229 **to the lynching of Emmett Till**: Clarence McKee, "Democrats Don't Care About the Presumption of Innocence," Newsmax, Sept. 26, 2018, https://www.newsmax.com/clarencevmckee/brett-kavanaugh-presumption-of-innocence-due-process/2018/09/26/id/883594/.

230 **senators were expressly political actors**: Adam Freedman, "Due Process for Judge Kavanaugh," *City Journal*, Sept. 25, 2018, https://www.city-journal.org/due-process-for-brett-kavanaugh-16192.html.

230 **"not going to ruin Judge Kavanaugh's life"**: Ian Kullgren, "Graham: Ford's Testimony Won't Change My Vote," *Politico*, Sept. 23, 2018,

https://www.politico.com/story/2018/09/23/kavanaugh-ford-lindsey
-graham-837391.

230 **Perhaps Feinstein truly wanted to respect:** Jodi Kantor and Meghan
Twohey, *She Said: Breaking the Sexual Harassment Story That Helped Ignite
a Movement* (New York: Penguin Press, 2019), 209; Nicholas Fantos,
"Dianne Feinstein Rode One Court Fight to the Senate. Another Has
Left Her Under Siege," *New York Times*, Sept. 21, 2018, https://www
.nytimes.com/2018/09/21/us/politics/dianne-feinstein-brett-kavanaugh
-sexual-misconduct.html.

233 **"willing to overthrow all of due process":** Ian Schwartz, "Kimberley Strassel: If We Are Willing to Overthrow Due Process, We've Got
Some Really Big Problems," *RealClearPolitics*, Sept. 30, 2018, https://
www.realclearpolitics.com/video/2018/09/30/kimberley_strassel_if_we
_are_willing_to_overthrow_due_process_weve_got_some_really_big
_problems.html.

233 **Trump issued his MRA-like warning:** Bump, "Trump Says It's 'a Very
Scary Time' for Young Men—but That Women Are 'Doing Great.'"

233 **he chose his boys:** David Martosko, "EXCLUSIVE: Donald Trump Jr.
Tells DailyMailTV in First-Ever Joint Interview with Kimberly Guil-
foyle That Sexual Assault Claims Make Him More Scared for His SONS
than His Daughters Following He-Said She-Said Kavanaugh Controversy," *Daily Mail*, Oct. 1, 2018, https://www.dailymail.co.uk/news
/article-6224635/Donald-Trump-Jr-Kimberly-Guilfoyle-DailyMail-TV
-Boys-harmed-said-said-cases.html?ito=social-twitter_dailymailus.

234 **"thinking of their husbands and their brothers":** Tal Axelrod,
"Trump: 'Hundred Percent' Ford Named Wrong Person," *The Hill*, Oct.,
6, 2018, https://thehill.com/homenews/administration/410253-trump-hundred
-percent-ford-named-wrong-person.

234 **held up Kavanaugh and Tom Robinson:** Daniel Buck, "The Me Too
Era Is Time to Revisit 'To Kill a Mockingbird's' Defense of Due Process,"
Federalist, May 7, 2019, https://thefederalist.com/2019/05/07/era-time
-revisit-kill-mockingbirds-defense-due-process.

235 **"less likely to believe women":** PerryUndem Research/Communication,
*The Immediate, Short-Term, and Long-Term Effects of the Kavanaugh Hearings
on the Electorate* 10 (Apr. 15, 2019), https://view.publitas.com/perryundem
-research-communication/kavanaugh-ford-survey-report_f/page/10.

CONCLUSION

239 **At least one court has concluded:** Lee v. Univ. of New Mexico, 449 F.
Supp. 3d 1071, 1102–03, 1129–32 (D.N.M. 2020).

239 **accusations of sexual assault demand extra care:** In the criminal context, a similar criticism can be made of sex offender registries, which treat
sexual harms as different from all others—one of many reasons to support registry abolition. See, e.g., Judith Levine and Erica R. Meiners, *The

Feminist and the Sex Offender: Confronting Sexual Harm, Ending State Violence (New York: Verso, 2020); Reina Gattuso, "Why Should Feminists Be Against the Sex Offender Registry?," Feministing, Dec. 21, 2018, http://feministing.com/2018/12/21/why-should-feminists-be-against-the-sex-offender-registry/.

240 **critics who demand exceptional procedures for sexual harassment:** In addition to the many examples throughout this book, see Jed Rubenfeld, "Mishandling Rape," *New York Times*, Nov. 15, 2014, https://www.nytimes.com/2014/11/16/opinion/sunday/mishandling-rape.html.

242 **sexual harassment plan was imposed from on high:** "We write to voice our strong objections to the Sexual Harassment Policy and Procedures imposed by the central university administration and the Corporation on all parts of the university, including the law school. . . . We also find the process by which this policy was decided and imposed on all parts of the university inconsistent with the finest traditions of Harvard University, of faculty governance, and of academic freedom." Elizabeth Bartholet et al., "Rethink Harvard's Sexual Harassment Policy," *Boston Globe*, Oct. 14, 2014, https://www.bostonglobe.com/opinion/2014/10/14/rethink-harvard-sexual-harassment-policy/HFDDiZN7nU2UwuUuWMnqbM/story.html.

242 **share as much information as it safely can:** Much of my thinking on this point is drawn from my collaboration with Judith Resnik and Claire Simonich, with whom I drafted an article in 2015. Alexandra Brodsky, Judith Resnik, and Claire Simonich, "Can Less Confidentiality Mean More Fairness in Campus Sexual Assault Cases?," *Nation*, Feb. 23, 2015, https://www.thenation.com/article/archive/can-less-confidentiality-mean-more-fairness-campus-sexual-assault-investigations/.

247 **excluded from Title VII, as are "independent contractors":** Meghan Racklin, Molly Weston Williamson, and Dina Bakst, "State Leadership on Anti-Discrimination Protections for Independent Contractors," A Better Balance, Apr. 22, 2020, https://www.abetterbalance.org/state-leadership-on-anti-discrimination-protections-for-independent-contractors/.

247 **isolated and particularly vulnerable:** Alexandra Brodsky and Elizabeth Deutsch, "The Promise of Title IX: Sexual Violence and the Law," *Dissent*, Fall 2015, https://www.dissentmagazine.org/article/title-ix-activism-sexual-violence-law.

247 **inclusion in existing antidiscrimination protections:** Anna North, "Democrats' Sweeping New Anti-Harassment Bill, Explained," *Vox*, Apr. 9, 2019, https://www.vox.com/2019/4/9/18300478/sexual-harassment-me-too-be-heard-democrats.

248 **"sought to transform the terms of debate":** Julie Goldscheid, "The Civil Rights Remedy of the 1994 Violence Against Women Act: Struck Down But Not Ruled Out," *Family Law Quarterly* 39 (2005): 157, 159, https://ssrn.com/abstract=925049.

248 **did not have a sufficient impact on the national economy:** United States v. Morrison, 529 U.S. 598 (2000).

ACKNOWLEDGMENTS

I am indebted to so many people without whom this book would either not exist at all or would be much worse. Thank you to my agent, Charlotte Sheedy, and to Ally Sheedy for believing in the book and me. Thank you to my editors, Sara Bershtel, Riva Hocherman, and especially Grigory Tovbis, and to the rest of the team at Metropolitan/Henry Holt. I am grateful for your thoughtfulness, precision, and care for this book during a tremendously trying time.

Thank you to everyone who spoke to me about their experiences regarding sexual harassment and allegations thereof. I am grateful for your trust. Thank you to the many attorneys, professors, and advocates who shared their insights. Thank you to the journalists, researchers, and theorists on whose work I drew.

Thank you to Grace Watkins, Mollie Berkowitz, Rita Gilles, Yao Lin, Kathryn Pogin, Pauline Syrnik, and the Yale Reproductive Justice Clinic for their research assistance. Thank you to Kayla Patrick for consulting on quantitative questions. Thanks also to Carrie Frye and Leah Finnegan for invaluable writerly guidance. And thank you to Maya Dusenbery for her expert fact-checking.

Thank you to my husband, Alec Schierenbeck, for encouraging me to take on this project, listening to me talk about it incessantly for years, helping me work through tough substantive and structural decisions, and spending the weeks before our wedding line editing my entire first draft. I am so grateful for our partnership in life and in thought.

Writing this book has been the most powerful, moving reminder of the generosity and brilliance of my community. Thank you to Katie Baker, Suzanna Bobadilla, Dana Bolger, David Chen, Elizabeth Deutsch, Jennifer Doyle, Max Ehrenfreund, Nia Evans, Seth Extein, Charlie Gerstein, Lucy Gubernick, John He, Rachel Kauder Nalebuff, Sarah Nesbitt, Kate Orazem, Kayla Patrick, Noah Rosenblum, Emma Roth, my sister Anna Schierenbeck, and my mother, Valerie Cooke, for reading and editing chapters—and even full drafts—of this work.

Thank you to Mike Wishnie, who supervised the law school paper that eventually became this book. Thank you to the many other professors whose teaching in college and law school also deeply influenced my thinking on this topic, including Michelle Anderson, Crystal Feimster, Julie Goldscheid, Ali Miller, Judith Resnik, and Reva Siegal.

Thank you to the Know Your IX organizers and other feminists with whom I grew up intellectually and politically. I am especially grateful to Dana, the most thoughtful partner a girl could have for such a wild, formative adventure. Thank you to Public Justice, and particularly Adele Kimmel, for righteous work and for encouraging me to use my voice in and out of the job.

Thank you to the feminist advocates, lawyers, writers, and scholars who made our lives possible and laid the groundwork, both practical and theoretical, for today's movements.

Thank you to everyone doing the hard work in good faith.

INDEX

ABOUT THE AUTHOR

ALEXANDRA BRODSKY is a civil rights lawyer and cofounder of Know Your IX, an organization devoted to ending gender violence in schools. A graduate of Yale Law School, she clerked for the U.S. Court of Appeals for the Ninth Circuit. Brodsky coedited *The Feminist Utopia Project* and has written about sexual violence for the *New York Times*, the *Guardian*, the *Washington Post*, and the *Atlantic*, among many other publications. She lives in New York.